SNEAKING INMATES DOWN THE ALLEY

Problems and Prospects in Jail Management

SNEAKING INMATES DOWN THE ALLEY

Problems and Prospects in Jail Management

Edited by

DAVID B. KALINICH, Ph.D.

Associate Professor, School of Criminal Justice
Michigan State University
East Lansing, Michigan

and

JOHN KLOFAS, Ph.D.

Associate Professor, Department of Criminal Justice
Illinois State University
Normal, Illinois

CHARLES C THOMAS • PUBLISHER
Springfield • Illinois • U.S.A.

Published and Distributed Throughout the World by
CHARLES C THOMAS • PUBLISHER
2600 South First Street
Springfield, Illinois 62708-4709

© *1986 by* CHARLES C THOMAS • PUBLISHER
ISBN 0-398-05264-6
Library of Congress Catalog Card Number: 86-5864

With THOMAS BOOKS *careful attention is given to all details of manufacturing and design. It is the Publisher's desire to present books that are satisfactory as to their physical qualities and artistic possibilities and appropriate for their particular use.* THOMAS BOOKS *will be true to those laws of quality that assure a good name and good will.*

Printed in the United States of America
Q-R-3

Library of Congress Cataloging in Publication Data
Sneaking inmates down the alley.

Bibliography: p.
1. Jails--United States--Administration. I. Kalinich,
David B. II. Klofas, John.
HV9469.S66 1986   365'.34   86-5864
ISBN 0-398-05264-6

CONTRIBUTORS

Paul S. Embert
Training Coordinator
School of Criminal Justice
Michigan State University

John J. Gibbs, Ph.D.
School of Criminal Justice
Rutgers University

David Kalinich, Ph.D.
School of Criminal Justice
Michigan State University

John Klofas, Ph.D.
Department of Criminal Justice
Illinois State University

Lucien X. Lombardo, Ph.D.
Department of Sociology/Criminal Justice
Old Dominion University

Edward Meister
Deputy Superintendent
Peoria County Jail

W. Ray Nelson
Director, Jail Division (retired)
National Institute of Corrections

Lesley I. Parsons
Graduate Student
Department of Criminal Justice
Illinois State University

v

Carl F. Pinkele, Ph.D.
Department of Political Science
Ohio Wesleyan University

Mark R. Pogrebin, Ph.D.
Graduate School of Public Affairs
University of Colorado-Denver

Eric D. Poole, Ph.D.
Graduate School of Public Affairs
University of Colorado-Denver

Robert M. Regoli, Ph.D.
Department of Sociology
University of Colorado, Boulder

Nancy E. Schafer, Ph.D.
School of Justice
University of Alaska-Anchorage

Beverly A. Smith, Ph.D.
Department of Criminal Justice
Illinois State University

Steven Smith
Superintendent
Peoria County Jail

Stan Stojkovic, Ph.D.
Criminal Justice Program
University of Wisconsin-Milwaukee

Ralph A. Weisheit, Ph.D.
Department of Criminal Justice
Illinois State University

DEDICATION

THE CO-EDITORS and Contributors have agreed to contribute all royalties from the sale of this book to the Midwest Criminal Justice Association (MCJA). For the past decade, MCJA has been dedicated to bringing criminal justice practitioners and scholars together to develop and share in a growing body of knowledge about the role and operations of the criminal justice system. Our reader is premised upon the need to add to the body of knowledge about the role and operations of the jail with contributions from scholars and practitioners presently active in the field. We, therefore, felt it appropriate to donate royalties forthcoming from our work to support the continuing contributions of MCJA to the field of criminal justice.

PREFACE

A CLICHE often applied to criminal justice management is that it is "reactive rather than proactive." A better depiction, especially of jail management, may be that it is "passive creative." Hence, the title of this book, *Sneaking Inmates Down the Alley*, depicts a creative method one jail administrator found to keep his jail below court mandated capacity. Like most jail administrators, he passively accepted his plight: the local criminal justice system was putting more inmates into his jail than the Federal District Court allowed. Being a good bureaucrat caught up in this dilemma, he obtained access to the local police lockup that had been closed, and snuck several inmates out of his jail, down an alley with their bed rolls, to the condemned lockup just before an official count.

A myriad of anecdotes could be told that all make the same point. We often choose to deal with our problems with a creative deviousness which allows us to get by for another day. This approach permits administrators and practitioners to maintain their appearance as good bureaucrats; somehow the storm is being weathered. With this perspective, administrators feel helpless, defining many current problems as imposed upon them as insolvable with the skills and resources available to them. Yet creativity abounds for clever, and even devious, maneuvers that enable survival for one more day. The question raised by this asks why policy problems aren't addressed with the same creativity used in response to crises. Our goal in this book is to describe the complexity of jail problems and to illustrate new ways of viewing them and new resources for addressing them.

Our book, therefore, is both descriptive and prescriptive. We hope that it will be useful to both students of contemporary jails and practitioners within them. With original research and analysis, several readings offer frameworks for understanding the complexity of jail problems. Other chapters provide illustrations of aggressive approaches to problem solving.

The book begins with a descriptive section. Here, the authors discuss the complexity of the functions of local jails as well as their social structure. Jails remain a catch-all for local social control and an institution whose inner workings for staff and inmates remain nearly unexplored. These chapters reflect efforts to organize our scant knowledge and view it within a context of an environment that is making new demands on local jails.

In the second section, we frame jail administration within this environment by looking more closely at correctional law as it applies to jails, the changing inmate population, and the links between the jail and its surroundings. Here we begin to examine and question the often passive nature of jail administration. Such a posture may hinder recognition of a changing population, impede responses to mandates for change and hide the tools needed for a rational response to a changing environment.

In the final section of our reader, we turn to prescriptions which emerge from a new perspective on jail problems. While the chapter on jail design clearly requires resources for a new facility, the other prescriptions require only a determination to break with routine passiveness and redefine problems as being within the scope of jail management. To us, this approach seems more productive than "sneaking inmates down the alley."

CONTENTS

SNEAKING INMATES DOWN THE ALLEY

Problems and Prospects in Jail Management

PART I

THE CONTEMPORARY JAIL
IN CONTEXT

ONE OF THE MOST thorough discussions of jails available carries the subtitle "An Unknown and Neglected Area of Justice" (Mattick, 1974). In the nearly fifteen years since that article was written little has been added which clarifies the status of American jails. They continue to be nearly ignored by scholars and attended to only begrudgingly by most policy makers.

To attribute this inattention to provincialism, however, would risk contributing to it. Neither academics nor policy makers are insensitive or uninterested in institutions which process over seven million Americans annually. Instead, we must look to the characteristics of jails themselves for the impediments to understanding them. The complexity of American jails makes them difficult to study or to change.

While jails process more people than most institutions in American society, their population is also a more diverse and complicated group. National surveys show that about half of jail inmates have been convicted and sentenced for crimes. The remainder is comprised of people awaiting trial and those caught somewhere in the judicial process. Even this cross-sectional division offers a deceptive oversimplification, however. Process studies indicate that the population of a local jail may completely turn over more than 30 times a year; furthermore, only a small number of jail inmates approach the hardened offender profile of many state prisons. Instead, those processed in jails reflect a diverse group of traffic violators, petty thieves, disorderly persons, civilly committed inmates and serious violators. Each category also contains both males and females as well as inmates of all age groups.

3

The complexity of jails is not only reflected in their populations but also in the organizations themselves. Facilities differ greatly in size and thus in staffing patterns, budgets and other factors. It is difficult to generalize about the experience of confinement when nearly two thirds of jails house less than fifty people but nine of ten inmates are housed in medium to large jails which range in size to over 5,000 beds. Finally, the political environment of jails complicates their understanding. Most often managed by local governments, jails differ depending on local tax base, spending priority and local expectations about the treatment of the confined.

The chapters in this section detail the complexity of the modern jail. In "An Historical View of the Multiple Roles of Jail," Beverly Smith traces the current complexity to the historical functions of a local jail in the midwest. While the jail remained a local facility, it functioned in an intricate network of local, state and federal agencies. The McLean County jail responded to local calls for order and morality by housing large numbers of women accused of being "insane" and a plentiful supply of men found to be drunk and disorderly. For many, their problems for the community were solved by transfer to state penal or mental health institutions. The federal government also influenced the roles of the local jail as the facility came to house violators of prohibition or other federal laws as well as AWOL soldiers and illegal aliens. As Dr. Smith points out, the unique roles of the McLean County jail were made possible by the unique qualities of the county and its resources. Other jails would develop their own unique constellation of roles.

In "Jails Versus Prisons," by Stan Stojkovic, the complexities of jail social structure are explored. The jail, with its diverse population and short stays by prisoners, is unique among correctional facilities. The combinations of sophisticated criminals, and naive first timers makes for a stressful and volatile environment. The rapid turnover of inmates creates a fluid and rapidly changing power structure. Levels of violence and victimization, the availability of contraband and the ascription of status within an institution will all depend on many variables relevant to students and managers of jails.

The dimensions of guarding in a jail environment are addressed by Regoli, Poole and Pogrebin. In an examination of guards' relationships with inmates, administrators and their peers, the authors describe the alienated work forces of four jails across the country. They attribute the demoralization of jail officers to their loss of a mission; their feelings of powerlessness to either control or treat effectively. As jails have become more complex with the intrusion of the courts, the professionalization of management and increasing numbers of inmates, it is the front line staff who appear to have suffered. Jail researchers and managers must take into account the pivotal position and the dormant resources of these staff.

The final article in the section is entitled, "New Rules and Old Rituals." In it, David Kalinich discusses the changing environment of jail management. Once secure in a predictable environment of power and patronage, jail administrators are facing new problems which include overcrowding, increasing levels of mental illness among prisoners and new demands for professionalism. Traditional attitudes and practices have made it difficult for jail staff to respond to the new requirements of courts and professional organizations. An effective response will require that administrators and staff approach jail management from a new perspective, one that will be explored later in this volume.

REFERENCES

Mattick, Hans. "The Contemporary Jails of the United States: An Unknown and Neglected Area of Justice," in Daniel Glaser (ed.) *Handbook of Criminology*, Chicago: Rand McNally, 1974.

CHAPTER 1

AN HISTORICAL VIEW OF THE MULTIPLE ROLES OF JAILS

The McLean County Jail Between the World Wars

Beverly A. Smith

IN THEIR STUDIES of incarceration as part of the criminal justice system, both criminal justicians and historians have concentrated on state and federal prisons. By contrast, criminal justicians, with a few exceptions (Wayson, et al., 1977; Moynahan and Stewart, 1980; Pogrebin, 1982), have slighted and historians (Rothman, 1980; Cahalan, 1979; Walker, 1982) have virtually ignored another category of institutions within the system — jails. Both our lack of knowledge and the generally poor conditions of jails may have arisen because until recently jails have been almost exclusively under local governmental and political control. This relative autonomy from state and federal supervision; their multiple roles; a detention orientation; changing and heterogeneous populations; largely untrained or even uneducated custodial staffs; few rehabilitative, job training, or recreational programs; inadequate or nonexistent medical care; and other factors have produced what are generally acknowledged as the worst living and working conditions of the criminal justice system (Mattick, 1974). Over the years, jails have come to represent "the perennial jail problem" (Robinson, 1945), "the jail blight" (Richmond, 1965), and "the ultimate ghetto of the criminal justice system" (Goldfarb, 1976). Most of our knowledge about jails has been based on scattered studies of big-city jails or on aggregate state or national data (USDC, 1933; USDJ, 1980). We know even less about

7

jails in rural or semi-rural counties both past and present (Handberg, 1982). For the important formative period between the First and Second World Wars, this study will provide a view of one such jail, the McLean County (Illinois) Jail, in relation to the populations it housed and the institutional network of which it was an integral part.

HISTORY OF ILLINOIS JAILS

The Illinois state legislature in 1827 passed "an Act Concerning Jails and Jailers," which provided that each county build and maintain a jail supervised by the sheriff. The law had general provisions about the separation of certain classifications of prisoners and the provision of edible food to prisoners who then had to pay for their own meals. Grand juries were to inspect the jails annually to insure humane treatment. The 1870 state constitution gave McLean county a board of commissioners whose duties included the general supervision of the operation and maintenance of the county jail, largely through its budgetary powers, including the provision of food. Revisions of the Illinois statutes in 1874 required greater degrees of separation in the inmate population. Witnesses, females, juveniles, and lesser offenders were to all be separate populations within the jail. The circuit court judge held the responsibility for enforcing those separation orders, and the grand juries reported to him on jail conditions. In 1917 the state made the last major change before 1971 in the laws directly affecting jails. In that year the state eliminated the fee system of paying the sheriff. Prior to 1917 the sheriffs had been paid by the county boards a per diem rate to feed each inmate. The State Board of Charities which inspected jails had argued for years that the fee system encouraged sheriffs to arrest the innocent or incarcerate lesser offenders to gain additional money, while at the same time scrimping on inmate meals for additional profits. According to the executive secretary of the State Welfare Commission (Hinrichsen, 1917-18:17), the county jails with their inadequate, unsanitary living conditions were "admittedly the disgrace of the state." The McLean County Jail, built in 1882, was certainly not one of the state's worst jails. The imposing nature of the jail's stone building made rennovations difficult, but its ventilation; indoor plumbing; windows; separate areas for young boys, the insane, and women; and the amount of space not taken up by cells made the McLean County Jail one of the state's better facilities.

MULTIPLE ROLES OF THE McLEAN COUNTY JAIL

The McLean County Jail had multiple roles largely determined by the many disparate groups of inmates processed in even this relatively small institution and by the institutional network of which the jail was an integral part. At the local level, the jail was one of several social control mechanisms used primarily with the disadvantaged, the disturbed, and the deviant, or, as Irwin (1985) repeatedly calls them, the "rabble." These groups included city ordinance violators, alcoholics, delinquents, prostitutes, gamblers, bad drivers, petty thieves, and the insane. Although these classifications of prisoners contained many cross-overs, i.e. alcoholics arrested for driving while intoxicated one day and for disturbing the peace the next, the classifications still represented different, often difficult tasks for the jail. In addition, the jail handled small numbers of more serious offenders, persons convicted or more often accused of larceny, assault, robbery/burglary, rape, and murder. Because of the statutory separation of sexes, the number of classifications was actually doubled.

The jail, of course, was one of the most impressive symbols of the political power wielded by the sheriffs. Jail patronage was sometimes hotly disputed among the sheriffs, the circuit court judges, and the county boards. The jail also served as the lockup for the police departments of both Bloomington and Normal. Throughout the time period in question, the combined population of the Twin Cities equalled that of the rest of the county for a total of 70,000 to 75,000. Those scattered communities that made up the other half of the county's population also used the jail to house the persons arrested by various town marshals or constables. By far, however, the jail housed a Bloomington/Normal-based population; a little more than three-fifths of the admissions reported their residence at admission to be within the two cities.

The jail provided interim housing for persons in transit to or from other local institutions. Adults arrived from and were sent to the county farm and local medical facilities. Delinquents who had escaped or runaway from local or state juvenile facilities were held in the jail awaiting return. Local juvenile facilities to which the jailed delinquents could be transferred included the Normal-based Illinois State Soldiers' and Sailors' Orphans (later Children's) Home and privately financed facilities for troubled youth.

The jail was also one of the ways in which the county reached out to the state along formal and informal lines. In other words, although the jail remained a local institution, it did become part of working relationships with state agencies, institutions, and personnel. Inmates were transferred to state prisons, reformatories, and mental facilities, and responsibility for those transfers lay in local hands. Deputies, matrons, and other persons with connections to the jail visited those facilities and the personnel who staffed them. The necessity of moving those inmates further depleted an already small staff. The state police, after its founding in 1922, brought admissions, largely driving cases or run-aways, to the jail. And the State Board of Charities also visited the jail during its non-compulsory inspections.

The inter-war years also saw the jail strongly affected by federal legislation, aimed not at improving jail conditions, but at regulating crime and/or social conduct. The Volstead Act (Prohibition) of 1920, the Mann Act of 1910, the Dyer Act of 1919, and the Harrison Act of 1914 all produced new inmate groups in the jail population. Although the most dramatic of these measures, Prohibition, was repealed in 1933 and the other measures brought in fewer inmates, the federal contacts remained tenuously in place, only to be revived in World War II when the jail served to house AWOL soldiers and suspect aliens for short periods and after World War II with increased federal funding and/or regulation.

The best way to investigate the various roles of the jail is to examine the populations which it held. From the end of 1918 to December 31, 1941, approximately 21,000 persons were jailed or housed in the facility. Existent jail registers provide demographic, offense, and processing information on each inmate. Because as Janet Connolly (1983: 99) has observed, jailed women are "an invisible gender in an ill-defined institution," all female admissions (1,765) for the entire twenty-four year period were collected first. The female figure for each year was then complemented by a randomly selected group of males equal in size, for a sample of 3,530 inmates or 17.02 percent of the total admissions for the period. The women made up 8.5 percent of the total admissions. Recent Department of Justice figures show that about 6.5 percent of the current jail population is female (USDJ, 1981), so the inter-war sample may seem large, but not necessarily indicative of a female crime wave. McLean County may have been subject to longterm and/or temporary shifts of the male, crime-prone age cohorts due to the seasonal nature and gradual mechanization of the chief industry, namely agriculture.

Possibly those shifts and the high number of insanity cases put female admissions higher than nationwide norms. With cell space relatively limited, periodically the number of female inmates presented problems to the jail administrators.

Despite fears of large numbers of incarcerated children, only a dozen of the females were under the age of twelve. This age group may have been informally controlled by the community or law enforcement agents. Teenagers (14.7%) made up the third largest group. As is largely the case today, almost all the teenagers were incarcerated for status offenses as runaways from home or school and as delinquents. Although jail records give little direct indication, undoubtedly many of these young women were jailed as much for, in Schlossman and Wallach's (1978) term, their "precocious sexuality," as for their actual criminal behavior. Indeed the two largest age groups (twenties = 32.2%; thirties = 20.9%) were also in their actively reproductive years. Altogether women under forty represented more than two-thirds (68.5%) of the total.

Three-fifths of the females were listed as housewives or employed in housework. Another fifth without a listed occupation were probably also housewives; at the time, it was assumed that most women worked within the family or parental home. Only 2.6 percent of the women were listed as factory laborers and 4.4 percent as office workers. Heavy industry was centered in nearby Peoria, and white-collar jobs for women did not become plentiful until the post-WWII growth of the insurance business and the local universities. White-collar crimes, like fraud and forgery, generally involved women who tried to cash checks with forged signatures or, more often, with insufficient funds (Steffensmeier, 1978).

Black women were disproportionately represented in the jail admissions. They made up 12.9 percent of the female admissions, while black women only made up a little more than one percent of the general female population according to both the 1930 and 1940 Censuses (USDC). Those blacks all lived in the crime-prone areas of Bloomington that consistently produced a disproportionate number of admissions, black and white. The more serious personal offenses, such as robbery and assault, tended to involve black admissions. Most of the assault charges involved female neighbors or residents of the same house who apparently had gotten into fights with one another. Jail provided a chance to calm down the parties involved as these black women often saw their cases dismissed or reduced to less serious charges resulting in jail time; none of them went to state prison. The percentage of black women remained stable for the first half of the twentieth century denoting a criminal sub-group, racism by court officials or arresting officers, the inability to pay fines or bail, or all of the above. Although records are incomplete, there is some indication that the jail, while holding these disproportionate numbers of black women, practiced racial segregation.

More than half (55.2%) of the females were born in Illinois. Only sixty (3.4%) were recorded as having been born outside the United States. The turn-of-the-century immigrant waves were never clearly reflected in the McLean County Jail population, although immigrant groups entered the communities and established ethnic neighborhoods that have existed to this day. By mid-century the systemic prejudices which might have been demonstrated in much earlier figures had lessened. Two-thirds of the female inmates (67.4%) were residents of Bloomington/Normal despite the fact that the cities only represented about half the county's population. This overwhelming majority of cases came from admissions for insanity, liquor violations, city ordinance violations, prostitution, and petty property crimes. Certain streets near the downtown were periodically raided for liquor violators, disturbers of the peace, and prostitutes. Other adjoining areas in the near southwest corner of Bloomington, between the downtown and the railroad station, were heavily represented. Certain outlying communities (11.8%) seemed to send their own types of female admissions. Chenoa, a center for bootleg whiskey during Prohibition, also sent several check forgers and bad-check writers. Women in small communities were picked up for disorderly conduct by local town marshals. Other women from the rural countryside or the small communities were arrested for shoplifting or petty theft during forays into the shopping areas of the two largest cities. This latter group would spend a night in jail pending disposition, while those living in town tended to be processed more quickly.

Insanity alone was the leading admission offense (25.6%). More than a quarter of the female admissions were sent to state mental facilities after a speedy commitment and one or two days in jail. Although such procedures limited stays in a jail clearly ill-equipped to deal with serious mental problems, such procedures undoubtedly meant that many women, even those undergoing relatively short periods of mental instability, found themselves labeled criminal by their jail experiences and then indeterminately sentenced to maximum security mental facilities (Fox, 1978). It should be noted that males were sent with the same alarming speed to asylums, but less than five percent of the male sample was admitted for insanity. The courts tended to send older women to the state hospital at Jacksonville, built in 1847, which customarily served an older population. By far, most insanity cases, male and female, were sent to the nearby Peoria State Hospital in the suburb of Bartonville. Created in 1895, this hospital with its relative newness, proximity to the courts and inmates' families, and the ease of transfer probably led McLean county justices to send more inmates (Scheff, 1964). But each new mental health facility, for example Manteno, soon found itself receiving McLean county women.

Ideally each of those women would have been accompanied by a deputy and the matron. However, the large number of insane admissions meant that often a single male deputy escorted one or more of these women to a state mental facility. The possibility for abuse is self-evident. The jail in employing a matron as early as the 1920s had been considered progressive, but the matrons' duties within the facility kept them from accompanying insane inmates and criminals to other state or county institutions. Although the employment of matrons removed the McLean County sheriffs' wives from any formal position within the jail staff, the sheriffs' wives sometimes informally took the matrons' place. Trips to Dwight Reformatory, the state prison for women, and other county jails, by both the matrons and the sheriffs' wives, maintained the informal, even familial ties that bound together many law enforcement personnel and their families. Use of the wives also denoted that the "family business" type of attitude was still prevalent in the counties.

At any one time, the matron, the sheriff's wife, the male deputies, and the sheriff himself were kept quite busy moving females. More than one fourth were sent to mental institutions or the county farm, essentially a public nursing home for the senile and disabled; several juveniles were shipped to the Lincoln State School and Colony created in 1865 as an experimental school for the feebleminded. Another 2.9 percent were returned to the institutions from which they had escaped (Lincoln in particular) and had been released (mental facilities). And 2.9 percent were sent to state prisons, first the State Reformatory at Joliet, attached to the male prison, and later to the Dwight Reformatory for Women opened in the early 1930s, and to the State Training School for Girls at Geneva, the female juvenile reformatory. Altogether about a third (29.2%) left the county jail for another institution, and that number excludes those moved to another jurisdiction's jail. The McLean County Jail was imbedded in the institutional network of Illinois. The ease with which certain cases could move through the institution may have falsely encouraged the community about how easily it could solve some of its problems and about how efficient the jail itself was as a handler of inmates.

Drunk and disorderly admissions together made up the next largest category of admissions (16.2%); related admissions for violations of city ordinances made up another 5.4 percent. It is difficult to estimate from these figures, or other available data, just how many of these incarcerations represented women with serious alcohol problems. What is clear is that McLean county and Bloomington/Normal law enforcement authorities used arrests of this type as a mechanism of social control. Monkkonen (1981) has clearly shown this mechanism at work in our largest cities during the nineteenth and twentieth centuries. Much less attention has gone to the use of such arrests in other than large urban settings.

Prostitution accounted for 10.8 percent, the third largest group of admissions. A large part of those admissions occurred in 1935 when the police apparently carried out an extensive campaign of raids against white brothels on Center Street near downtown Bloomington. Several women were arrested more than once during a single month for prostitution and had to pay increasingly higher fines to gain their releases. The prostitution figure does not include the eight admissions for violation of the Mann or White Slavery Act (1910). All but one of those Mann Act admissions took place in 1931, but they do not seem to indicate discovery of an organized ring. Arrest rates for prostitution tapered off towards the Second World War. Other sex-related crimes played very minor roles. Adultery, performing/obtaining an illegal operation (abortion), and bigamy together account for one percent of the total female admissions. Less than half that amount were admitted for child abuse/neglect. However, it should be noted that abuse and abortion were probably two of the most hidden crimes in the period.

Prostitution is an age-old offense, but some authorities have pointed to newly enacted statutes as having "created" the female crime wave of the first part of the twentieth century, especially as reflected in the growth of federal prison populations (SchWeber, 1980). Some of these statutory changes seem to have had limited effects on the nature of the female jail population. As previously noted, few women were jailed for violations of the Mann Act. Only five females were admitted for violating the Dyer Act (1919), stealing a car. Most were teenagers obviously caught joy-riding. Violations of the Harrison Act of 1914 and subsequent narcotics statutes made up less than one percent (0.6%) of the total female admissions. Offenders ranged in age from 18 to 45, were all white, and listed housewife as their occupation. More than twice as many women than men were jailed for narcotics violations. In other words, the female addicts of McLean county probably fit the nationwide picture of a female-dominated addict population: mature, conservative, rural women addicted by physician prescription or through the use of narcotic-laden patent medicines (Courtwright, 1982; Cuskey, et al., 1972). These narcotics violators were turned over to federal agents. It is unclear, however, whether those men engineered the women's arrests or merely appeared to carry out their transfer to federal jurisdiction (Kinsella, 1933). There were no admissions, male or female, for narcotics offenses in this sample after 1928. In 1897 Illinois had become one of the first states to limit the non-prescription sale of narcotics. The state's pioneering efforts may have led to a relatively early drying out of its original addict population. And before mid-century, the jail did not have to deal with a drug-addicted population.

Probably the most interesting offense category is that of violations of the Volstead Act of 1920, which enacted national prohibition of the manufacture, sale, and transportation of liquor. Volstead Act violations accounted for 8.2 percent of the total female admissions, 1918-1945, despite the fact that Prohibition was repealed in 1933. Although this was predominantly a white, male offense, violations ranked fourth for females. Women had been involved in the illegal sale of untaxed liquor before the enaction of Prohibition. A number of violators had Southern states like Kentucky and Tennessee listed as their birthplaces; those women may have brought the moonshiner subculture with them to the North. Several women listed the rural McLean community of Chenoa as their birthplace or residence. That town may have been the rural manufacturing center for moonshine in the county, and it certainly had many of the county's most popular roadhouses on its outskirts. However, most admissions took place as the result of raids conducted from 1929 to 1931 in the cities of Bloomington and Normal. Then and in other years, raids centered around the holidays, Christmas Eve and New Year's Eve, when the level of patronage was at its height. Center Street in Bloomington apparently contained a number of brothels and/or speakeasies. The madams were arrested on prohibition charges and had to post bonds of $1,000 to $2,000 for each offense. Their "girls," though most were certainly older than that, were admitted as inmates of a disorderly house. Their fines were generally under twenty dollars each. Servants in the brothels, frequently black women, were admitted, then quickly released. These women, with their ready supplies of cash, did not spend long periods in jail despite the relative seriousness of their crimes. The speakeasies and roadhouses remained in business and provided ready targets for periodic police raids. Most of the other women admitted for Volstead Act violations were probably pedlars selling their own or others' liquor on a more informal, periodic basis "as a form of work relief" (Herbert, 1983: 337). When Prohibition ended, some of the women continued to produce liquor for family use and/or illegal sale, but their market largely disappeared.

Property-related offense (robbery, burglary, larceny, grand larceny, and fraud) together made up a low percentage (7.1%) of the female admissions, especially considering the fact that the Great Depression severely hurt agriculture, the county's chief industry. Prior to the economic downturn, women's work had been insecure and underpaid, and the Great Depression meant real hardships for working women. However, the number of female admissions for property offenses, with the possible exception of larceny, did not seem to rise with the onset or the continuation of the Depression. It appears that women were committing traditional or sex-role stereotyped property offenses. The economic plight of some women may have been a factor in the bulge in prostitution rates in the late 1920s and the high number of Prohibition admissions. The women were selling their bodies or liquor instead of stealing.

The male population was a somewhat more troubling population, because of its larger size and slightly more violent character. Males made up 91.5 percent of the total admissions to the jail during the interwar years. The male cases collected for this sample represent 9.3 percent of the total male cases; therefore, the male data are not as reflective of true patterns as the more complete female data, which included every female admission. Although the male admissions were more than nine times the females, it should be remembered that the jail was built to accommodate greater numbers of males; and issues of same-sex supervision in the institution and during transfer were much simpler.

Blacks made up 1.2 percent of the males in the 1940 Census, but 9.1 percent of the male admissions, a figure similar to that for black females. Fifty-one percent of the males were laborers or factory workers, while another 9.1 percent were skilled workers and 7.4 percent were independent males or less often merchants or professionals. Another 8.7 percent were farmers or farm workers. As expected, McLean County Jail admissions show the customary urban-rural differences. Males from outside the cities tended to be arrested at night and on the weekends for drunk and disorderly, gambling, Prohibition, and driving offenses. In other words, the revelers who came into the "big" city for fun and frolic often also got arrested.

Slightly more than half (55.2%) of the males were born in Illinois, and only 3.2 percent were born outside the country. The males probably represented a more mobile work force. Indeed some are recorded as working for the railroad or living on armed forces bases in nearby counties. One half (54.5%) lived in the Twin Cities, while another 14.2 percent lived in McLean county outside those cities. The crime "problem" was "home-grown."

The leading admission offense (23.7%) was drunk, drunk and disorderly, and disorderly conduct combined. Even with random sampling it is clear that the group included many chronic alcoholics who spent one night to two weeks in the jail sobering up. Sometimes the same individual was jailed more than once in a single week. These chronic drunks were a source of amusement and disgust for the jail officers, who realized along with most of the community that jail offered little to the alcoholic beyond a place to sleep it off (Deutscher, 1953; Brown, 1955; Price, 1946). The chronic drunks also meant a passive, somewhat consistent workforce to be used in jail maintenance.

Without other alternatives for housing alcoholic, older, unemployed males, the jail remained the catch-all institution for those arrested by the police. The second-ranked offense was violation of city ordinances (15.8%); "other" ranked fourth (6.6%); and suspicion was sixth (4.5%). Half of the male admissions then represented attempts, largely by city officers, to rid the streets of troublesome populations. Although males showed higher percentages of certain violent crimes (robbery—4.1%, ranked 7th; assault—2.8%; rape—0.5%; and murder—0.5%), they hardly threatened the fabric of society or the peace of the jail. Only eight rapists were admitted, but the conservative nature of the communities may have precluded the commission and certainly the reporting of such a crime. Gambling was 1.2 percent of the male admissions, yet it was non-existent among the female admissions. It is apparent that those males picked up in prostitution raids and in certain drinking cases were cited for gambling. When prostitution and Prohibition raids tapered off, so did the gambling arrests. Considering the lack of recreational facilities in the jail, the male inmates undoubtedly continued their games, with or without money bets, on the inside.

There were two other interesting groups in the male jail population. Prohibition arrests were 7.4 percent of the admissions for third place among male offenses. Although males probably dominated the manufacture and transportation of illegal liquor, most of these arrests were for lesser acts. It is in the area of Prohibition that recently enacted federal legislation had its only real impact on male admissions. The ninth-ranked admission offense for males was non-support (2.9%). Assuming that husbands/fathers have never been punished by the criminal justice system, feminists in recent years have argued for legal means to make the indigent or the unwilling support their families. Goldfarb (1976: 75) notes that non-support or contempt cases form large parts of urban jail populations today. But he also states, based on scattered studies, that rural jails had few, if any, such admissions. This is not true for McLean county. Current jail officials note that until the 1970s non-support cases made up one-third to one-half of the jail admissions at certain times in the conservative, family-oriented environment of McLean county. The jail reflected community standards.

For males, the jail was the primary and virtually the only form of institutionalization. About 3.5 percent of the males went to state mental facilities and the Lincoln State colony. Another 1.5 percent returned to institutions. More than women, men were sent to the state prisons (Pontiac, Joliet, and Menard, in that order) or Vandalia, housing younger males with shorter sentences (4.4%). About 6.9 percent left jail almost immediately having paid fines, while another 14.4 percent spent 8 to 14 days in the facility, two times the female percentage serving that length of sentence.

Male adolescents were admitted for delinquency, but their figure (0.8%) is far below that of young women. The difference represents pre-trial screening and the community's general willingness to see female delinquency as more dangerous despite the greater severity involved in male actions. Delinquent males in McLean county also had more alternatives for their safe housing than just the jail. A primary example of alternative housing was Victory Hall, established by several society matrons who hoped to curtail what they saw as a rising tide of delinquency. Certainly in the twentieth century the Illinois Soldiers' and Sailors' Home at Normal was taking more than orphans. And a Child Guidance Clinic sponsored by the Chicago-based Institute for Juvenile Research opened in 1927.

The male population of the jail was by far the larger, and its sheer size presented problems to jail administrators. But the more diverse, and in many ways the more troubling, female population may have presented even more problems as the jail tried to respond to roles placed on it by the local community, to its position in local and state institutional networks, and to changes in the law, even at the federal level. During the inter-war years the McLean county jail seems to have responded reasonably well, even if perfunctorily, to the demands which these roles placed on the institution. It is clear, however, that by the end of World War II, the McLean county jail was facing problems that would continue to plague its operation. The jail population was so heterogenous and changable as to make the longterm planning or innovative programs virtually impossible and the provision of basic services difficult. The relative success that the McLean county jail had in carrying out its functions may lie, not in the administrative acumen of the sheriffs, but in the relationship between the county and the institution. In other words, jail may be an impractical institution for more populous areas such as Chicago's Cook county whose jail population outnumbers the total incarcerated population of some states. Other counties that are smaller and more rural than McLean, such as nearby Livingston, may not have the interest, the money, or the "crime problem" to justify a county jail which meets even minimal standards. Indeed, the current Livingston county jail was built in 1839 and has survived numerous adverse evaluations. By contrast, McLean county has a large enough population, tax base, and interest in local crime control to support a jail. At the same time, its low crime rate and political stability make the management of the jail possible, if not necessarily without problems.

Our knowledge of jails, past and present, is so limited that we tend to make sweeping generalizations or to attach blame indiscriminately. No single jail nor set of problems is completely like any other. With additional studies of differing institutions over time we can better understand what longstanding pressures face all jails, how some jails differ in both their problems and their solutions, and how some jails have achieved relative success in meeting or avoiding certain problems. By recognizing the individual nature of jails and the longevity, yet complexity, of certain problems we can take the first step understanding the issues facing today's local institutions.

REFERENCES

Brown, P.R. "The Problem Drinker and the Jail." *Quarterly Journal of Studies on Alcohol* 16 (September 1955): 474-83.

Cahalan, M. "Trends in Incarceration in the United States Since 1880: A Summary of Reported Rates and the Distribution of Offenses." *Crime and Delinquency* 25 (January 1979): 9-41.

Connolly, J.E. "Women in County Jails: An Invisible Gender in an Ill-Defined Institution." *The Prison Journal* 63, 2 (1983): 99-115.

Courtwright, D.T. *Dark Paradise: Opiate Addiction in America Before 1940.* Cambridge, MA: Harvard University Press, 1982.

Cuskey, W.R., Premkumar, T., and Sigerl, L. "Survey of Opiate Addiction Among Females in the United States between 1850 and 1970." *Public Health Reviews* 8 (1972): 8-39.

Deutscher, I. "The White Petty Offender in the Small City." *Social Problems* 1,2 (October 1953): 70-73.

Fox, R.W. *So Far Disordered in Mind: Insanity in California, 1870-1930.* Berkeley, CA: University of California Press, 1978.

Goldfarb, R. *Jails: The Ultimate Ghetto of the Criminal Justice System.* New York, NY: Doubleday Press, 1975.

Handberg, R. "Jails and Correctional Farms: The Neglected Half of Rural Law Enforcement." *Journal of Correctional Education* 32 (1982): 20-23.

Herbert, J.R. "An Oral History of the Prohibition Era, Indiana County, Pennsylvania" *Western Pennsylvania Historical Magazine* 66, 4 (1983): 335-46.

Hinrichsen, A. "The New Jail and Almhouse Laws." *Blue Book of the State of Illinois,* 1917-18.

Irwin, J. *The Jail: Managing the Underclass in American Society.* Berkeley, CA: University of California Press, 1985.

Kinsella, N. "County Jails and the Federal Government." *Journal of the American Institute of Criminal Law and Criminology* 23 (July-August 1933): 428-39.

Mattick, H.W. "The Contemporary Jails of the United States: An Unknown and Neglected Area of Justice, in Glaser, D. (ed.). *Handbook of Criminology.* Chicago, IL: Rand McNally, 1974.

Monkkonen, E.H. "A Disorderly People? Urban Order in the Nineteenth and Twentieth Centuries." *Journal of American History* 68, 3 (December 1981): 539-59.

Moynahan, J.M. and Stewart, E.K. *The American Jail: Its Development and Growth.* Chicago, IL: Nelson-Hall, 1980.

Pogrebin, M. "Scarce Resources and Jail Management." *International Journal of Offender Therapy and Comparative Criminology* 26 (1982): 263-74.

Price, C.F. "The Jail's Responsibility Toward the Chronic Alcoholic." In *Proceedings of the 76th Annual Congress of Corrections of the American Prison Association.* New York, NY: American Prison Association, 1946.

Richmond, M.S. "The Jail Blight." *Crime and Delinquency.* 11,2 (April 1965): 132-41.

Robinson, L.N. "The Perennial Jail Problem." *Journal of Criminal Law and Criminology* 35,6 (March-April 1945): 369-74.

Rothman, D.J. *Conscience and Convenience: The Asylum and Its Alternatives in Progressive America.* Boston, MA: Little, Brown, 1980.

Scheff, T.J. "Social Conditions for Rationality: How Urban and Rural Courts Deal with the Mentally Ill." *American Behavioral Scientist* 7 (March 1964): 21-24.

Schlossman, S. and Wallach, S. "The Crime of Precocious Sexuality: Female Juvenile Delinquency in the Progressive Era." *Harvard Educational Review* 48,1 (1978): 65-94.

SchWeber, C. "Pioneers in Prison — Inmates and Administrators at Alderson, the Federal Reformatory for Women: 1925-39, The Founding Years." *Federal Probation* 44 (1980): 30-36.

Steffensmeier, D.J. "Crime and the Contemporary Woman: An Analysis of Changing Levels of Female Property Crime, 1960-75." *Social Forces* 57 (1978): 566-84.

U.S. Department of Commerce, Bureau of the Census. *County and City Jails: Prisoners in Jails and Other Penal Institutions under County or Municipal Jurisdiction*, 1933.

———— *Fifteenth Annual Census of the United States, 1930, Population.*

———— *Sixteenth Annual Census of the United States, 1940, Population*, Vol. 2.

U.S. Department of Justice. "Profile of Jail Inmates: Sociodemographic Findings from 1978 Survey of Inmates of Local Jails." Washington, DC: U.S. Government Printing Office, 1980.

———— "Jail Inmates, 1982." Washington, DC: Bureau of Justice Statistics Bulletin, February, 1983.

Walker, S.E. *Popular Justice: A History of American Criminal Justice*. New York, NY: Oxford University Press, 1982.

Wayson, B., Funke, G., Familson, S., and Meyer, P. *Local Jails*. Lexington, MA: Lexington Books, 1977.

CHAPTER 2

JAILS VERSUS PRISONS

Comparisons, Problems and Prescriptions
on Inmate Subcultures

Stan Stojkovic

PAST RESEARCH on the organization of the prison has focused on the relationship between the inmate social system and prison stability. Beginning with Clemmer's (1940) formulation of the "prisonization" hypothesis, researchers interested in the origins of the inmate social system have focused on the relationship between the prisoner social world and internal control to the prison organization. As a result, much literature has addressed the subcultural elements of the inmate social system and their influence on the direction of the prison organization. Sykes (1958), for example, discusses the solidarity of the "inmate code," and in addition, how the "pains of imprisonment" are mollified by a visible and somewhat cohesive inmate organization.

What has not been thoroughly examined, however, is how these subcultural elements are instrumental to jail administration. More importantly, there has been very little research developed to examine if a jail subculture exists, and what, if any, role it plays in the administration of the jail facility. While there has been voluminous research conducted with prison settings around this theme (Sykes, 1958; Sykes and Messinger, 1960; Irwin, 1970; Jacobs, 1977; Irwin, 1980), very little has been done to investigate the nature of jail subcultures, along with their many complexities and diversities. Thus, much of our knowledge is limited at best and detrimental to any sufficient understanding of the jail as a series of complex interactions among many actors (Rottman and Kimberly, 1975).

If the prisoner subculture of the jail is crucial to our collective understanding of the environment of jail, it is essential that more data be gathered on how the socialization of jail inmates influences jail operations. Past prison research, for example, has examined how "institutional careers" are developed within prison structures (Wheeler, 1961), the subcultural roles within the prison environment (Garabedian, 1963; Bartollas, 1982), and how disparate goal structures within differing prison organizations engender a differential attachment to an inmate social structure (Berk, 1966; Street, Vinter and Perrow, 1966; Akers, Hayner and Gruninger, 1977). Even more recently, research has discovered how subcultural elements with the prison setting influence, in a direct fashion, the operation of the organization. Such items as violence (Bowker, 1977), adaptation to stress (Toch and Johnson, 1982), contraband markets (Kalinich and Stojkovic, 1985), sexual relations (Wooden and Parker, 1982), race relations (Carroll, 1974, 1982), and power relations (Stojkovic, 1984), are all relevant qualities to a prisoner social system. As a result, it is imperative that these subcultural themes be examined within the context of the jail, and more importantly, how they may influence the management of the jail deserves attention by those interested in jail administration.

Thus, the purpose of this paper will be threefold: First, to describe the relevant aspects of the prison setting and how they are relevant to an understanding of jail structures. Second, to explore what is currently known about the subcultural context of the jail, and how our current understanding of jails is limited in comparison to traditional prison structures. Finally, to provide some prescriptions for future research in jail settings.

Prison Subcultural Context

Past research into the social organization of the prison has examined a number of topics which influences the direction and purpose of the prison structure. For our purposes here, we can identify five basic subcultural themes which are relevant to an understanding of the inmate social system and their affect on the prison setting.[1] They are violence and stress, contraband, sexual relations, race relations, and power relations. We begin our discussion with prison violence and the adaptive strategies among prisoners when dealing with institutional stress.

Violence

Bowker (1979) has described the concept of violence inside prison facilities, employing a model of victimization as a way of understanding prison violence. According to Bowker, victimization can include four general types: physical, psychological, economic, and social. Concomitantly, he suggests that there are a number of factors associated with victimization in the prison environment: inadequate supervision, architectural designs which promote victimization, easy availability of deadly weapons, the housing of violence-prone prisoners with weaker victims, and a generally high level of tension produced by close living quarters (Bowker, 1982). In addition, it is his belief that a number of intervention strategies can be implemented to reduce violence in prison, along with guaranteeing greater security to the environment.

With respect to jail violence, it seems we know very little, and as a result, we are not able to formulate a rational policy to deal with the situation. According to the Bureau of Justice Statistics (1984), the principle cause of death among jail inmates is suicides, with natural causes ranking second, and injury to a prisoner by another prisoner being third. While death by violence among inmates is rare in jails (1 in every 50 fatalities), we know very little about the specific factors which may cause violence in our jails. Moreover, many policy prescriptions are not based on any empirical evidence indicating causes, either attitudinal or structural, which create conditions for violence. Additionally, it is not clear whether or not violence is related to the subcultural context of the jail, and whether jail violence is institutional specific or imported into the jail by individual offenders. Consequently, we not only have very little information about the jail subculture, but in addition, we know nothing about its correlates to an identifiable social system within the jail.

Related to this issue is how jail prisoners cope with the stressful environment of jail, where violence may be imminent. Gibbs (1982) suggests that jail environments can be structured to be less stressful places for many prisoners, and what is essential is that more research be conducted to differentiate the environments of jails and how jail inmates cope with the stressful conditions of facilities. Relying on the early work of Toch (1977), Gibbs suggests that not only can jail environments be differentiated, but in addition, it may be more relevant to examine "subenvironments" or "niches" within the inmate social system that provide "ameliorative qualities" to those prisoners experiencing stressful conditions within the prison. This same perspective is relevant to our knowledge of the jail subculture; however, at present, this knowledge is not available, and it would seem imperative that this information be created for proper administration and management of the jail.

Contraband

Much of the research on socialization in prison suggests that illegal markets are an essential component of the prisoner social system. Williams and Fish (1974) have argued that the prisoner sub rosa economic system is of extreme relevance to a majority of prisoners, and a component of the inmate social hierarchy, which many prisoners identify with. As a result, the delivery of goods and services by prominent inmate leaders provides many prisoners with the ability to cope with the pains of imprisonment, while simultaneously relieving the tension and stress produced by a potentially volatile environment. Moreover, as suggested by Irwin (1980), the prison contraband system provides often hostile inmate gangs or groups a stage upon which interaction is controlled. In other words, the illegal market structure of the prison engenders a system of rules and regulations, all at the informal level, that maintains peace between often conflicting inmate bodies.

This position is further developed by Kalinich and Stojkovic (1985) in their discussion of legitimate power and prisoner economics. According to their position, not only are informal rules and regulations among prisoners reinforced through the contraband market structure, but more importantly, the influencial leaders of such a system are viewed as legitimate by a majority of prisoners, enabling pivotal distributors of goods and services power to stabilize the prisoner social system. Consequently, prisoner economics are much more than the provision of products within the inmate social arena—they are a crucial element toward long-term stability within that environment. In turn, prison administrators are required to monitor the market structure of the sub rosa system to ensure long-term prison order. Moreover, sudden alterations in this market place, such as an increase in supply of goods and services, would produce deleterious effects in the prisoner social system (Stojkovic and Kalinich, 1986). Hence, prison control, in part, is influenced by the subcultural context of the prisoner economic structure.

As with the element of violence, this area of illegal economic systems in jail facilities has been virtually neglected by researchers. While Irwin (1985) has done some excellent work in describing the composition of the contemporary jail, not much is devoted to the idea of production of goods and services in the jail, and more importantly, the relationship between prisoner economics and jail stability. In fact, what is known is that illegal market structures do exist in many jail facilities, but very little is known about the diversity of goods and services in these institutions and their relative price structure. Kalinich (1986) has examined these important questions with respect to prison systems, yet this is not evidenced in the literature on jails. If jail subcultures are relevant to jail administration, and sub rosa economic systems are an important component of jail subcultures, a more detailed knowledge base on this area is required. Presently, we know very little which would guide rational policy development in this area.

Sexual Relations

Much of the contemporary prison literature has examined the nature of sexual relations behind bars, particularly the violent nature of these relationships (Lockwood, 1980). As a result, this literature has focused on the nature of sexual violence (Bowker, 1982; Parisi, 1982), its form and expression (McGrath, 1982; Nacci and Kane, 1982; McNamara and Karmen, 1983), and the myths of prison sex (Lockwood, 1983). Additionally, current research has developed models or typifications of prison sexual roles.

Wooden and Parker (1982), for example, distinguish the various "sexual scripts" within a prison community. Based on their research, they identify four predominant patterns of sexual behavior in prison: the **kid** or **punk** who has been "turned out" or forced into a sexual encounter, a **jocker** or **stud** who has sex with homosexuals or punks and typically assumes a masculine role in the relationship, the **queen** or **sissy** who adopts effeminate mannerisms and plays predominantly the submissive sexual role, and the **homosexual** or **gay** who exhibits diverse sexual scripts while assuming both active and passive roles in the various sexual encounters. Furthermore, much research has also identified the characteristics associated with both the offender and the victim (Lockwood, 1980; Bartollas and Sieverdes, 1983).

As is evidenced, there is much literature describing the nature, type, and expression of sexual relations in the prison environment. Such is not the case in jail facilities. The delineation of forms and types of sexual activities among jail prisoners would enhance the jail administrator's ability to cope with the problems surrounding sexual encounters among prisoners. It is a very common occurrence inside jails to hear about sexual assaults, but the relevant question becomes what can be done to segregate those prisoners who are sexually aggressive from the general population. We, at present, cannot even identify them, let alone understand that behavior within the context of a prison social system. Further, the multiple sexual roles exhibited within jail structures may be helpful to jail administrators for control purposes. Many prison administrators, for example, identify the various forms of sexual scripts within their institutions and segregate those that cause violence among inmates. It is common to hear within institutions how prisoners may fight over the ownership of a known homosexual. On many occasions, disturbances arise among inmates over questions as to who has exclusive rights over a particular "sissy" or "punk." Thus, prison officials are required to take administrative action which diminishes the possibility of violence among prisoners.

Some prison administrators, in fact, have suggested that the various sexual scripts among prisoners need to be proportioned throughout the prison environment for stability reasons, particularly known homosexuals who can provide multiple services to a wide variety of prisoners.[2] In this way, the violence attributed to sexual behaviors in prison may be reduced, at least kept to a minimum if the sexual scripts were divided equally among the prisoner body. These suggestions are tentative at best, and future research in both jails and prisons would want to examine the plausibility of this position. Nevertheless, what is essential in future research is how sexual behavior is expressed in the jail environment, and the implications of these findings for jail policy development and the long-term management of these types of correctional settings.

Race Relations

Researchers of the modern prison have become aware of the effect race relations has on the environment of prison (Jacobs, 1977; Carroll, 1982). A consensus among this research has been that race relations is a significant factor to understand the existing climate of today's prisons (Carroll, 1982). Carroll (1974), in his seminal piece **Hacks, Blacks, and Cons**, explores the relationship between race relations and prison control. Jacobs (1977) describes the influx of racially oriented gangs in the social structure of the Stateville penitentiary and how this racial perspective altered the organization of the prison. Additionally, Irwin (1980) discusses the evolution of a social reality within our prisons among incarcerated blacks, fostering a new identity and increased violence: "As black prisoners developed their new identities, experienced new levels of rage, and steadily asserted themselves more and more in the prison public life, racial hostilities and eventually racial violence increased" (p. 72).

Thus, race relations is an important aspect to understanding the contemporary prison social system and prison control. While Irwin (1985) suggests that the modern jail has as its primary objective the management of society's underclass, very little is available to examine who composes this category of offenders, and what role underclass values of many prisoners are a representation of beliefs, attitudes, and values imported from the city streets. Furthermore, the relevancy of these values in the development of a jail culture is not known at all. Consequently, we are not sure of the importance of race with reference to the development of the jail subculture, even though we do know that roughly 58 percent of all jail inmates are white, with 40 percent being black and 2 percent persons of other races (Bureau of Justice Statistics, 1983). With respect to how race may be crucial to prison control, we do have some research evidence from prison settings.

Spencer (1977) has shown the tenuous relationship between custodial staff and inmates in terms of prison control, and moreover, the development of inter-racial hostility as a control mechanism by correctional administrators. This issue deserves attention in the jail subculture research literature. Finally, we need a deeper understanding as to the role race plays in the division of the jail subculture and what management strategies would be productive in promoting more peace, order, control and security in the jail environment.

Power Relations

Past literature on prison organizations has suggested that prison society and control in prison were largely dependent upon the symbiotic relationships between prisoner and guard (Sykes, 1985; Sykes and Messinger, 1960; Cloward, 1960). In fact, traditional organizational theory literature suggests that prisons employ coercive power to effectuate order goals (Etzioni, 1961). In addition, much of the traditional prison literature on power has concluded that it operates in a coercive fashion and often produces identifiable divisions in the roles assumed by administrators, officers, and inmates.

Current prison literature, however, suggests that the power relations within today's prisons have changed over the years. Some have suggested that the modern prison is influenced by the interests of multiple interest groups, e.g., prisoners, courts, legislatures, mass media (Stastny and Tyrnauer, 1982), segregated by the interests of many inmate groups, whereby a "pluralistic prisoner community" exists in the prison setting (Fox, 1982), diversified and more problematic to control because of an infusion of racially motivated "gangs" or "cliques" (Jacobs, 1977), and stabilized by administrative officials through a maintenance of balance among the various prison groups and their competing demands (Berkman, 1979; Carroll, 1982).

More current research suggests that disparate forms of power exist among the competing prisoner groups, and that prison equilibrium is largely determined through the interaction of types of power among the differing interests groups within the prison structure, e.g., prisoners, officers, and administrators. Stojkovic (1984, 1985, 1986) has described the various forms of power among prisoners, officers, and administrators, arguing that each group relies on different forms of power to accomplish its own objectives. Relying on a typology of power developed by French and Raven (1968), Stojkovic argues, with respect to prisoners, that five basic forms of power exist in the prison social system: coercive, referent, providing of resources, expert, and legitimate. Moreover, Stojkovic suggests that the providing of resources type of power is the most influential in the prisoner social world, enabling key inmates much influence if they are able to acquire, market, and distribute scarce products in the prison environment. This form of power, therefore, is crucial to an understanding of the prison subculture.

More importantly, how the various forms of power interact with competing types of power among officers and administrators is what determines prison stability. As a result, an understanding of the types of power among competing groups within the prison and their dispersion throughout the prison social environment is crucial to prison management and administration. This position is just as relevant to jail administration as prison administration. Nevertheless, there is a dearth of material in this particularly important area. As suggested by Irwin (1985), what is produced in many jails is an overt process of "degradation" for many jail prisoners. What becomes significant is that the jail obtain what it requires from prisoners in a clear and efficient manner, usually relying on coercive power to effectuate its own goals. Irwin (1985) states:

> What is needed and wanted in a jail are prisoners who will wait obediently wherever they are placed (in a cell, on a bench, or against a wall), who will make no demands (or few), and who will willingly perform the few required jail procedures, such as returning to their cells, standing for a count, coming to the front when called (for a visit, release, bail, or transfer), and following the procedures required when

being delivered to court. Generally, the method used to convert free adults into this compliant and passive state is to give commands — either short and polite orders or shouted threats — and to back them up by applying whatever force is required to immobilize a person (p. 69).

While coercion is at the base of every correctional institution's compliance structure, it is not clear if the other forms of power discussed with respect to prison settings are applicable to jail facilities, and if an identifiable subculture, whatever its origin, does not facilitate the development of other types of power to deal with the various situational aspects many jail inmates experience. It may be (this will be addressed later with respect to all the subcultural themes mentioned) that the transient nature of the jail population precludes development of an identifiable subculture within the context of the jail. This remains to be investigated by future jail research, as it is not possible to conclude whether or not time is a crucial variable to an understanding of both jail subcultures and the dispersion of social power within the contextual environment of the jail among disparate groups.

Jail Subcultural Contexts

As is evidenced in the above sections, there is definitely much literature focusing on the prison subculture and its relationship to the dynamic operation of the prison. Additionally, it is apparent that such material is scant at best and limited in the jail literature. The relevant question, therefore, is what do we know and how can we enhance the existing body of knowledge on jail subcultures to understand the vicissitudes of the jail setting, along with proper management and administrative techniques to provide a more secure, safe, and humane jail environment. First, much of the information we have on jails is demographic in nature, such as race, sex, population growth, percent of juveniles in jails, and size of jails. Very little information is available with respect to how these demographic characteristics shape the social system of the jail. In short, there has been very little integration of what we do know about jail populations and how they influence the operation of the jail.

Second, we do know, in spite of the above statements, that the jail population is divided between convicted and unconvicted, housed in larger jails which are above occupancy standards, and very expensive to control, with the cost of jail operations reaching the two billion dollar mark for the fiscal year 1983 (Bureau of Justice Statistics, 1984). Beyond this, we know very little on the prevalence of a social system behind jail bars and its origins. While our knowledge in these areas is limited, we do have data on issues that have always plagued jail administrators. Overcrowding, for example, is still a perennial problem for many jails. Accordingly, the Bureau of Justice Statistics (1984) reported that almost one in every five jails (17%) had inmates backed up because of overcrowding elsewhere in their respective systems. While this has been an ubiquitous problem for jails, it is more positive in the area of inmate deaths. Recent research suggests that jail deaths decreased 9 percent for the fiscal year 1983 as compared to data compiled in 1978 (Bureau of Justice Statistics, 1984).

As discussed earlier, suicide remained the principle cause of death, with natural causes and fatalities ranking second and third, respectively. Yet, beyond this information, we, surprisingly, know very little about the interactions of the people we confine in our jails. Some research is being developed in this area, however. Garofalo and Clark (1985) have begun preliminary research which suggests that if a subculture does exist in jail, and this may be questionable, it seems that positive orientations toward inmate subcultural norms in jail settings are mostly attributable to experienced inmates who are familiar with the social expectations of the jail subculture and who "readapt" after determining they will be in jail for a period of time. In addition, the authors argue that time as a variable is crucial to an understanding of the jail subculture, since many prisoners turnover with such rapidity that it is difficult for an identifiable subculture to develop, unless the subculture is imported into the setting by "carriers" who have experienced jail during earlier periods of incarceration. Thus, a possible interpretation of the origin of the jail subculture may closely align with the importation model of subcultural systems in the prison literature. At present, this conclusion is tentative at best.

Future research in the subcultural context of jail settings would have to compare facilities where sentence length is short for many prisoners with jails that incarcerate for longer periods of time. It may be hypothesized that the subcultural elements discussed earlier in this paper with respect to prison social systems are largely contingent upon the variability of sentences among incarcerated prisoners. We would expect, as a result, that longer time among prisoners produces more of the subcultural themes identified earlier and clearer normative rules and regulations among prisoners. This, too, is only speculative and it deserves attention by future researchers.

Finally, we can deduce that since our understanding of jail subcultures is circumscribed, management techniques of jail administrators, are, for the most part, antiquated and not suitable for contemporary jail operations. Despite poor conditions and out-dated jail facilities, jail managers need to be sensitive to the demands of a subculture within their facilities. Moreover, this area of jail management requires more attention on the part of not only the immediate administrators of the local jail, but include the sheriff, usually the individual in charge of the jail in a formal sense, and community leaders who devise budgets for the jail. If, as we described earlier, the jail houses more long-term, sentenced prisoners, and in addition, is forced to accept more prisoners from overcrowded state institutions, then administrators are going to have to respond with management strategies that are cognizant of and sensitive to the demands of jail subcultures. If, however, sentenced prisoners to the jail are occupying space for shorter periods of time, the subcultural themes may be moot in the context of the jail. However, it would seem that the former interpretation is more probable rather than the latter, since invariably an overcrowded state system has always relied on local facilities to handle its overflow of offenders. The role of proper management techniques, therefore, is crucial to effective jail administration when confronting more certain and stabilized prisoner populations.

Recommendations for Future Jail Research

A theme which has directed this essay has been the dearth of research literature on jail subcultures. The purpose of this concluding section is to provide some suggestions for future research in jail environments, specifically the types of investigation required for a more complete understanding of jail subcultures. It is hoped that these suggestions will spur researchers interested in correctional organizations to pursue the jail as a domain which will enlighten us about the influence jail subcultures have in the management and administration of these types of correctional settings.

Accordingly, Garofalo and Clark (1985) suggest that the subcultural context of jail requires investigation into the qualities of the environment and how it influences normative rule development among jailed prisoners. We can, thus, suggest a number of themes endemic to prisoner subcultures that are relevant to an understanding of jail subcultures and deserve attention by future researchers interested in the jail.

First, all of the subcultural elements discussed earlier—violence and stress adaptation, sexual relations, race relations, contraband markets, and power relations—require thorough investigation. There has been

virtually no research done in any of these areas with respect to jail subcultures, and it is essential this information is gathered and analyzed, for
without this data, management and control of more serious, long-term,
and problematic prisoners in the jail setting will be difficult to say the
least. At present, this lack of information is hampering our ability to run
an efficient and effective jail.

Second, future research should focus more specifically on the origins
of the prisoner subculture. As was examined earlier, there are major theoretical models which prison research has developed with reference to
subcultural development among prisoners. This same type of research is
needed to direct future jail administration, particularly if the subcultural
context of the jail is largely contingent upon the functional characteristics of the jail. If so, it may be possible to identify those structural qualities which influence origination of prisoner subcultural systems in the
jail and to modify them toward the goals and/or direction of the jail organization. Currently, this is problematic with respect to prison subcultures, yet the knowledge base is evident and prescriptions can be formulated. We cannot say the same for jail organizations.

Third, the language and roles employed among prisoners within the
context of the jail deserve attention by future researchers. Sykes (1985)
was the first to coin the nature of "argot roles" behind prison bars and
their relevance to an understanding of prison societies. A similar approach needs to be adopted in our investigation of the jail subculture.
Additionally, the level of attachment to these roles over time should be of
interest to jail researchers, and more importantly, to those who administer and manage the jail. Role diversity, differentiation, and stratification
are crucial elements to any society, and there is every reason to believe
that jails do not differ in this regard.

Finally, jail research requires more comparative examinations of facilities of differing size and structure. As described earlier, our understanding of jail demographics is extensive; nevertheless, we have no
integration of this data into a comprehensive theory of socialization
among jail prisoners. Large jails, for example, may have stronger indicators of subcultural developments within the inmate body when compared to smaller facilities, e.g., violence, contraband, race relations. If
this is the case, proper management strategies are essential to cope with
a more diverse prisoner population. Presently, this is not possible with
our limited base of knowledge about inmate socialization behind jail
bars. As suggested by Garofalo and Clark (1985), an important contribution that jail subcultural research can make to the extant literature on

prisoner socialization is that in most of the cases jail prisoners graduate into prison inmates. Thus, the knowledge learned from the jail experience can be expected to have effects on adaptations to prison. We concur but would like to suggest one other contribution of jail subcultural research: a knowledge base upon which rational policy development can be pursued in the context of the jail and can be of benefit to all those concerned with making jails more efficient and effective, items which currently elude contemporary jail administrators.

NOTE

[1]These "themes" were chosen because of the voluminous amount of research which has been conducted in these areas. Obviously, others could be included; for example, inmate-staff relations are crucial to an understanding of prisoner social systems. It was felt, however, that these five elements were more widely accepted and represented in the current research literature.

[2]See Stojkovic, Stan, "Homosexuality in a Prison Community." Paper presented at the *Academy of Criminal Justice Sciences Meeting*, Las Vegas, Nevada, March, 1985, for a further discussion of this topic.

REFERENCES

Akers, R.L., Hayner, N.S., and Gruninger, W. (1977). "Prisonization in Five Countries: Type of Prison and Inmate Characteristics. *Criminology*, 14, 527-554.

Bartollas, C. (1982). "Survival Problems of Adolescent Prisoners." In R. Johnson and H. Toch (Eds.), *The Pains of Imprisonment* (pp. 165-179). Beverly Hills, CA: Sage.

Bartollas, C. and C.M. Sieverdes (1983). "Sexual Victim in a Coeducational Juvenile Correctional Institution." *Prison Journal*, V. 63, No. 1., (Spring/Summer: 80:90).

Berk, B.B. (1966). "Organizational Goals and Inmate Organization." *American Journal of Sociology*, 71, 522-534.

Berkman, R. (1979). *Opening the Gates: The Rise of the Prisoners Movement*. Lexington, Massachusetts: D.C. Heath.

Bowker, L.H. (1977). *Prisoner Subcultures*. Lexington, Massachusetts: Lexington Books.

Bowker, L.H. (1979). "Victimization in Correctional Institutions: An Interdisciplinary Analysis." In J.A. Conley (Ed.) *Theory and Research in Criminal Justice: Current Perspectives*. Cincinnati: Anderson, 1979.

Bowker, L.H. (1982). "Victimizers and Victims in American Correctional Institutions." In R. Johnson and H. Toch (Eds.) *The Pains of Imprisonment*. Beverly Hills: Sage.

Bureau of Justice Statistics Bulletin (1983). "Jail Inmates 1983." Washington, D.C.: National Bureau of Justice Statistics.

Bureau of Justice Statistics Bulletin (1984). "The 1983 Jail Census." Washington, D.C.: National Bureau of Justice Statistics.

Carroll, L. (1974). *Hacks, Blacks, and Cons*. Lexington, Massachusetts: D.C. Heath.

Carroll, L. (1982). "Race, Ethnicity, and the Social Order of the Prison." In R. Johnson and H. Toch (Eds.) *The Pains of Imprisonment*. Beverly Hills: Sage.

Clemmer, D. (1940). *The Prison Community*. New York: Holt, Rinehart and Winston.

Cloward, R. (1960). "Social Control in Prison." In Lawrence Hazelrigg, (Ed.) *Prison Within Society*. New York: Doubleday.

Etzioni, A. (1961). *A Comparative Analysis of Complex Organizations*. New York: Free Press.

Fox, J. (1982). *Organizational and Racial Conflict in Maximum-Security Prisons*. Lexington, Massachusetts: D.C. Heath.

French, J. and B. Raven (1968). "The Bases of Social Power." In Cartwright and Alvin (Eds.) *Group Dynamics*. (3rd ed.). New York: Harper and Row.

Garabedian, P. (1963). "Social Roles and Processes of Socialization in the Prison Community." *Social Problems*, 11, 139-152.

Garofalo, J. and R. Clark (1985). "The Inmate Subculture in Jails." *Criminal Justice and Behavior*, Vol. 12, No. 4, December: 415-434.

Gibbs, J.J. (1982). "The First Cut is the Deepest: Psychological Breakdown and Survival in the Detention Setting." In R. Johnson and H. Toch (Eds.), *The Pains of Imprisonment*, 97-114: Beverly Hills: Sage.

Irwin, J. (1970). *The Felon*. Englewood Cliffs, NJ: Prentice-Hall.

Irwin, J. (1980). *Prisons in Turmoil*. Boston: Little, Brown.

Irwin, J. (1985). *The Jail: Managing the Underclass in American Society*. Berkeley: University of California Press.

Jacobs, J. (1977). *Stateville: The Penitentiary in Mass Society*. Chicago: University of Chicago Press.

Kalinich, D. and S. Stojkovic (1985). "Contraband: The Basis for Legitimate Power in a Prison Social System." *Criminal Justice and Behavior*, Vol. 12, No. 4, pp. 435-451.

Kalinich, D. (1986). *Power, Stability, and Contraband: The Inmate Economy*. Prospect Heights, Illinois: Waveland Press.

Lockwood, D. (1980). *Prison Sexual Violence*. New York: Elsevier.

Lockwood, D. (1983). "Issues in Prison Sexual Violence." *Prison Journal*, Vol. 63, No. 1, (Spring/Summer: 73-79).

McGrath, G.M. (1982). "Prison Society and Offense Stigma—Some Doubts." *Australian and New Zealand Journal of Criminology*, Vol. 15, No. 4, (December: 235:244).

McNamara, D.E.J. and A. Karmen (1983). *Deviants—Victims or Victimizers?* (Eds.), Beverly Hills: Sage.

Nacci, P.L. and T.R. Kane (1982). *Sex and Sexual Aggression in Federal Prisons*. Washington, D.C.: U.S. Department of Justice Federal Prison System.

Parisi, N. (1982). *Coping With Imprisonment*. Beverly Hills: Sage.

Rottman, D.B. and J.R. Kimberly (1975). "The Social Context of Prisons." *Sociology and Social Research*, 59, pp. 344-361.

Spencer, E.J. (1977). *Social System of a Medium-Security Women's Prison*. Unpublished Ph.D. Dissertation, University of Kansas.

Stastny, C. and G. Tyrnauer (1982). *Who Rules the Joint: The Changing Political Culture of Maximum-Security Prisons in America.* Lexington, Massachusetts: D.C. Heath and Company.

Stojkovic, S. (1984). "Social Bases of Power and Control Mechanisms Among Prisoners in a Prison Organization." *Justice Quarterly*, Vol. 1, No. 4, December: 511-528.

Stojkovic, S. (1986). "Social Bases of Power and Control Mechanisms Among Administrators in a Prison Organization." *Journal of Criminal Justice*, Vol. 14, No. 2.

Stojkovic, S. (1986). "An Examination of Correctional Officer Power and Compliance Structures." *Justice Quarterly*. (Forthcoming).

Stojkovic, S. and D. Kalinich (1986). "Prison Contraband Systems: Implications for Prison Management." *Journal of Crime and Justice*. (Forthcoming).

Street, D., R.D. Vinter and C. Perrow (1966). *Organizations for Treatment.* New York: Free Press.

Sykes, G. (1958). *The Society of Captives: A Study of a Maximum-Security Prison.* Princeton, NJ: Princeton University Press.

Sykes, G. and S.L. Messinger (1960). "The Inmate Social System." In R.A. Cloward et al. (Eds.) *Theoretical Studies in Social Organization of the Prison.* New York, NY: Social Science Research Council, pp. 5-19.

Toch, H. (1977). *Living in Prison.* New York: Free Press.

Toch, H. and R. Johnson (1982). *The Pains of Imprisonment.* Beverly Hills: Sage.

Wheeler, S. (1961). "Socialization in Correctional Communities." *American Sociological Review*, 26, pp. 697-706.

Williams, V. and M. Fish (1974). *Convicts, Codes and Contraband.* Cambridge: Ballinger.

Wooden, W.S. and J. Parker (1982). *Men Behind Bars: Sexual Exploitation in Prison.* New York: Plenum.

CHAPTER 3

WORKING IN JAIL

Some Observations on the Work Relations of Jailers[1]

Robert M. Regoli,
Eric D. Poole, and
Mark R. Pogrebin

ABSTRACT

In this article we shed light on how jail guards view their role with special attention being given to their relations with inmates, administrators, and fellow officers. Data for the project were derived from sixty (60) interviews with jailers who represented four custodial institutions. Our findings are numerous. Most noteworthy, however, is, for jail guards many institutional changes have been disastrous. They have become frustrated and demoralized by the apparent futility of their efforts.

JAILS ARE peculiar institutions. Most Americans are unaware of their deteriorating conditions and confuse them with prisons. Perhaps this is because there are so few reports on jails, a dozen or so, while there are hundreds of studies on prisons (Irwin, 1985). It is ironic that so little has been published on jails, because the jail, ". . . not the prison, imposes the cruelest form of punishment in the United States" (Irwin, 1985:xi). One of the most penetrating accounts of U.S. jails has been offered by Richard Verde, a former director of the Law Enforcement Assistance Administration:

> Jails are festering sores in the criminal justice system. The result is
> what you would expect, only worse. Jails are, without question, brutal,
> filthy cesspools of crime — institutions which serve to brutalize and em-
> bitter men, to prevent them from returning to a useful role in society
> (Allen and Simonsen, 1985:405).

More than 250,000 persons are detained in county jails each year
and 3 to 7 million people pass through the jail annually (Irwin, 1985).
Most are restrained in small structures designed for 20 occupants or
fewer. Contrary to popular belief, the typical jail is not a massive, imposing building. Of the 3,493 jails in the United States that hold persons
for longer than 48 hours, only 3 percent keep 250 inmates or more (Pogrebin and Regoli, 1985).

Jails house persons who have been convicted of crimes and persons
who have not. Irwin (1985) has labelled them "rabble," meaning that jail
residents represent the "disorganized" and "disorderly," "the lowest class
of people." Thirty-five percent of the jail population are persons who are
awaiting trial. Nearly four-fifths of this group sit in jail not because of
the seriousness of the offense charged or because of their prior arrest re-
cord, but because they cannot make bail. Thus, many jail residents are
poor and uneducated persons. In 1978, approximately 60 percent of jail
residents had not completed high school and 43 percent were without a
job when they were arrested. The median income of all jail inmates in
1978 was only $3,255 in the year prior to their arrest (National Criminal
Justice Information and Statistics Services, 1979).

The Role of the Jail Guard

Although there exists an extensive literature on the sociology of corrections, very little serious attention has been paid to jails, and particularly to jail guards. A systematic bias of the vast majority of jail studies,
including the most recent one (Irwin, 1985), has been the selective inattention to the guard's perspective of social structure and organization of
jails.

Perhaps part of the reason for the neglect of jailers has been the tendency to stereotype them almost exclusively as a homogeneous, undif-
ferentiated lot — as cogs in the custodial machinery who follow uniformly
an explicit blueprint of institutional rules and regulations in supervising
and controlling jail residents. This narrow perspective of jailers has serious consequences when inferences are drawn about the nature of jails,
because it distorts or suppresses the dynamics of their organizational
role. In examining the role jailers play, as well as the adjustments and

adaptations reflective of their "working ideologies" (Jacobs and Kraft, 1978), we must focus on the nature of the relations between jailers and those who occupy similar (other jailers), subordinate (jail residents), and superordinate (administrators) positions within the jail.

Jailers occupy a central role in the administration of justice. They are managers of people, and thus, their duties extend far beyond custodial and security duties. Our view is that the jail officer is the single most important and influential agent within the jail system. More than any other jail personnel, the jailer affects inmates' resocialization. It would be a mistake to conceptualize jailers as responsible only for custodial and security tasks. Rather, their impact upon correctional operations extends to subtle definition and communication of correctional policy and jailers are the intermediaries between higher echelon managers and the inmate population. What is problematic for us in this paper is to shed light on how jailers view their role with special attention being given to their relations with others in the jail setting.

METHODOLOGY

Data for the project were derived from interview responses of jailers in four different types of jails (N = 60). Subjects were guaranteed that their responses would be anonymous and confidential. Formal interviews were conducted with a stratified sample of selected jailers (n = 15 per jail) based on demographic characteristics of officers. The focus of the interviews was to obtain jailers' views about their working relations and their judgments of institutional policy. The four jails we studied were located in Ventura County (California), Contra Costa County (California), Lane County (Oregon), and Jefferson County (Kentucky).

FINDINGS

Relations With Inmates

In jails, officers function as social control agents whose primary duties involve custody, security, and discipline. This was true even for the most treatment oriented jail we investigated (Contra Costa County). Jail residents view the officers as agents of repression or oppression, often expressing open contempt and defiance of their authority. The relationship between the two groups is one of "structured conflict" (Jacobs and Kraft, 1978). This conflict situation puts emphasis on the anticipation and prevention of discipline problems. The officer must maintain a constant vigil, alert and ready to respond to potential as well as actual trouble. One guard put it this way:

> The goals are to provide a secure environment for prisoners, where they can't get out; to provide for their safety and the safety of the community and we take away their freedom. The purpose is to punish. All I'm here for is to provide security. We are here to keep order, not to be their buddies.

The threat of danger fosters a defensive posture toward inmates, who are viewed with a mixture of suspicion, fear, and hostility. This state of tension further produces a psychological segmentation of the jailers from the jail residents and promotes a protective isolation within their organizational role. One jailer said to us,

> I have seen some (jailers) who are hostile with inmates. I think the jail has got to them. They told me that I would become hardcore like them after I have seen a lot, but I do not think I am going to change or act any differently. I know how to act aggressively with inmates if I have to.

And,

> I talk to inmates a little bit, but I do not get involved with them. I have to communicate a little, but as far as sitting down and being chums, I don't do that. I have nothing in my life that relates to theirs. . . I don't trust them. They are lying to me most of the time. Most of the guys in here are professional cons, a good percentage are; I would say fifty percent have been back several times. They know the ropes, and they are going to do everything they can to get as much for themselves as possible.

To the jailers the institutional atmosphere of tension and fear has been further exacerbated as a result of jail policy changes circumscribing their handling and control of inmates. Consequences of humanitarian reforms (e.g., limiting the use of solitary confinement) and the prisoners' rights movement (e.g., establishing formal grievance procedures) have undermined the coercive control traditionally exercised by the jailers, while providing inmates with the opportunity to develop considerable countervailing power. The jailers thus view such institutional reforms to protect the inmate as detrimental to their own interests and welfare. To put it differently, jailers, those front line workers, feel the brunt of inmate demands more than their superiors due to the fact that they are in more frequent contact with prisoners. Often, prisoner demands are perceived as having diminished officer authority and has caused jailers to believe that in their quest to avoid legal action, superiors have sold out to prisoner demands at the jailers' expense.

Relations With Superiors

Having to accommodate their security and control functions to comply with organizational safeguards for prisoners' rights also fosters the general feeling among jailers that they are not supported by their superiors. We were told,

> The administration does not back officers in the decisions they make concerning reports they write about inmate misbehavior. I feel that when an officer is on a particular post, and that post changes or any post rules and regulations change, officers should be included for their input. I am the officer that works forty to fifty hours a week on the floor. But the administration seldom includes us in any policy making. They should ask us for our opinions on what needs to be changed.

As Jacobs and Retsky (1977:34) observe in the prison setting, "administrators and professional personnel feel more respect and greater affinity for the inmate than they do for the guard." In fact, the social distance between line staff and administrators parallels, if not exceeds, that between the guard and the inmates. According to one guard,

> At times I actually feel I'm almost like an inmate. I really feel that the lieutenants on up and some of the sergeants subconsciously view us as inmates with the tactics they use in relating to us.

The paramilitary organization subjects guards to the same scrutiny by higher exchelon personnel as the inmates under custodial supervision. In addition to jailers facing inspection, shake-downs, write-ups, and disciplinary actions for their rule infractions, they have trouble communicating their needs and concerns to supervisors.

> We do not have two-way communication whatsoever. If you have got a problem you talk to your sergeant. You have to follow a chain of command. If you have a problem and there is no immediate supervisor around, and if your captain is not here, you can't talk to anyone else, because if you do break the chain of command you get written up.

Relations With Fellow Officers

Thus far we have noted the organizational chasms that existed between jailers and inmates and between jailers and jail administrators. It may be anticipated that such disaffection from these two groups would support the emergence of a tightly knit occupational subculture among jailers, much like that noted among police (Skolnick, 1966; Barker and Carter, 1986). This has not been the case, however. Two features of the jailer's role preclude the development of extensive work camaraderie and in-group solidarity.

First, interaction with fellow officers is minimal, usually limited to brief periods of contact at the end of a shift or during staff meetings. The jailer works alone in his or her particular area of assignment. Second, the expectation is that the guard performs the functions of the job alone. Any tendency to depend on colleagues would give jail officials the impression that the jailer is deficient in self-reliance and autonomy. Whenever the jailer needs fellow officers "to pull his chestnuts out of the fire," questions concerning his competence to manage or control inmates are raised (Korn and McCorkle, 1959:490-491). Collegial isolation of the jailer is thus supported by organization role prescriptions that stress personal accountability rather than cooperative and collective responsibility.

Role Relations and Alienation

The above examination of the jailer's role relations with inmates, administrators, and fellow officers presents a bleak picture. Jailers feel threatened by inmates, unsupported by their supervisors, and isolated from fellow officers. Such conditions have fostered experiences of work alienation among the jailers, who find themselves having to manage an exceedingly complex set of expectations regarding their working relationships and job performance (Carroll, 1974; Duffee, 1975; Jacobs, 1977).

Alienation as a consequence of the organization of work has received extensive attention in the literature. In his early writing, Marx illustrated several facets of alienating experiences including alienation from the work process, alienation from the products of work, alienation from other workers, and alienation of the worker from himself. While Marx's discussion of alienation applied primarily to the manual factory worker under capitalism, Weber later extended Marx's view to all bureaucratically organized work settings and forms of bureaucratization.

Since the work of Marx and Weber, the concept of alienation has taken on a variety of meanings. Seeman (1959) attempted to clarify the term, distinguishing five varieties of alienation: powerlessness, normlessness, meaninglessness, isolation, and self-estrangement. While not all of the meanings of alienation identified by Seeman are equally applicable to every work context, each type appears to be salient to the bureaucratically organized jail. Below we examine how the jailer's role is subject to these five types of alienating experiences.

Powerlessness

The jail incorporates a structure of authority in which decisions are made at the top with orders passed down through several managerial and supervisory levels to the jailers. A bureaucratic hierarchy of ranks operates through an established set of rules that regulates the behavior of both inmates and staff. In short, inmates are expected to obey institutional rules, jailers are expected to ensure inmate compliance with the rules, and administrators are expected to see that jailers enforce the rules. With respect to prisons, Cressey has noted:

> Guards manage and are managed in an organization where management is an end, not a means (1965:1024). Guards were expected . . . to place themselves completely at the disposal of the administrators to be used as the latter saw fit (1959:7).

In addition to the regulation of his work from above, the ability of the jailer to control the content and pace of his activities is in part determined by inmates. Simply, rule enforcement by its very nature tends to be ex post facto. Yet the jailer must be ready to respond not only to actual infractions but also to potential violations. The jailer, therefore, must maintain a state of constant alertness geared to the possibility of trouble in which the initiative rests with the inmates. The work behavior of the jailer is, to a great extent, a function of the decisions and actions of others occupying subordinate, as well as superordinate positions in the jail. For these reasons powerlessness would appear to be a fundamental feature of the officer's work experience.

The argument can further be made that specific institutional changes and reforms have also generated feelings of powerlessness among the jailers. The implementation of policies embracing concerns for humanitarian treatment and prisoners' rights has eliminated many of the rules and procedures by which inmate behavior was regulated. To the jailers, such reforms have undermined their authority and thus their capacity to maintain discipline. One jailer told us:

> I feel there is a lot of disregard from the inmates towards the deputies due to the fact that the jail is run so leniently. Since there is so little contact with prisoners, whenever we do have some contact with them, and we instruct them to do anything, we always catch flack.

Jailers feel sold out, viewing their superiors as aloof and unconcerned with the problems that they must deal with.

Normlessness

There is also evidence to indicate that organizational concerns for re-formation and rehabilitation of inmates have generated feelings of normlessness among jailers. The irony here is that jailers only believe a handful of inmates will change. Thus, believing as they do, jailers some-times express confusion about what their exact role ought to be. We were told,

> Probably about three percent will change. Very few will change their behavior. It's their environment. One time, before I went to the police academy, I asked one of the inmates if I would see her in the new jail. She said, "Probably." I asked her, "Why? You're going to get out of here. Why not change?" She said it was her way of life.

The introduction of treatment goals within a traditionally coercive insti-tution has resulted in ambiguous and contradictory role definitions for the jailer. They walk a thin line between maintaining discipline and con-tributing to a rehabilitative atmosphere. Decisions as to what types of inmate behavior constitute a threat to custody concerns must be left to the common sense and discretion of the jailer. Consider that,

> It states in our rules that there will be no gambling. There were three officers working the dorms for about three months. They were working on this one gambling ring that was in operation. They gathered all the information and documented everything in order to make their case. They then wrote up the conduct adjustment report and nothing hap-pened. The inmates involved were not rehoused or anything. The whole thing was a waste of time. There are a lot of situations like that. For example, we have housing rules that state that all socks and T-shirts and proper clothing will be worn in the dayroom. If a guy comes into the room without socks I'm not going to write a report on him, be-cause I know nothing will happen. Why have rules in the first place if they are not going to be enforced. We write reports, but the adminis-tration ignores them. All they do is give inmates a warning and it re-sults in the officer looking bad in front of the inmate.

Given the inherent ambiguity, and, to some extent, conflict in the jailers' role expectations, in his study of prison guards, Carroll (1974:57) con-cluded that "there has developed among the officers a state of normless-ness regarding their job performance." We also found normlessness in jails. One officer stated to us that,

> I would like to see more trust of the officers on the part of our supervi-sors. I would like to see us have more responsibility in making deci-sions about the inmates we are working with. I would like the administration to say, . . . its your post, let us know what you are

going to do and do it on a trial basis and if it works, fine, and if it doesn't work try something different. They need to allow us more flexibility in making decisions.

Meaninglessness

For a variety of reasons, meaninglessness might also be expected to be endemic to the work experience of jailers. Working in jails is dull and monotonous. With few exceptions, one day's routine is like the next.

There is more, however, to the jailer's predicament than just the routine and boredom of the job. Feeling that they are abused by inmates, unappreciated by superiors, unsupported by colleagues, jailers tend to think they are fighting a lost cause. There is a pervasive feeling that their best efforts are wasted. They realize no sense of accomplishment or purpose. In effect, their daily work is rendered meaningless. We were told,

> Regardless of what I do, nothing here will change. The inmates, most of them would not change despite any program that was offered. Maybe two percent we could help. I very seldom see guys that are in here . . . that have any class or that won't be here again.

And another jailer told us,

> I do not think it is enjoying the job that keeps officers here. It actually is a shit job.

Social Isolation

Frequently accompanying these feelings of futility in jail work have been the shirking of duties, on-the-job absenteeism, buck-passing, and a progressive paralysis of decision-making. As noted earlier, in attempting to minimize their own personal risk and trouble, jailers come to define their roles in a highly individualized manner, essentially detached from overall institutional concerns.

But the individualization of the jailer's role serves to isolate the jailers from one another so they cannot help or depend on colleagues. Unable to rely on fellow officers, jailers make their own accomodations in the dorms to ensure their own safety and security. In short, jailers maintain a defensive posture in the social organization of the jail, working neither for the administration or the inmates but for themselves. Said one of our interviewees,

> I do not take the tough approach. I can't. When I just started working here, I saw officers who seemed to be pretty tough guys. I thought that if that's the way I have to be then I can't do this job. I didn't want to be like some of the other officers. I hoped they did not expect me to act

tough. It was not until I worked with other people and tried to evaluate several different styles of dealing with prisoners, that I finally decided that I was going to have to just work my own way and not try to be somebody I am not. When I developed my own style, I began to be comfortable on the job.

This condition thus hinders the development of a sense of solidarity or community among guards.

Self-Estrangement

The final type of alienation, self-estrangement, also is typical in jails. In common with most workers, jailers try to make their job more pleasant, less laborious, and more endurable. But, as noted earlier, the existence of threats to the physical and psychological integrity of the jailer may force him to subordinate other goals to his interest in self-protection. With self-preservation in the jail as the focal concern, jailers engage in patterns of work relations geared more for their extrinsic than for their intrinsic value. This situation evolves from the jail environment itself. One guard told us,

> A lot of people think that it is dangerous for police to work the streets, but they do not stop and think what types of situations officers find themselves in, in the jail. I have had people come in here with knives and guns. Had it happen to me one night when I was out on the grill in the booking area with a female officer I was helping. A woman prisoner the city police brought in was not searched by them. I guess, because she was female the two male cops did not want to pat her down. It was winter and the prisoner had on a pair of gloves. She took her gloves off and sticks a gun in my chest, and says, "Here, take this." She was handing the gun to me, but it was pointed right at me. She could very well have shot it off right there.

We may conclude that the nature of the work and work relations effectively denies the jailer several opportunities for intrinsically rewarding experiences. Jailers feel little pride in their work since the public imbues the job with such negative attributes. He feels his work is unappreciated by superiors since they seem to show greater concern for the interests of the inmates. And since his immediate associates cannot be counted on, the jailer enjoys no spirit of teamwork. These conditions create few incentives for the infusion of the worker's self in his work and consequently results in self-estrangement.

Perhaps we in the academic field of corrections have, for too long a period of time, neglected to study the importance of the jailer. Hawkins (1976:105) best discusses the absence of research.

One of the most curious features of the whole history of modern imprisonment is the way the custodial officer, the key figure in the penal equation, the man on whom the whole edifice of the penitentiary depends, has with astonished consistency either been or ignored or rarely taken seriously as an instrumental factor in correction.

Apparently, jailers, too, have recognized that they have been the victims of benign neglect.

SUMMARY

The purpose of this article has been to examine the work relations of jail guards and their impact on experiences of alienation. We derived our data from sixty intensive interviews with jailers working at four separate facilities. With their traditional status and role altered by institutional reform policies, jailers feel threatened by inmates, misunderstood by superiors, and unsupported by fellow officers. The weakening of their position vis-a-vis inmates has fostered a sense of powerlessness, meaninglessness, and isolation; the ambiguous and contradictory nature of the operational directives of superiors has generated sentiments of normlessness, powerlessness, and isolation; and the deterioration of the working relations among the guards has contributed to feelings of normlessness, isolation, and self-estrangement.

To the guards many institutional changes have been disastrous. They can no longer do their job because they feel they are no longer in control. The institution is viewed as disordered and adrift, failing to either keep or treat inmates effectively. They have become frustrated and demoralized by the apparent futility of their efforts. They further find themselves working alone, able to count on no one. With little sense of accomplishment or satisfaction in their work, coupled with its stigmatization, the personal commitment of jailers to their job is minimal. As one guard put it, "We put up with a lot of bullshit."

NOTE

[1]Authors are listed in reverse alphabetical order. Our contributions to the manuscript have been equal.

REFERENCES

Allen, Harry and Clifford E. Simonsen, 1985. Corrections in America. New York: Macmillan.

Barker, Thomas and David L. Carter, 1986. Police Deviance. Cincinnati: Pilgrim-
    age Press.

Carroll, Leo, 1974. Hacks, Blacks, and Cons: Race Relations in a Maximum Secu-
    rity Prison. Lexington, Mass.: Lexington Books.

Cressey, Donald, 1965. "Prison organization," pp. 1052-1055 in J.G. March (ed.),
    Handbook of Organizations. Skokie, Ill.: Rand-McNally.

_____ 1959. "Contradictory directives in complex organizations: The case of the
    prison." *Administrative Science Quarterly* 3:1-19.

Duffee, David, 1975. Correctional Policy and Prison Organization. New York:
    Halsted.

Hawkins, Gordon, 1976. The Prison: Policy and Practice. Chicago: University of
    Chicago Press.

Irwin, John, 1985. The Jail: Managing the Underclass in American Society. Berke-
    ley: University of California Press.

Jacobs, James B., 1977. Stateville: The Penitentiary in Mass Society. Chicago: Uni-
    versity of Chicago Press.

_____ and L. Kraft, 1978. "Integrating the keepers: A comparison of black and
    white prison guards in Illinois." *Social Problems* 25:304-318.

_____ and H. Retsky, 1977. "Prison guard," pp. 47-65 in R. Leger and J. Stratton
    (eds.), The Sociology of Corrections: A Book of Readings. New York: John Wi-
    ley.

Korn, R. and L. McCorkle, 1959. Criminology and Penology. New York: Holt,
    Rinehart and Winston.

National Criminal Justice Information and Statistics Services, 1979. Census of Jails
    and Survey of Jail Inmates. Washington, D.C.: U.S. Government Printing Of-
    fice.

Pogrebin, Mark R. and Robert M. Regoli, 1985. "Mentally disorder persons in jail."
    Journal of Community Psychology 13 (4):54-57.

Seeman, Melvin, 1959. "On the meaning of alienation." *American Sociological Review*
    24:783-791.

Skolnick, Jerome, 1966. Justice Without Trial. New York: John Wiley.

CHAPTER 4

NEW RULES AND OLD RITUALS

Dilemmas of Contemporary Jail Management

Dave Kalinich

CONTEMPORARY jail management is trapped between a new set of rules and traditional jail and criminal justice system practices. A set of unexpected, complex, and often non-negotiable rules has been imposed upon the operation of jails within the last decade. The new set of rules basically requires the assurance of constitutional rights for inmates as well as a higher standard of care for their physical and psychological well-being than past practices could achieve. However, the practices and technology with which jails have traditionally operated have not been modified to an extent great enough to fully or even partially implement the new rules. Currently, jail management problems have been exacerbated by an increase of inmates who formerly would have been classified as mentally ill and dealt with by the mental health system. It is also common for jails to suffer from overcrowding (Jail Census, 1983). In spite of the myriad of problems faced by jails, the Criminal Justice System, for which the jails act as a catchall and storage bin for pending work, continues to perform in its time-consuming manner, clinging to its procedures and rituals, indifferent to the problems of its jails.

The Evolution of New Rules for Jails

The new rules for jails developed from both standards promulgated by professional organizations and case law emanating primarily from Federal Courts. The new rules include the guarantee of certain constitutional rights for inmates such as due process review prior to punishment, censor-free mail, and standards of care such as adequate diet, protection from assault, adequate medical treatment, etc. Comprehensive standards for corrections were put forward as early as 1870 by the National Congress on Penitentiary and Reformatory Discipline. Called Principles, the National Congress put forward thirty-seven concise statements prescribing prison design, health care, prisoner programs, administrative reforms, and personnel management.

The promulgation of standards began again in the nineteen thirties with the appearance of the Wickersham Report, followed

> in 1939 [by] the National Probation and Parole Association (now the Council on Crime and Delinquency) which produced model acts that detailed conditions for the operation of probation and parole services. These model acts continued through the mid-sixties with publication by the National Council and the American Correction Association of Standard Acts for State Correctional Institutions (Perspective, 78/79).

In 1946, the American Correctional Association published a **Manual of Suggested Standards for a Correctional System** and revised it intermittently through 1959. Since then, a number of groups have begun to prescribe standards: The American Bar Association (1968), National Commission on Criminal Justice Standards and Goals (1973), National Sheriffs' Association (1970/1974), American Public Health Association (1976), American Institute of Architects (1977), American Medical Association (1977), and the Commission on Accreditation for Corrections (1977/1978) (Perspective, 78/79).

Prior to the seventies, the focus of correctional standards had been primarily on prisons and reformatories. Local detention facilities began receiving more attention through standard promulgation from the National Sheriffs' Association in 1970. In 1972, the **Manual of Correctional Standards,** published by the American Correctional Society, dedicated a section to standards for local detention facilities. Concern for professional jail management and operations was manifested by the production of lengthy training manuals on jail operations and management by the Federal Bureau of Prisons (Jail Operations, a Training Course for Jail Officers, edited by Nick Pappas, and Jail Management, a Course for Jail Administrators, developed by Alice Howard Blumer, 1971).

The focus on standards for jails continued to expand. In 1974, the National Sheriffs' Association published manuals on Jail Security, Classification, and Discipline, and on Inmate Programs. The Nebraska State Bar Association Committee on Correctional Law and Practice published a 300 page document titled **Jail Standards** in 1977. Again in

1977, the American Correctional Association published the **Manual of Standards for Adult Local Detention Facilities.** This work was revised as **Standards for Adult Local Detention Facilities** in 1981 with the cooperation of the National Jail Association and National Sheriffs' Association, and updated in 1984 with the Standards **Supplement.**

While the standards promulgated by the various groups are not mandatory, Federal Courts have intervened actively in corrections during the last 20 years. The Courts, through their decisions on cases emanating from corrections, have created a set of fairly clear and non-negotiable rules for jail operations. Sechrest (1978) argues that the evolution of standards for corrections by professional groups and the intrusion of courts into corrections were interdependent. However, he contends that the new legal requirements make up only a part of standards promulgated by the American Correctional Association:

> What about the standards? How many were drawn from case law? And how far beyond the courts did the Commission and the ACA go? Of 465 standards for adult correctional institutions, at least 100, or almost one of every five, are based on specific case law generated by courts at all levels, and every major area of concern of the courts is addressed (Sechrest, 1978, pp. 183).

While correctional case law from the Federal Courts comprises only one-fifth of the standards promulgated by 1978, rules put forward by court cases, unlike remaining standards, are non-negotiable. Traditionally, the courts were reluctant to intervene in the administration of corrections. However, in the early sixties, the court began to look into the operations of correction (Place, Sands, 1975). In October of 1973, the United States Supreme Court decided four cases that had more impact on inmates' rights than any previous term. The landmark corrections cases were:

Wolff v. McDonnell (discipline)
Procunier v. Martinez (mail censorship)
Wolff v. McDonnell (mail inspection)
Pell v. Procunier (media access to specific cases)

Other cases which opened the floodgates:

Holt v. Sarver (1970 cruel and unusual punishment)
Palmigiano v. Trasisano (1970 mail)
Clutchette v. Procunier (1971 due process)

These cases together determined that certain constitutional rights are fundamental and apply to inmates, and existing correctional procedures abridged those rights. In addition, substantive changes in operational procedures in institutions had to be made.

Based on the following cases that emanated from the United States Supreme Court, premised upon the principles of the Eighth Amendment, standards of care for inmates were defined at law and upgraded:

Rhodes v. Chapman, 1981, and Bell v. Wolfish, 1979 (shelter)

Penn v. Oliverton, 1971, and Laaman v. Helgemore, 1977 (personal safety)

McIntosh v. Haynes, 1977 (sanitation)

Landman v. Royster, 1971, and Holt v. Sarver, 1970 (diet and exercise)

Wolfish v. Levi, 1978 (clothing)

Estelle v. Gamble, 1976 (medical care)

Wyatt v. Stockney, 1972 (mental health care)

Palmigiano v. Garrahy, 1977 (classification)

Essentially, the court decisions shown, which scratch the surface of Corrections Law, declared that inmates retain the majority of their constitutional rights, and correctional systems are obliged to provide inmates with sufficient care and supervision to protect them from psychological and physical harm that can arise from conditions in traditional correctional environments. Current standards, whether from court decisions or from standard setting groups, mandate jail practices which require that inmates be provided with active and reasonable care while in custody, rather than treated with indifference (Perlman, Price, and Weber, 1983).

New Rules and Civil Liability

Standards and goals on their own are not enforceable. However, the new rules promulgated by court decisions are enforced with some frequency. Courts have taken actions against local detention facilities ranging from taking them over to writing policy and procedure manuals for jails through court orders and consent decrees (Jones v. Wittenburg, 323 F. Supp. 93 [N.D.O. 1971]). In addition, civil suits filed by inmates, or their families, claiming to have been harmed as a direct result of poor jail practices and lack of standards of care for inmates are rather routine and often successful. Currently, the liability for poorly operated jails may extend to governmental officials who knew of the conditions but did nothing to alleviate them (Parnell v. Waldrop, U.S. District Court, W.D., North Carolina, May 1982).

Civil suits against correctional facilities are usually brought under the Civil Rights Act of 1871, 42 U.S.C. 1983. Under this act, courts can recognize damages and award relief to plantiffs who have been harmed as a consequence of a violation of their basic constitutional rights. This procedure allows individuals in an organization to be held personally liable for damages, both actual and punitive, suffered by a plaintiff. During such suits, courts look to previous cases and standards promulgated by professional organizations, such as the American Correctional Association, to determine standards of care and proper correctional policies and procedures.

Rather large settlements have resulted from such suits against local detention facilities, especially those surrounding physical harm or death of an inmate. For example, liability can accrue to jail personnel or administrators in the event of an inmate suicide if the correctional officer staff knew or should have known an inmate was suicidal and failed to prevent his/her suicide. This type of suit will be brought under 42 U.S.C. 1983 which will circumvent limited governmental immunity usually granted to correctional officers. The rationale for this high standard of care for inmates is well summarized in concluding remarks of the case in Wayne County, Michigan:

> When government imprisons people, it deprives them of freedom to look after their own health and safety. In the free community the man may run from his assailant, In the jail, flight is not possible. In the free community, a man may see a doctor at his own convenience. In jail, he must see the jail physician under the rules prescribed by the institution. In the free community he is not exposed to the hardships of confinement which may bring out suicidal tendencies. Since the prisoner is very much at the mercy of his jailers, no one should be surprised that the common law recognizes the duty on the part of the jailer to give confined persons reasonable protection against assault, suicide, and preventable illnesses. **(Wayne County Jail Inmates v. Board of Commissioners of Wayne County,** Wayne County, Michigan, Circuit Court Opinion of May 17, 1971, p. 32)

New Rules and Old Rituals, Problems of Implementation

Providing current standards of care for jail inmates requires active and skilled supervision of inmates rather than the passive custody role traditionally taken (Cromwell, 1975). To update jail operations first requires an understanding of the problem. The current standards are complex and often foreign to jail administrators as well as governmental attorneys who should be abreast of changes in the law. Experience in Michigan, where the State Department of Corrections through administrative law has promulgated jail rules and standards and has had inspection authority since 1975, suggests a strong resistance on the part of local authorities to accept current standards. Successful civil suits and active court intrusion in several jurisdictions has seemingly little impact on resistance to accept new standards. Once the problem is known, a positive commitment to change must be made by jail personnel and administrators and especially on the part of local governmental officials to provide resources for change. Given usual economic constraints, it is comfortable, at least in the short run, for local governments to prefer traditional jail operations (Richmond, 1975).

The traditional role of the jail correctional officer was to keep the jail reasonably clean and quiet, feed inmates, keep them from escaping, and get the pretrial inmates to court on schedule. To see to the health and well being of inmates under current standards requires a highly trained cadre of correctional officers as well as auxiliary personnel with medical and psychiatric skills. This is in sharp contrast to traditional personnel procedures in county jails run by a sheriff—a police-oriented official— whose personnel priority was on road patrol, placing trainees and malcontents in correctional officer positions. Michigan, for example, has pre-service training requirements for police officers but none for jail correctional officers. (In 1986, Michigan will require state certification by training for jail correctional officers.) Finally, the traditional physical plant structure of jails systematically limited visual and audio contact between inmates and correctional officers. The active type of supervision that is required to provide inmates with protection from themselves and others in an effective and efficient manner is almost impossible in the traditionally constructed jails that make up the majority of today's local detention facilities (Kerle, Ford, 1982).

Those jail administrators who have come face-to-face with the new set of rules that have been imposed upon them are well aware of the problems they face. If their reaction is passive and they truly view their systems as trapped between contradictory forces, change will be imposed by external forces and interests and will be painful. If, however, local officials take an active approach to the problems they face, then jail administrators may develop options with which to bring the philosophy and technology of jail management current with contemporary standards. To begin with, current standards must be taken as a given. Once this important step is taken, then an operational philosophy that can facilitate change will be developed. Once a proactive posture is taken by jail administrators, then options can be considered to bring operations in line with standards. Options can be developed within the most antiquated jails, and options that are not based upon physical plant renovation or new jails should be the first considered. Options such as on-the-job training, policy and procedure revisions, and better personnel management can be developed with existing resources. Inmate programs can be developed by utilizing public and private community resources. In addition, local officials who are concerned with improving jail operations can make it clear that the Criminal Justice system and the public share the responsibility for the problems faced by jails as well as for many of the solutions. Jail administrators are not in a position to be passive curators of the local dumping grounds.

Both the philosophy and operations of jails are beginning to change. New jail designs have been developed, and new jails are continually being constructed (albeit many based upon traditional designs), training standards for jail correctional officers are being mandated in several states, and, in Michigan and New York, The State Mental Health Bureaus are beginning to take an active role in providing assistance to the mentally ill inmate. The new rules are being accepted by local officials, however begrudgingly.

REFERENCES

American Correctional Association. *Manual of Standards for Adult Local Detention Facilities*, 1977.

American Correctional Association. *Manual of Correctional Standards*. College Park, MD, 1972.

American Correctional Association. *Standards for Adult Local Detention Facilities*, 1981 (Standard *Supplement*, 1984).

Bureau of Justice Statistics Bulletin, "The 1983 Jail Census," U.S. Dept. of Justice — Bureau of Justice Statistics, Washington DC, 1983.

California Probation and Correction Association, "The Power of Public Support: A Handbook for Corrections." Sacramento, CA, California Probation Parole, and Correction Association, 1984.

Cromwell, Paul F., "Jails: 200 Years of Progress" from *Jails and Justice*. Edited by Paul F. Cromwell, Jr., Charles C Thomas, Publisher, Springfield, Illinois, 1975.

Federal Bureau of Prisons, edited by Nick Pappas, *Jail Operations, a Training Course for Jail Officers*, 1971.

Ford, F.R. and Kerle, K.E., "State of Our Nation's Jails." Document #87298 in

National Institute of Justice/NCJRS, National Institute of Justice Library, Washington, DC, 1982.

"History of Standards in Corrections for Adults," in *Perspective,* Crime and Justice Foundation, Winter 1978, 1979, Vol. III, Number 1.

National Congress on Penitentiary and Reformatory Discipline. *Proceedings.* Weeds Parsons and Company, 1971, Cincinnati, OH.

National Sheriffs' Association. *Manual on Jail Security, Classification and Discipline,* 1974.

National Sheriffs' Association *Manual for Inmate Programs,* 1974.

National Sheriffs' Association. *Manual on Jail Administration* (1970). In *Compendium of Model Correctional Legislation and Standards,* U.S. Department of Justice, 2nd Ed., 1975.

Nebraska Bar Association Committee on Correctional Law and Practice. *Jail Standards,* U.S. Department of Justice, 1977.

Perlman, E., Price, A.C. and Weber, C., "Judicial Discretion and Jail Overcrowding," *Justice System Journal,* Vol. 8, No. 2 (Summer 1983) pp. 222-223.

Place, M. and Sands, D., "The Evolution of Judicial Involvement," *Jails and Justice,* edited by Paul F. Cromwell, Jr., Charles C Thomas, Publisher, Springfield, Illinois, 1975.

Richmond, M., "Prisoner Management and Control," *Jails and Justice,* edited by Paul F. Cromwell, Jr., Charles C Thomas, Publisher, Springfield, Illinois, 1975.

Sechrest, Dale, "The Legal Basis for Commission Standards," in *Proceedings of the American Correctional Association,* 1978.

PART II

RESPONDING TO THE CHANGING
ENVIRONMENT

A N IMPORTANT perspective in the study of organizations has focussed on the significance of organizational environments. Successful organizations tend to respond easily to changing environments and, at times, even to influence those environments. In Section I of this book the authors described the complexity of the jail and its environment. In this section we will examine the problems in responding to that complexity.

Until recently the environment of local jails has been relatively stable and predictable. Local administration and the rapid turnover of the jail population appear to have insulated jails from some of the pressures which effected prisons during the past decade. While overcrowding and poor conditions have been constant criticisms of local jails during this century, only recently have these charges had a dramatic impact on jail management.

Throughout most of the seventies the jail population remained stable at approximately 155,000. In the late seventies, however, the population increased dramatically to nearly 225,000 in 1983. During the same period, state and federal courts began to turn their attention to local jails. Caps have been placed on local jail populations and programs and services have been judicially mandated.

The first chapter in this section discusses the legal environment of local jails. In "Correctional Law and Jails," Paul Embert traces the influence of state and federal courts into the local jails. Courts first made significant intrusions into correctional management in the nineteen sixties. These early cases were filed by state prisoners and their applicability to local facilities remains uncertain. While prison staff are now

guided by a fairly clear set of legal standards, no such security is available for jail administrators.

In "Overcrowding and the Jail Budget," Dave Kalinich suggests the
application of management information systems to the problem of jail
overcrowding. While private sector approaches may suggest the utility
of a space renatal model as a method of addressing resource allocation,
the political realities of local jails may mitigate against such an approach. Instead, systematizing data on jail use by the police, judges and
probation officers may provide the information base necessary to address overcrowding from a rational perspective.

A different element of the jail environment is the focus of the next
chapter by Ralph Weisheit and Lesley Parsons. Because of their small
numbers, female inmates have traditionally been regarded as a special
needs population who have received little attention. Increases in the
numbers of women coming to jail are catapulting concern for meeting
the needs of female inmates into the mainstream of jail management.
This study uses data from a national survey of jail inmates to describe
the unique problems of female inmates. While male and female inmates
may be incarcerated for similar offenses their program needs may differ
significantly. As jails look to the provision of inmate services they must
deal with the limited work experience and reduced income of female inmates all within the context of their family responsibilities. Likewise,
women in jail present unique health problems and histories of substance
abuse. Overall, the research illustrates the importance of empirical in-
quiry to guide program development as jails respond to increasing numbers of female inmates.

In "Jails: An Invisible Political Issue," Carl Pinkele suggests some of
the difficulties that jails may have in responding to their environment.
In a theoretical analysis, he focuses attention on the jail in a political
context. Hidden from the public in both a physical and psychological
sense, there often is no significant constituency supporting jail reform.
Public ambivalence and autocratic leadership insulate local jails and
make them politically invisible. The solution to this, suggests Pinkele, is
the politicalization of the local jail issue. Even reformers, however, may
be unwilling to widen the conflict.

In the final chapter of this section, Nancy Schafer presents a case
study of judicially mandated jail reform. In "Jails and Judicial Review"
the success of courts at requiring significant change is brought into question. Bound by local tradition, jails are unprepared to respond to outside
demands for reform. At the Marion County Jail (Indianapolis) twelve

years elapsed between the filing of a lawsuit and full compliance with the court's orders in the case. The time was marked by efforts to ignore and sabotage the mandate and by intense conflict between the jail and the court, The bitter episode, however, cannot be attributed simply to reluctant individuals. Instead, local jails lack the professional network necessary for effective response. Isolation, restrictive budgets, and local politics hampered the jail's ability to deal effectively with this influence from its environment.

CHAPTER 5

CORRECTIONAL LAW AND JAILS

Evolution and Implications for Jail and Lockup Administrators and Supervisors

Paul S. Embert

THE PRIMARY purpose of this chapter is to present some implications of correctional law for jail administrators and staff. Broadly, the chapter describes the evolution of correctional law, outlines inmates' and jailers' rights, and discusses the implications. Since a significant portion of the law of corrections is Constitutional Law, evolution of Constitutional Law is addressed to put correctional law in its proper perspective. Similarly, some of the differences between prisons, large jails, small jails, and lockups (police-operated temporary detention facilities) are also noted.

The chapter is organized around five major topics: (1) the various types of law impacting on jail personnel; (2) the evolution of correctional and Constitutional Law; (3) the Civil Rights Act of 1871; (4) jail inmates' rights; and, (5) implications for jail personnel.

TYPES OF LAW IMPACTING ON JAIL ADMINISTRATORS AND STAFF

There are at least four types of law that impact on personnel charged with operating a jail or lockup: criminal (penal) law, civil law, correctional law, and Constitutional Law. Each type of law has its own inherent philosophies and trends, and is often treated in isolation from the others. Yet, each is intertwined with the others to the extent none can be ignored by practitioners. Each must be viewed in terms of its impact and restraints on the other types of law.

Criminal (Penal) Law: For county and city governmental leaders and jail employees, criminal or penal law is relatively straightforward. This law defines offenses, prescribes punishments, and governs trial procedures and the methods of obtaining court convictions. It is the law that peace officers tend to be most knowledgeable of, as well as the law which brings jailers their clientele.

In the total criminal justice process, application of criminal law may pose significant problems for those who operate a jail or lockup. Criminal law enforcement, prosecution, and court sentencing philosophy impact on the inmate population size and character. This often becomes a significant factor, contributing to crowded jails and lockups. Crowded and overcrowded confinement facilities, in turn, frequently lead to managerial policies, procedures, and other actions that may result in correctional law violations, civil suits, and Constitutional issues the local jail administrator may not have anticipated. At the very least, the process may present major budgetary problems, which many jail administrators cannot deal with effectively. (Kalinich, Chapter 6; Schafer, Chapter 9, address fiscal issues in greater depth.)

The major implication of the criminal law enforcement, prosecution, and sentencing process seems to be the need for jail administrators to initiate a meaningful dialogue between county (or city) administrators, judges, prosecutors, and other participants in the local criminal justice system. Without this dialogue and a serious, resultant commitment to resolve the **shared** problem of crowded jails and lockups, prosecutors may well label minor offenders as habitual felons rather than misdemeanants; judges may sentence nearly all convicted offenders to jail (typically for the maximum allowable time); community alternatives to incarceration may go unused; and, the body politic may not financially support the facilities or staff needed to operate a humane, Constitutional jail within this type of environment. Without a humane, Constitutional jail, civil suits are bound to be filed and won. Yet, in conducting a series of training programs dealing with jail management issues, the writer has detected a consistent reluctance to initiate this type of dialogue and commitment. Instead, jail personnel frequently express the opinion that they cannot talk to prosecutors, judges, or county commissioners; hence, they are resigned to civil suits.

Civil Law: Civil law, generally in the form of tort action, has not been a major concern to governmental leaders or jailers until recent years. With the exception of civil rights cases, most jail administrators and staff have paid little attention to the broad area of torts. Yet, there is a growing body of literature that equates tort philosophy with the philosophy found in civil rights cases. Plaintiff tactics and jail defenses are similar, as are court philosophies and reasoning. Some legal experts now believe that the criminal justice system will see increasing numbers of general tort actions and fewer civil rights suits (e.g., Avery and Rudovsky).

A tort (from the Latin TORTUS, meaning twisted conduct) is a noncriminal, noncontractual suit wherein a plaintiff may collect damages as the result of **an act or failure to act** (negligence) in carrying out a legal duty (Spain). Some people refer to this duty as the "duty of care." Essentially, it is a duty similar to that imposed on homeowners to provide reasonable safety and security for others—household residents, invited guests, and trespassers; or, as motorists, the duty owed to passengers, other motorists, and pedestrians. A key element in tort suits is the expectation of those with a legal duty to **foresee** problems that might result in injury or harm to persons or property. In the context of a jail, this might involve foreseeing that overcrowding may result in increased assaults, riots, etc.

The implications of civil law, as well as civil rights litigation, are apparent. Either an **act or failure to act** may subject governmental entities, jail or lockup administrators, and employees to litigation. The expectation for jail personnel to **foresee problems** that might result in injury or harm to persons or property will become increasingly critical. Those who ignore potential problems, or who lack the professional ability or training to reasonably foresee injury or harm, will be an increasing liability to the government entity responsible for a jail or lockup.

Correctional and Constitutional Law: Correctional law, or prisoners' rights law, is a body of law that was largely non-existent until the past few years. As a result, many criminal justice practitioners are not fully aware of the law, choose to ignore the consequences of litigation (see Schafer, Chapter 9), or perhaps, assume that the law does not apply to them. Others seem to believe that the law will disappear as quickly as they perceive it has come to pass. None of this is a correct response to the problem. Political leaders, jail administrators, and jail staff must recognize correctional law for what it is—a part of Constitutional Law. Like the broader body of Constitutional Law, correctional or prisoners' rights law did not develop in a vacuum. It evolved in conjunction with social and philosophical changes, standards promulgated by professional

groups (see Kalinich, Chapter 4), and through judicial re-examination
of issues. These factors combine to make our Constitution a "living document." It is, therefore, important to put correctional law into its Constitutional context.

EVOLUTION OF CORRECTIONAL AND CONSTITUTIONAL LAW

For many years our courts did not appreciably involve themselves in
corrections or criminal matters. It was not until the 1960s and '70s that
court decisions were rendered in great numbers and with significant impact on our overall criminal justice system. While many have decried
this change in judicial involvement, evolving social conditions, professional standards, and philosophies merged at the same proximate time
to virtually mandate a shift in court activity and judgments. To put this
shift into perspective, it is useful to briefly consider the evolution of
penal theory and practice in relation to Constitutional theory and practice. Neither was the same in 1789 as it is today.

When our Constitution was written, it became the document by
which the people drew the line on **federal** intervention in their lives;
only by exception could these rights and privileges be restricted. Yet, this
philosophy has not always been fully accepted or extended to all classes
of people.

In the unamended Constitution, where our concern was **federal** intervention with rights, slaves were regarded as little more than valuable
property, with no legal status or rights. On the eve of the Civil War this
concept was sufficiently viable that Justice Taney could declare that
whether emancipated or in slavery, Blacks could not be entitled to the
rights and privileges of the Constitution (Dred Scott v. Sandford, 19
How. 393; 1857). Penal philosophy was similar; criminals had no legal
status or rights and were, indeed, "slaves of the state" (Ruffin v. Com-
monwealth 62 Va.; (21 Gratt) 790, 796; 1871). Transportation, gaols, use
of hulks, and death as punishment for most crimes were public expectations for dealing with criminals. Neither accused nor convicted had reason to even contemplate humane or Constitutional treatment! But penal
theory, like Constitutional theory, was about to undergo major changes.

The Reconstruction Amendments to the Constitution recognized
former slaves as people and expanded the protection of the Constitution
so that it protected **all** people against governmental deprivation of their

rights at **both federal and state level.** In penology, the reformatory model, built in Elmira, New York, in 1876, sowed lasting ideas of humane treatment and rehabilitation in corrections. The Civil Rights Act of 1871 (42 U.S.C. Section 1983) created a civil cause of action against any person acting "under color of law" who deprived another of Constitutionally guaranteed rights.

True, these changes did not take instant effect. As it took nearly 100 years and the Reconstruction Amendments (1865-'70) to extend the philosophy of the Constitution to **state** government acts, nearly a second century would pass before attorneys, libertarians, professional groups, and the courts would use the Amendments and Civil Rights Act of 1871 to give meaningful substance to the ideals expressed in the Constitution.

CIVIL RIGHTS ACT OF 1871
(42 U.S.C. SECTION 1983)

History: From post Civil War through 1936, only 19 decisions involving civil rights abuses were decided in our courts (Strom). As recently as 1961, the Supreme Court ruled that governments were not individuals, hence not liable to suits through the tort concept of vicarious liability (Monroe v. Pape, 365 U.S. 167). Prison and jail administrators were allowed wide latitude in dealing with their charges and the concept that prisoners were slaves of the state was commonly accepted. Yet, these philosophies (similar to Justice Taney's) were also held on the edge of major social changes, including the so-called Supreme Court Revolution of the 1960s (and '70s).

The court began to closely scrutinize state government, police and correctional practices. By 1978 it ruled that civil rights violations did, in fact, involve vicarious liability, and that governmental agencies could be sued vicariously for the acts of their employees (Monell v. Department of Social Services, 436 U.S. 658). In 1982 it expanded civil rights litigation without exhausting all remedies in state courts (Patsy v. Florida Board of Regents, 102 S. Court 2557).

Now, through Constitutional Amendment, accompanying Congressional legislation, changes in social values, standards promulgated by professional groups, and court decisions, a whole body of philosophy is embraced as Constitutional rights—to include prisoners' rights. The Civil Rights Act of 1871 is the basic tool which gave meaning to a philosophy contained in the Constitution itself.

Provisions: For jailers, the important part of the Civil Rights Act is Section 1983. That section provides that: (1) **any** public officer, (2) who violates **any** person's Constitutional rights, (3) **under color of law or custom,** (4) **is liable** for actions at law (suits).

Because the courts largely ignored these provisions for 65 years, a series of qualifiers, defenses, and interpretations were almost a necessity once the courts began to address the act's requirements. For jailers, the decisions changed their traditional ways of doing business, and provided some leeway in dealing with prisoners—without which jails probably could not function.

Some Defenses: One of the more important defenses relevant to the operation of jails is found in Bell v. Wolfish (441 U.S. 520; 1979), wherein the court ruled that "rational basis," not "compelling necessity," is the proper test or standard in determining whether regulations and practices in a jail amount to punishment.

The implications of this decision rest primarily in the unique population incarcerated in jails and lockups, as compared to prisons. Jail populations typically consist of both sentenced prisoners and pretrial detainees. In the latter case, the defendant might even be free, except for a lack of funds for bail. Because they have not been convicted, it is axiomatic that they should not be punished. Somewhat logically, courts tended to conclude that nearly any restrictions or privations which were not inherent to confinement, or necessary to ensure the defendant's appearance at trial, were unconstitutional unless justified by the "compelling necessities" of jail administration.

Under the rigors of this test, federal courts logically invalidated numerous jail regulations where they found no "compelling necessity." **Wolfish** relaxed this "compelling necessity" standard to one of "rational basis," thereby largely, but not completely, eliminating the distinction between pretrial detainees and convicted inmates. To a degree, the decision gave greater deference to the judgment of local officials than the courts. Yet, it also contained a caveat—whether pretrial or convicted, each prisoner has certain Constitutionally protected rights (Clute; Goodson v. City of Atlanta, CA 11, June 25, 1985).

In another ruling, the Court determined that public administrators are not vulnerable to suit where there is no violation of "clearly established law or custom" (Wood v. Strickland, 420 U.S. 308; 1975). In practice, this decision implies that jail administrators should look beyond local laws and custom to regional and national "established laws and customs." One need look no farther than to **Garner** (Tennessee v.

Garner, 710 F. 2d 240, 6th Cir. 1983) to see the impact of national laws and customs, as opposed to local or state laws, customs, and standards.

Rulings such as **Wolfish** and **Wood** have other significant implications: First, reasonable or rational policies and procedures **can** be developed; Second, established law and custom (on a **national** basis) provide the foundation for these policies and procedures. They provide tools with which jailers can do their jobs without having to be god-like in their wisdom!

On the other hand, the courts have indicated that certain defenses for policies, procedures, actions, and facilities are clearly **not** acceptable when civil rights violations occur. These include clearly outrageous conduct (conduct that violates clearly established law, and which a reasonably competent public official **knew or should have known**); deliberate or calloused indifference; and the budgetary defense.

"Knew or should have known" equates to the tort concept of foresight, and implies that jailers must have a corrections orientation and training. Deliberate or calloused indifference speaks largely for itself, but does have implications for pre-employment screening and personnel retention. The budgetary defense, however, warrants particular discussion.

The Budgetary Defense: The budgetary defense is an issue in most jails and lockups. With rare exception, the writer has heard jailers consistently raise budget constraints in protest of reasonable actions to prevent jail suicides, provide inmate medical care, provide adequate staffing and training, and virtually every other concern inherent to a humane, Constitutional jail. Yet, the courts have clearly ruled that an inadequate budget is no defense for unconstitutional jails. For example:

> If the State cannot obtain the resources to detain persons awaiting trial in accordance with minimum constitutional standards, then the State will simply not be permitted to detain such persons (Hamilton v. Love, 328 F. Supp. 1182, 1184; 1983).

> Let there be no mistake in the matter; the obligation of the respondents' government to eliminate existing unconstitutionalities does not depend upon what the legislature may do, or upon what the Governor may do, or upon what the respondents may actually be able to accomplish . . . it is going to have to be a system that is countenanced by the Constitution (Hutto v. Finney, 437 U.S. 678, 1978).

The implication of this philosophy is plain: find the funds to run a Constitutional jail or close the jail. Admittedly, this may not be an option. For example, in Michigan, sheriffs are mandated to operate jails (Michigan Compiled Laws Annotated). However, other jails and lockups are being run for a variety of reasons other than legal mandates. Regardless, in all cases the jail administrator must convince the political leadership to provide funds necessary to do the job or consider closing the facility. Dialogue and commitment by all who **share** in the problem is essential.

The Shared Problem: Several references have been made to jail problems being a shared problem. Sheriffs and police chiefs have borne the problems of jails and lockups for many years. Twenty-odd years ago, as a young military police officer, the writer shared a view frequently voiced in training seminars: "jails are our problem." Jails and jail problems are no longer the jail administrator's problem. Indeed, it can be argued that they never were. The problems of jails and lockups are a shared problem.

The general public shares. They decide, to a large extent, the amount of tax revenues that will be collected and how they will be allocated. They influence political leaders and judges. The overall political process has an influence.

For example, the sheriff, who tries to accommodate all the police chiefs and city administrators, and thereby overloads the jail, may be politically motivated. Similarly, the prosecutor who campaigns on a "get tough with crime" platform, subsequently files the most serious charges possible, and asks the courts for the maximum jail or prison sentence, may also be politically motivated. Both may envision an easy path to reelection. Yet, dialogue with the public may be more effective in the long run. A major civil suit will probably cost an election, but dialogue may bring public realizations that there are no alternatives beyond running a humane, Constitutional jail, or closing the jail. There are numerous ways of operating a legal jail, which the public will accept, and still reelect the judge, prosecutor, or sheriff. These are discussed later in the chapter.

Rights and Liabilities of Correctional Officers: Before leaving the general topic of the Civil Rights Act, some mention of correctional officers' basic rights and liabilities is warranted. To a degree, one basic right and one basic liability balance the rights and privileges of jail inmates with those of the jail staff.

Generally, correctional officers have the right to use force; however, there is the potential for civil damages. **Excessive** force is normally the issue in suits. The courts have usually ruled that a jail employee is permitted to use as much force as is "reasonably necessary" to perform his or her duty. The use of deadly force and the **improper** use of restraints (handcuffs and leg irons) can be serious problems. The vagueness of terms like "excessive force" and "reasonably necessary" dictate adequate policies, clear procedures, proper supervision, and meaningful training.

On the opposite side of the coin, correctional staff and jail administrators are liable for negligence in tort or in a civil rights suit. Negligence can be classed gross, wanton, intentional, or reckless (Smith v. Wade, 103 S. Ct. 1983). The overall topic of negligence, like the use of deadly force, is most complicated and dictates precise policies, comprehensive procedures, viable supervision, and supportive training. Negligence suits will generally fall in the area of failing to protect prisoners: (1) from themselves; (2) from other inmates; and (3) from other staff members. Included in this problem area are suicides, assaults, and excessive use of force by staff members. Either negligence or excessive use of force can lead to litigation.

In cases of willful or wanton use of excessive force or negligence, liability will normally fall on the individual officer. Most cases, however, involve an issue of inadequate training, policy, or procedures, and raise the question of vicarious liability—"respondeat superior."

Doctrine of Respondeat Superior: Under this doctrine, an employer is vicariously liable for the acts and omissions of its employees if the employee is acting within the scope of his or her employment (Spain). In most jail cases, the employer (city or county) or supervisor has been vicariously liable for such reasons as: (1) lack of adequate pre-employment screening; (2) negligent assignment of personnel; (3) lack of adequate policies and/or procedures; (4) failure to supervise; (5) failure to train; and (6) failure to protect. Obviously, these suits dictate that more time, effort, and dollars be spent on pre-employment screening, policy and procedure development, supervisory training and development, and training of jail staff. Many jail administrators do not seem to fully appreciate these implications. Others seem thwarted by fiscal constraints, which, as previously discussed, is no defense.

Possible Remedies: Not every civil rights or tort judgment has resulted in million dollar judgments. Some result in the award of monetary damages to compensate for the actual harm. Some result in declaratory or injunctive relief. Others result in punitive monetary damages. Of particular concern to jail administrators and staff are punitive damages. The Supreme Court has held that a municipality cannot be held liable for punitive damages (City of Newport v. Fact Concerts, Inc., 101 S. Ct. 2748; 1981). This means that where a jail administrator or staff member is guilty of a civil rights violation (to the extent punitive damages are appropriate), the city or county will not pay the damages. Neither will insurance companies. The implications of this are apparent. Every person working in a jail or lockup should be trained to recognize that deliberate, calloused ignoring of Constitutional rights is liable to cost the employee directly and personally. Each jail administrator and staff employee must ask if he or she is willing to pay out of their pocket, perhaps over a lifetime, for reckless or calloused indifference to a federally protected right (Smith v. Wade, 103 S. Ct.; 1983).

Summary: The Civil Rights Act of 1871, through Supreme Court decisions, has provided reasonably clear guidance for jail administrators and staff. The guidance includes who may be sued (any officer or administrator), possible defense (money is no defense), and the fact that individuals may have to pay out of their own pockets. Yet, the Court has not been one-sided. It has recognized that jails are different, that correctional officers may need to use force, and that some inmates' rights must be restricted. For jail administrators, the implications include a need to learn and comply with the court philosophies, and then take a pro-active approach to protecting the inmates, employees, department, and governmental agency. Inherent in these implications is a need for improved policies, procedures, supervision, and training, as well as a clear understanding of jail inmates' rights.

JAIL INMATES' RIGHTS

Having discussed inmates' rights in general, it is appropriate to reiterate that there are no special or different rights for prisoners beyond those possessed by free persons. As noted in Wolff v. McDonnell (418 US 539; 1974) "there is no iron curtain drawn between the Constitution and the prisons of this country." The same rights that apply outside prisons and jails apply inside; however, both the rights of free persons and the rights of prisoners may be restricted **if justified.** It is the lack of adequate justification for restricting prisoners' rights that has created the majority of problems for correctional administrators.

Prisoners' rights are largely the same whether an inmate is confined in a prison or in a jail; only the problems of protecting the rights are different. Yet, some practitioners seem to feel that "prisoners' rights" do not apply to the jail setting because of the differences between prisons and jails.

Prisons are obviously different than jails, but large jails are different than small jails, and small jails are different from most lockups.

Differences include clientele; staff; fiscal bases; extent of "corrections" versus "law enforcer" orientation; professional affiliations; and local, as opposed to national, mores (Schafer, Chapter 9, expands on these differences). Yet each **must** be managed in a humane manner. Each **must** be run in a way that will minimize successful litigation. Jail administrators must pay particular attention to the following **potential** problem areas (the expectation to foresee):

1. Cruel and unusual punishment.
2. Personal safety (suicide potential, fire and safety hazards, etc.).
3. Adequate medical and mental health care.
4. Sanitation.
5. Overcrowding.
6. Abuse of force by correctional staff.
7. Assault by other inmates.
8. Due process in disciplinary actions.
9. Right to mail, phone calls, and visitations.
10. Freedom of religion.

The broad category of cruel and unusual punishment addresses inadequate conditions, such as plumbing, lighting, nutrition, etc. A Section 1983 suit can prevail for **one** inadequate condition if it is "gross" or "clearly outrageous" (i.e., a condition which would shock the conscience of a reasonable and prudent person). Cruel and unusual punishment can also be based on the "totality" of several less severe conditions that add up to an unconstitutional jail. The totality of conditions might include physical plant deficiencies, improper policies and procedures, or a combination thereof. Many cases seem to address problems in policies and procedures because of a failure to differentiate between rights and privileges.

Rights Versus Privileges: Constitutional rights are basic to human rights, but they are not an all-or-nothing situation. Some may be more fundamental than others. But even fundamental rights may be restricted—both in free society, and in jail. The key to restrictions is a rational basis for the restriction. In jail this usually involves procedures aimed at security, management and custody, or order and discipline. Procedures which are clearly designed to prevent escapes, riots, suicides, and assaults, or which are necessary to utilize space and staff personnel, will normally be upheld. The problem appears to come when procedures have not been reviewed and changed; instead, the procedures have been perpetuated and lack rational basis for achieving these kinds of goals. For example, a haircut restriction probably could not be rationally defended in terms of preventing escapes. On an individual basis, it might be rational in the interest of health standards.

The key implication is that jail administrators need to constantly evaluate local policies and procedures and ask three questions about restricting rights: (1) is a Constitutional right involved? (2) can, or should, the right be restricted? and (3) what is the real or proper reason for restricting the right? (Clute).

In contrast to Constitutional rights, jail rules may grant, abridge, or deny privileges which are not subject to scrutiny by the courts. For example, a jail may grant late-evening television privileges but deny the privilege if the inmate fails to clean his or her area each day. Here, there is probably no Constitutional right involved; there is rational reason for denying the privilege (to encourage sanitation standards); and, most privileges can be denied. This is clearly different from basic Constitutional rights.

Basic Constitutional Rights: Constitutional rights stem largely from the First, Fourth, Eighth, Tenth, and Fourteenth Amendments to the Constitution. Some have a foundation in the preamble to the Constitution. In some cases, jail administrators have a legal duty to protect a right because it is a Constitutional right; in other cases, they have an equal duty to protect the right under civil tort concepts. The right to life is the most fundamental right protected under both Constitutional and civil law.

Right to Life and Duty to Protect: Without life, one cannot ". . . secure the Blessings of Liberty to ourselves and our Posterity. . ." (preamble to the Constitution). The right is protected in the Fourteenth Amendment: ". . . nor shall any State deprive any person of life . . . without due process. . ." Jail personnel have a legal duty to protect the lives of inmates against assaults by others, as well as against suicides. Yet, many jail and lockup administrators have yet to come to grips with the threat of in-custody suicides. Classification (screening) procedures are often lacking, or do not assess the threat of suicide; policies and procedures for dealing with high-threat inmates are deficient; and, facilities and staffing are often inadequate to prevent an inmate from committing suicide. In some cases, administrators cite a lack of funds for adequate staffing or facility modification; inadequate funding is no excuse in litigation. In other instances, jail administrators dismiss the potential of the problem because they have never had a suicide in their facility (failure to foresee). In both instances, the absence of a successful in-custody suicide may well reflect luck, rather than the presence of adequate facilities, staffing, or policies and procedures.

The implications of this major problem are many. If a jail or lockup administrator cannot operate a facility in a manner that will prevent inmate suicides, the jail may be a candidate for closure. If the staff cannot develop adequate policies and procedures for coping with this critical threat, there is a serious question concerning the ability of the staff and facility to comply with other Constitutional mandates.

First Amendment Rights: This amendment restricts government from either establishing a religion or restricting its free exercise. Religious practice can only be curtailed when it affects the good order and security of the jail or places an "unreasonable" hardship on the administration. Issues involving religion tend to focus on: (1) whether a belief is a religion; (2) access to services; (3) access to ministers; (4) access to religious writings; (5) special diets; (6) personal appearance and hair style; and (7) religious medals. Every jail needs clearly defined policies and procedures dealing with these and other religious issues (Clute; Kalinich and Postill).

Other First Amendment rights include speech, press, publications, mail, and associations. Restrictions in these areas generally must be made using tests such as the "clear and present danger" test or "rational reason." In general, restrictions on mail, visitations, and telephone use must be no greater than necessary to protect the government interest involved. Relevant policies and procedures must be carefully developed and specific. Regulations stated in vague and general terms are bound to be challenged.

Fourth Amendment Rights: In general, the courts have held that prisoners have no reasonable expection of privacy anywhere in a jail. Yet, the courts expect jailers to show that the right to privacy is being restricted in light of security measures (Travers v. Paton, 1966). Similarly, the courts have given officials reasonably broad rights to search prisoners. The key is to avoid arbitrary, harassing, or unnecessary searches (Moore v. People, 1970). "Pat Downs" and Strip Searches have been found reasonable if conducted according to **documented** procedures.

Eighth Amendment Rights: The underlying principle of the Eighth Amendment is the concept of the "dignity of man" and draws its meaning from evolving standards of decency that mark the progress of a maturing society. Areas of concern for jail administrators include: (1) shelter (Rhodes v. Chapman, 1981); (2) personal safety (Penn v. Oliverton, 1972, and Laaman v. Helgemore, 1977); (3)sanitation (McIntosh

v. Haynes, 1977); (4) diet and exercise (Landman v. Royster, 1971); (5) medical care (Estelle v. Gamble, 1976); and (6) mental health care (Wyatt v. Stockney, 1972). The implications of this brief listing are that jail administrators must keep up with litigation; work actively with local attorneys to insure the facility conforms to new decisions; and continuously review and revise established policies, procedures, and training.

Summary: This brief discussion of the more basic inmates' rights has served to stress the need for current legal knowledge, as well as for adequate policies and procedures. Certainly the jail administrator must also have knowledge of other legal requirements: state housing laws setting living space requirements; health and fire codes; and, standards dealing specifically with jail or lockup operations. Failure to comply with any of these may result in the issue of "failure to protect." Failure to protect, in turn, may be **the** critical concept with implications for most jail and lockup administrators today.

IMPLICATIONS FOR JAIL PERSONNEL

The need to protect jail inmates is crucial. This includes protecting inmates against themselves (suicide attempts), from other inmates (assaults), from staff members (assaults, harassment, and negligence), as well as against inhumane or unconstitutional conditions. Failure to provide this protection may result in either tort or civil rights suits.

Ideally, jail administrators should focus their efforts on running a humane, Constitutional jail. Realistically, the writer's experience suggests that many jail and lockup personnel are more concerned with limiting successful litigation. This, perhaps, is not surprising, for the number of prisoner petitions increased from 218 in 1966 to more than 10,000 a year by 1980 (Clute). Resultant court decisions added exponentially to an already highly stressful work environment and compounded fiscal problems. Somewhat appropriately, some jail personnel have looked for ways to avoid being sued, rather than for ways to operate a humane, Constitutional facility. Ironically, attempts to operate a humane, Constitutional jail, are mutually complimentary to the goal of limiting **successful** litigation. Accordingly, this chapter has focused on implications for jail administrators and staff that will help achieve the goals of a humane, Constitutional jail. Each will, however, simultaneously reduce the threat of successful suits.

Before expanding and summarizing the implications raised in this chapter, it should be noted that in today's litigious society, it is somewhat naive to expect a jail or lockup to totally escape litigation. It is a fact that jail personnel and their responsible governmental entities are going to be sued (Clute). The goal is to prevent successful litigation, or at a minimum, to reduce the impact of successful litigation.

The starting point in running a humane, Constitutional jail, is for every staff member to have a firm concept of the evolution and philosophy of correctional law. This implies training. It also implies that jail administrators must tackle difficult tasks — tasks that criminal justice practitioners have not handled well to date. These include engaging in dialogue and forcing commitments from other people (judges, prosecutors, county commissioners, etc.); improving policies and procedures; improving training; and, improving supervision. These tasks, in turn, require a pro-active, rather than reactive, approach to jail administration.

Each of these tasks is easier to prescribe than accomplish. They were challenges to the writer twenty years ago. They are problems in most criminal justice agencies today. They are, however, challenges that must be undertaken. The alternatives — numerous suits, shattered personal and professional lives, injury and death, stress-induced physical and mental ailments, rapid and increasing personnel turnover, court appointed masters, and large dollar settlements — in reality, are not alternatives at all.

Throughout this chapter two implications of correctional law were raised and reiterated: (1) the concept that jail administration is a shared problem, and (2) the fact that a limited budget is no excuse for an inhumane, unconstitutional jail or lockup.

Jails do not exist in a vacuum. The clientele is "input" by the collective actions of prosecutors, judges, local citizen mores, independent police agencies, probation officers, and state corrections systems. There is a strong tendency on the part of each of these various participants in the total criminal justice process to operate as a separate entity, unmindful of the impact on other parts of the system. In Michigan, for example, where the state prison system is overcrowded, judges have resorted to sentencing people to jail rather than prison; legislators have introduced bills to allow longer periods of confinement in jail to alleviate prison overcrowding; and, some prosecutors have taken a hard-nosed approach toward offenders, further adding to the jail population. The jail administrator in this type of environment must take forceful, pro-active

steps to generate dialogue with these other people in the system who are
contributors to the jail crowding problem.

True, there are political problems involved. It is difficult for a sheriff
to tell a judge or prosecutor that no more prisoners will be taken at the
jail. It is equally difficult to reconcile differences between county commissioners, who have voters clamoring for reduced governmental expenditures, with the judge who wants to send all felons to jail for the
maximum period possible. Yet, open discussion and consensus-building
can help resolve these inherent systemic conflicts. The key ingredient
seems to be for each participant to develop a system and process orientation, and get past traditional, narrow, and parochial perspectives. The
jail administrator who understands court mandates and the need for humane, Constitutional jails, appears to be the logical person to initiate the
dialogue necessary to resolve this common and shared problem.

Another implication of correctional law is the need for jailers to expand their knowledge of the law. Most peace officers learn a significant
amount of criminal law in basic police academies. Relatively little attention is paid to tort law, Constitutional Law per se, or correctional law.
For example, in Michigan, the Michigan Law Enforcement Officers
Training Council (MLEOTC) standard for police academies requires
56 hours of training on substantive and procedural criminal law; only
two hours are mandated to cover correctional law (MLEOTC). Yet, police officers run lockups, some deputy sheriffs start their careers in the
county jail, and many personnel are often thrust into the position of
jailer after years of law enforcement duty as a "street" officer or "road"
officer. Somehow, usually through osmosis, these officers are suddenly
expected to supervise a jail or lockup operation. The same is often true
of the chief jail administrator. He or she may have had a brilliant career
as a law enforcer; suddenly, she or he is responsible for a jail or lockup,
yet has no background in correctional law, penal theory, or jail management. All jail personnel need a thorough grasp of Constitutional Law,
particularly those aspects affecting the operation of a Constitutional jail.
They need a thorough understanding of the implications of correctional law as a legal basis for inmate management (such as prescribed by
Kalinich and Postill). Training in this area cannot be superficial (Chapter 12 addresses training goals, techniques, and evaluation criteria).

A fourth implication for jail administrators is the need for **adequate**
policies and procedures. This means **written** policies and procedures
that are followed in practice, and supported by adequate training. Adequate policies and procedures are the backbone upon which supervision

and training should be attached. In the writer's former career as a military police officer and, more recently, in training and researching problems related to jail management and liability, no area seems more important.

Some agencies lack written policies or procedures. Others have them in two or three versions (depending on which copy of "the book" one removes from the shelf). In still other cases, the policies and procedures in "the book" are not the policies or procedures followed by supervisors and subordinates. Written policies and procedures vary from actual practice because the policies are not clear, procedures for implementing the policies are lacking, or because personnel are not trained on the policies and procedures.

A policy might read like this: "It is the policy of this agency to exert every possible effort to prevent jail suicides, including careful intake screening, and constant surveillance of persons identified as potentially suicidal. To insure that this policy is carried out, the shift commander will personally review the intake screening process and take such other actions as may be needed to assure inmates identified as a suicide threat are given constant supervision and observation." The procedures would be much more comprehensive and specific. The one on constant supervision might include provisions for the shift commander to authorize overtime payments so that an additional officer would be available and able to personally "eyeball" an inmate on a 60 second per minute basis until competent authority (clearly defined) determines that the suicide threat has subsided.

Next to a lack of adequate, written policies and procedures, inadequate training appears to be the single most important aspect of running a humane, Constitutional jail. Typically, training efforts are fragmented, sporadic, undocumented, and unmeasured. Research shows that most jail officers are undertrained and underutilized, and that most training programs lack a needs assessment to start, learning measurements at the end, and do not link with job requirements (e.g., see Lombardo, Chapter 12).

In some cases the training officer is appointed to the job because he or she cannot be trusted out on the road or in the jail. In other instances, the training officer may be a highly qualified officer, but one whose background does not equip her or him to teach every possible subject. Perhaps the officer has always been a road officer, rather than a jailer, yet is expected to teach others how to function in a jail. In other cases the officer's background may be so limited that his or her thinking does not extend beyond the agency's geographical boundary.

On the other side of the coin, the training officer, pressed for time, will often task supervisors to train—without providing clear-cut objectives, topical guidance, or measuring standards. Training may consist of a memo such as "conduct a class on the application of handcuffs." Almost every supervisor will teach something different; perhaps none will address the critical issue of double-locking the handcuffs (or leg irons) so as to prevent the serious, permanent injuries that have resulted in civil judgments against some departments and officers.

Another common training technique is the "train by memorandum" or "read and initial" concept. This approach poses problems in the event of a suit. Did the employee actually read the memo? Did the employee understand the memorandum? Was the employee able to do what the memo required?

These examples of "training" have been seen by almost every criminal justice practitioner. They have been defended in the name of fiscal constraints, time limitations, or because the chief administrator never developed an understanding of meaningful training. For jail administrators, the budgetary excuse is no defense. Adequate training **must** be conducted and documented. The alternative is poor performance and, perhaps, civil judgment based on inadequate training. Adequate training, like the other implications raised in this chapter, requires above all else, pro-active management and administration.

The jail administrator who sits back and waits for something to happen, and then reacts to it, will likely not be disappointed. Something will happen, a suit may follow, and someone will have to react. One need only read some of the legal authors, such as Avery and Rudovsky, to understand plaintiff tactics in litigating a civil suit. Once an incident occurs, a search will begin to place blame on someone. Full discovery may take place, including examination of the jail's operation, policies, procedures, training records, etc. Experts in the field may analyze the incident, including a history of prior incidents. Documentation will become crucial.

Pro-active management, on the other hand, requires the jail administrator to evaluate the jail operation, note problems, and begin making improvements. This will probably satisfy the legal duty to foresee. The jail must be evaluated against state requirements, Constitutional standards, and current professional standards, not just local standards.

Where there is a problem, the issue must be documented to those above the jail administrator. The pro-active administrator will not deny the existence of problems. In civil cases the concept of "knew or should have known" will come back to haunt the jail administrator who denies knowing about a problem or potential problem. Professional jail administrators are expected to know every problem in their jail.

Closely aligned to self-evaluation and documentation in pro-active management is the need to keep current. The rules under which jails and lockups are operated constantly change. The city attorney or county prosecutor should be challenged to keep the police chief, sheriff, and jail administrator constantly updated **on a timely basis.** Many do not, especially on a timely basis. Sometimes this is because administrators do not push the issue. Other times the chief administrator may not relay the information to the jail administrator. Regardless, without staying current, the jail administrator is likely to have outdated policies, procedures, or training materials.

In the long run, the pro-active jail administrator who engages in dialogue with other criminal justice system participants, who is current on the laws affecting the jail, and who has adequate policies, procedures, and training, is almost certain to operate a jail that is humane, Constitutional, and relatively immune to successful litigation.

The alternative, reactive approach, has been well-documented in terms of suits addressing negligent hiring, retention, supervision, direction, and training.

SUMMARY AND CONCLUSIONS

This chapter traced the evolution of correctional law. Correctional law does not exist in a vacuum. It includes Constitutional Law, civil law, and criminal law. Once understood, correctional law mandates that jail administrators initiate a dialogue and commitment with other participants in the local criminal justice system, for the problem of operating a humane, Constitutional jail is a shared problem. Open dialogue and shared commitment may generate funds and other support needed for a proper jail. If it doesn't, pro-active management will have documented the problem and at least shifted the burden in a civil suit, or possibly resulted in closing the jail.

While this seems somewhat simplistic, county commissioners, city council members, sheriffs, and police chiefs seem to understand the dilemma and the solution once they have lost a significant suit. The unfortunate aspect of the issue lies in the fact that it is all too easy to visit jails and lockups and hear such comments as "We've never had a jail suicide," "The county won't give us the funds," and "We understand, but the rules don't apply to us; besides, folks around here don't sue."

The literature involving the evolution of correctional law is replete with examples of similar comments. So too, are media accounts of court cases successfully litigated against governmental agencies and jail personnel!

As more and more jail administrators use the implications of correctional law to become pro-active managers who document their problems, develop adequate policies and procedures, and initiate viable training programs, those who cling to the old philosophies will assuredly become more and more at risk in civil court actions.

On balance, this seems to be the ultimate implication of the evolution of correctional law for jail administrators and supervisors.

REFERENCES

Allen, Harry E., and Clifford E. Simonsen, *Corrections in America: An Introduction.* 4th ed. New York: MacMillan, 1986.

Alpert, Geoffrey P., ed., *Legal Rights of Prisoners.* Beverly Hills: SAGE, 1980.

American Correctional Association, *Correctional Officer Resource Guide.* College Park, Md.: American Correctional Association, 1983.

Avery, Michael, and David Rudovsky, *Police Misconduct Law and Litigation.* New York: Clark Boardman, 1985.

Black, Henry Campbell, *Black's Law Dictionary.* 5th ed. St. Paul, MN: West, 1983.

Clute, Penelope D., *The Legal Aspects of Prisons and Jails.* Springfield, IL: Charles C Thomas, Publisher, 1980.

Eimermann, Thomas E., *Fundamentals of Paralegalism.* Boston: Little, Brown, 1980.

Embert, Paul S., *Optimizing The Cost Effectiveness of Military Corrections.* Washington, DC: Defense Documentation Center, 1978.

Hobbs, Douglas S., and Martin Shapiro, *American Constitutional Law Cases and Analyses.* Cambridge, MA: Winthrop, 1978.

Kalinich, David B. and Frederick J. Postill, *Principles of County Jail Administration and Management.* Springfield, IL: Charles C Thomas, Publisher, 1981.

Krantz, Sheldon, *The Law of Corrections and Prisoners' Rights; Cases and Materials.* 2nd ed. St. Paul, MN: West, 1981, as supplemented.

Law Offices of Craig, Farber, Downs, and Disc, P.C., "Client Update," Vol. I, No. 3, December, 1985.

Lewis, Peter W., and Kenneth D. Peoples, *The Supreme Court and the Criminal Process.* Philadelphia: Saunders, 1978.

Lund, Lynn J., *Liability in Personnel Management.* Salt Lake City: Corrections and Enforcement Training Associates, 1983.

Michigan, *Compiled Laws Annotated.* St. Paul, MN: West, 1968.

Michigan Law Enforcement Officers Training Council, *Basic Police Training Program; Basic Training Module Specifications*. Lansing, MI: State of Michigan, September, 1984.

Nagel, Stuart S., ed., *The Rights of the Accused in Law and Action*. Beverly Hills: SAGE, 1972.

Nahmond, Sheldon H., *Civil Rights and Civil Liberties Litigation*. New York: McGraw-Hill, 1979.

National Sheriff's Association, *Inmates Legal Rights*. Washington, DC: National Sheriff's Association, 1983.

National Street Law Institute, *Curriculum Materials Practical Law for Correctional Officers*. Washington, DC: National Institute of Corrections, 1978.

O'Brien, Edward; Margaret Fisher; and David T. Austein, *Practical Law for Correctional Personnel*. St. Paul, MN: West, 1981.

O'Brien, John P., and William C. Voigt, *Michigan Law Enforcement Manual*. Lansing, MI: Michigan Sheriff's Association, 1982.

Palmer, John W., *Constitutional Rights of Prisoners*. 2nd ed. Cincinnati: Anderson, 1977.

Rohde, David W., and Harold J. Spaeth, *Supreme Court Decision Making*. San Francisco: W.H. Freeman, 1976.

Sechrest, Dale, "The Legal Basis for Commission Standards," in *Proceedings of the American Correctional Association*. 1978.

Spain, Norman MacArthur, *Civil Law for Security Managers*. Pittsburg, PA: Norman MacArthur Spain, JD, CPP, Workbook, 1985.

Strom, Fredric A., ed., *Civil Rights Litigation and Attorney Fees Annual Handbook, Vol. One*. New York: Clark Boardman, 1985.

CHAPTER 6

OVERCROWDING AND THE JAIL BUDGET
Addressing Dilemmas of Population Control

Dave Kalinich

INTRODUCTION

IN TWO EARLIER articles in this reader, it was argued that jail officials should actively share the responsibility for problems within their
jail to the users of the jail facility: the local criminal justice system and
the community. In his article on the legal aspects of running a jail, Paul
Embert prescribes that jail administrators actively pursue assistance
from the local courts and prosecutors office in keeping up with the legal
changes (which consistently change), training of staff, as well as
cooperation on all other dimensions of jail management. Similarly, in
discussing the dilemmas of contemporary jail management earlier, I
propose that if jail operations are to improve, the criminal justice system
and the public must be influenced to share the responsibility for the
problems facing their jails and make substantive contributions to many
of the solutions. The problem addressed in this chapter is jail overcrowding.

The dilemma implicit in jail overcrowding is that Federal Courts
are defining and attempting to control overcrowding in local jails while
the local courts and criminal justice system continues to operate with
traditional practices, often utilizing the jail without regard to jail capacity limits (Taft, 1979; Flinn, 1984). The jail takes the burden of the
blame and responsibility for overcrowded conditions while having no
control over its population (Cromwell, 1975; Perlman, 1983). In this
chapter, methods to place the responsibility for jail overcrowding on the

criminal justice agencies are discussed. What is proposed are accountability systems that would manifest the use of jail space by criminal justice agencies in dollar terms. The first is a budgeting approach that would actually cause the local courts and criminal justice agencies to be debited for using the jail from their budgets. This is an unlikely scenario, but its presentation here provides a clear picture of the lack of accountability of criminal justice agencies for their use. The second approach, a realistic scenario, develops from the former budgeting approach as an accountability method, can provide a new feedback loop into the criminal justice process which can provide at least political incentives for criminal justice agencies and its actors to be more parsimonious with the use of the local jail facility. Presently, no measurable incentives exist for criminal justice system agencies to minimize their use of jail facilities. An accountability system that places at least some of the responsibility for overcrowding on criminal justice agencies may provide those agencies with incentive to process offenders more efficiently and maximize the use of alternatives to incarceration (Dale, 1980).

THE OVERCROWDING PROBLEM

Overcrowding has been a consistent problem for prisons and jails for the last decade, and has been considered a national epidemic (Allison, 1982). According to the 1983 Jail Census unused bed space decreased between 1978 and 1983 as occupancy rose from 66 percent to 81 percent. In large jails housing the majority of inmates, the occupancy rate rose from 77 percent to 96 percent within those years. In particular regions, occupancy rates peaked at 102 percent (U.S. Department of Justice, 1983). During 1982, correctional facilities operated from four to twenty percent above capacity (New York State Commission of Correction, 1983). Overcrowding was found to have negative physiological and psychological effects upon inmates (Paulus and McCain, 1983).

Overcrowding of jail facilities is not just a current problem. Barns and Tetters (1959) discuss this problem in their classic work and include a photo of jail inmates sleeping on the floor of an overcrowded jail in the midwest during the mid 1930s. The authors iterate recommendations put forward by the National Jail Committee of the American Correctional Association in 1937 that focused on the problem of jail overcrowding:

I. Measures to Keep People Out of Jail

    1. By law direct that the Courts adopt a more extended use of bail, recognizance, and other approved measures of release from custody.
    2. Secure a law providing for collection of fines by installment and sufficient personnel to enforce it.
    3. Develop an approved probation system, not only to prevent people from getting into jail, but to supervise and guide offenders released from custody.

In addition, the National Jail Committee recommended shorter sentence, and regional work camps as alternatives to traditional jail facilities.

Current prescriptions do not differ substantially from the general recommendations put forward by the National Jail Committee in 1937 (currently, offenders are not usually jailed in lieu of fines or restitution). Prescribed methods of dealing with pretrial offenders include a myriad of diversion programs, appearance tickets, and liberal bonding programs. Programs to impose some control or limits over convicted offenders have been work release, weekend custody, and population caps imposed by accepted systems-wide policy or court orders. Some jurisdictions have created central intake centers to screen out bond-eligible offenders upon their "intake" into the system without the usual time-consuming red tape that holds most systems hostage. The Law Enforcement Assistance Administration (LEAA) funded a series of programs aimed at reducing jail overcrowding in 1979 and 1980. Basically, an array of pretrial release programs, similar in essence to those mentioned, were developed in the various jurisdictions involved (Blumenthal, Neubaum, 1979, 1980; Neubaum and West, 1982).

In areas with overcrowded jails, informal and ad hoc measures are often taken in response to the population problem. Some judges appeared to be sensative to jail population in sentencing and setting bonds. In a particular jurisdiction in Michigan, judges were spending 60 to 70 percent of their time on the criminal docket in contrast to typical past practices of spending 60 to 70 percent of their time on the civil side of their case loads in an effort to process offenders quickly. Sheriffs often rent jail space at adjoining counties with available bed space in their jails.

Based upon legislation or practice, many jurisdictions require inmates to be housed in single cells. There are arguments that allowing double rather than single celling of inmates would quickly lead to adequate jail and prison space. However, many jails have ignored past practice and even state jail rules in favor of double bunking to deal with overcrowding (Lafay, 1983). Yet, double celling has been a short term solution for many of those jurisdictions as the influx of inmates has driven them beyond capacity provided by double celling.[1] Some more imaginative jail administrators have used storage space, class rooms — when available — or acquired space in motels or other private housing to deal with the numbers. In two jurisdictions familiar to this writer that had capacity caps imposed upon them by court decree, inmates were kept in transportation vans during the inmate count. One sheriff "sneaked" inmates out of his jail to the local city lock-up that had been officially closed. It must have been a delightful sight watching inmates sneaking deftly in line through an alley with bed rolls on their backs.

It is difficult to categorically discuss success or failure of any of the discussed attempts to alleviate or control overcrowding. The evaluation of LEAA's pretrial overcrowding program (1981) concluded that the average population of jails involved in the program had not been observed to decrease. However, this lack of reduction when viewed against increasing arrests and bookings may not necessarily be pessimistic. Most jurisdictions familiar to this writer usually scramble to develop programs aimed at releasing offenders after those forces which contribute to overcrowding have gathered momentum. Like the jurisdictions evolved in the LEAA program, they manage to keep even through developing programs, ad hoc efforts of the systems practitioners, and "sneaking" inmates down an alley to other sleeping accommodations with their bed rolls on their backs. Basically, when systems are faced with pressures that create jail overcrowding they will make those changes that are the least cost economically and politically and that, at least hopefully, will keep jail facilities at no more than 100 percent capacity. Given the criminal justice system tradition of reactive rather than proactive management, it is easy to surmise that overcrowding is only a problem when it is at hand. Thus, programs to deal with overcrowding are usually limited, being born of immediate needs, and not considering of long term systems alterations that can lead to proactive ways of recognizing and dealing with jail overcrowding before the fact (Garry, 1984; Dale, 1980).

What is initially being proposed here is a budgeting process that makes criminal justice system agencies and their sub-agencies accountable for their use of the jail facility on a per diem basis. Presently, jail administrators submit line item budgets, or in rare cases some form of program budget, for the forthcoming fiscal year. The budget, of course is an estimate of cost the jail will incur for housing and maintaining inmates as well as other peripheral costs such as building repair, etc. Other criminal justice system agencies similarly submit budgets to county governmental bodies based on projects of their operating needs for the forthcoming fiscal year. For the most part, each criminal justice system component submits a budget, including the jail, independent of other components. Some interdependent considerations can exist. If a component estimates its work load will increase because of the activity of other criminal justice system components, it will reflect that estimate in its budget. Thus, if a jail administrator predicts increased inmate population for the forthcoming year, additional resources may be requested during the budgeting process. However, no system-wide coordinated program budgeting takes place. Each component of the criminal justice system passes units of work forward to other components and all use and depend upon the jail to house inmates who are being processed and sentenced. Component agencies use the jail while expenditures for their use of the jail are extracted from the jail budget. Therefore, those criminal justice agencies that routinely utilize jail space, have no economic incentive to be sensative or efficient with the use of the jail. A budgeting process that imposes a per diem cost on criminal justice system components for their use of the system's jail would provide an economic incentive for those agencies to make efficient use of jail space. In addition, such incentive may cause components to review their methods and work habits and perhaps lead to greater efficiency in general in the processing of criminal cases.

THE BUDGET AS A MANAGEMENT TOOL

Most jails and criminal justice system agencies submit "lump sum" budgets or "line item" budgets to their funding authorities. Lump sum budgeting, which was prevalent around the turn of the century and still exists in many jurisdictions today, means simply that the operating agency would ask for and be given a "lump sum" of money for its fiscal period. The only link between lump sum budgeting and planning is the need for an agency to calculate how much the lump sum has to be to operate during its fiscal time period. The calculations would likely be based upon past expenditures. Line item budgeting is probably the most common form of budgeting used by criminal justice system agencies (Kramer, 1976). This form of budgeting is a step up from lump sum budgeting as it requires that items required for the operations of an agency be listed by category and a price tag placed on the items categorized to prepare a budget based upon a summary of projected needs. Line item budgeting requires an analysis of needs by listing the items that are required for each category of operation. However, if agencies simply show previous years' budgets with inflation factored in, such a submission becomes, in effect, a lump sum budget.

As the art of budgeting evolved, the notion that budgets could be used as management tools became popular. Three forms of management budgets have been developed: (1) Management or performance budget planning; (2) planning, programming and budgeting (PPB); (3) zero based budgeting. The first form considers efficiency by comparing dollars spent to work performed. However, the measure of efficiency is no guarantee that what is produced has any value (Hudzik and Cordner, 1983). The second approach, PPB, requires that the agency develop its budget based upon the agency's objectives and goals. Hence, an attempt is made to link the agency's resource distribution programatically to the agency's desired output. Zero based budgeting, developed in the early 1970s goes beyond PPB in an attempt to make budgeting a planning and management tool. Zero based budgeting requires that the submitting agency start the budgeting process from a zero base. Starting from the zero base, all programs must be re-examined and rejustified (Hammond, Thomas, Knotts, 1980). In addition, a "decision package" must be prepared for all individual activities however limited in scope. The decision package requires a description of the activity being proposed, an explanation of how the activity relates to the agency's objectives and goals, an analysis of the alternative way the activity can be achieved with a cost benefit statement attached to each alternative, and a statement of how performance can be measured (Hudzik and Cordner, 1983). For the criminal justice system, it is conceivable that each agency could submit zero based budgets based on their agency's goals and objectives, and each agency's goals and objectives could be dictated by a set of operational goals and objectives promulgated by some overriding authority for a community's criminal justice system. Using a management budget technique for a criminal justice system could promote systems-wide planning, which could include parsimonious use of the system's jail facility. It is not likely, however, that a system will move from traditional line item budgeting to a complicated and time consuming management budget approach just to protect the interest of the jail. In addition, agencies that have been required to move from line item budgeting to PPB have been accused of submitting basically line item budgets with a PPB format. In other words, agencies would rationalize line item submissions rather than think programatically when developing their budgets (Wildavsky, 1979). Hence, what is being suggested here is not a sophisticated budget technique, rather, what is prescribed is a modification of the variable cost budgeting approach that has been traditionally used for jails.

TRADITIONAL JAIL BUDGETING PRACTICES

Jails have traditionally been funded through a combination of line item/lump sum budgets and per diem allotments for variable costs of housing inmates. For items such as vehicles, maintenance equipment and maintenance expenses, personnel and related costs, utilities, paper and pencils, are usually submitted with line item/lump sum budgets. However, there are variable costs that are related to inmate maintenance and vary with inmate population that have been funded to the jail on monthly or weekly basis. The variable cost are computed on a per diem basis: the greater the inmate population, the more funds received by the jail from the county governmental treasury. The per diem costs usually include food items, clothing, laundry services, basic medical supplies, etc.

The system of per diem funding has its roots in the jail fee system established in the early English jails (Barnes and Tetters, 1959). The inmates were provided with less than basic goods and services by the crown. Any additional amenities such as adequate food or clothing had to be paid for by the friends or relatives of the inmates to the jailor who took his cut or fee before providing the inmate with additional goods. This cut or fee was the legal income of the jailor. Higher inmate populations, especially those with friends or families who could afford to assist them, would increase the jailor's wages. The fee system in its crass sense is no longer prevalent. However, if the present per diem system can be manipulated legitimately, or illegitimately, to the benefit of those who administer jails, incentives may exist to encourage a high jail population. At least little incentive exists to work toward lowering jail populations short of law suits that spring directly from overcrowding or indirectly from ineffective management of inmates that relates to crowded conditions. What is proposed below is a modification of the per diem system that creates criminal justice systems-wide incentives to use the jail parsimoniously.

SYSTEMS ACCOUNTABILITY AND JAIL USE:
THE BEST CASE SCENARIO

The budgetary process prescribed here requires first a comprehensive assessment of inmate per diem cost, and second, a method of charging criminal justice agencies for placing and keeping offenders under their jurisdiction in the jail facility. The charge to the criminal justice agencies would be tantamount to rental charged on a per diem basis for the inmates they are processing or have sentenced. This is obviously easier to prescribe than to implement. However, I will start with the unrealistic scenario—being that a criminal justice system would willingly set aside a decade of budgeting tradition including the self-interest that goes with it in favor of the jail rental scheme. I will attempt to sketch out the format for the jail rental scheme as well as discuss the legitimate problems that would be created if a criminal justice system willingly accepted such a scheme. The value of discussing the best case scenario is that it leads logically to a discussion of a system of accountability for jail space use which is a realistic scenario. While the second approach will appear to be less powerful than a jail space rental system in controlling jail population, its implementation is more likely, and it can be a powerful political tool which may point out the misuse of the jail facilities.

The premise for the prescriptions presented here is not an effort to reduce jail populations without regard to the legitimate need for incarceration for particular pre- or post-adjudication offenders. Rather, it is to eliminate the misuse of a criminal justice systems jail facility based on standards that are held as legitimate by members of a criminal justice system being subjected to accountability tests. Misuse of a jail facility is defined here as inefficient processing of incarcerated offenders, and inefficient use of credible community alternatives to incarceration.

In the ideal scheme of jail budgeting being proposed here, jail space would literally be rented to the agencies that have jurisdiction over offenders while they are in custody. The rental would be a per diem charge paid to the jail by the agencies of jurisdiction by a transfer from that agency's budget to the jail budget. To achieve this, two primary determinations must be reached within a criminal justice system. First, a per diem cost or charge for incarcerated offenders must be established; and, secondly, in the sometime fuzzy offender flow, identifying which agency has jurisdiction over incarcerated offenders at a particular time during the process.

Determining per diem cost is more than a matter of cost accounting. Typically, per diem costs funded from the county treasury to jail

operations were based upon those costs noted above that are clearly variables; that is, additional cost necessary to house one more offender.
However, if one were actually renting space in a physical facility, the
owners of the space would need to recuperate their capitol investment,
maintenance, and personnel costs in order to maintain ownership and
operate the facility. It can be argued then that per diem rental cost for
jail space should include all personnel, maintenance, and housekeeping
costs incurred in running a jail, as well as the cost of the physical plant
amortized over a period of years as well as variable cost. Actual capacity
should be used in the per diem calculation. In short, all costs of running
the jail divided by capacity should determine the per diem rental.

Assigning jurisdiction over offenders is often vague if we are attempting to identify what sub-agency is actively working on a case and, hence,
responsible for the efficiency or inefficiency with which a case is processed. For example, the prosecutor may be moving slowly to facilitate
plea bargaining, yet the court will be charged with delayed case processing. Probation officers may delay in producing presentence investigations which will create a backlog of cases pending sentence.
Concurrently, probation officer delays may be due, in part, to a lack of
cooperation by the jail staff in facilitating interviews between offenders
and probation officers. In addition, delays may be created by the usually
forgotten clerk of courts office in passing the paperwork from one jurisdiction to the next. This is especially true when lower courts bind felony
cases over to the higher courts. The offenders bound over may sit in jail
for a number of days before the higher court is made aware, through
court entry, that the offenders are within the higher court authority. In
addition, I have even witnessed examples of offenders spending a number of days in jail after their release has been effected by the court as the
clerk's office took days to process and forward the release order to the
jail. This section can't be left without recognizing the impact defense attorneys can have on slowing the process by delays and continuances.

There is a web of influences and sub-agencies involved in the processing of offenders. To attempt to identify all of the various sources of
influence clearly would be a difficult task that would undoubtedly produce erroneous assignments of responsibilities to particular sub-agencies
or support services. The more realistic approach recommended here is
to make each local court responsible for renting jail space while it has offenders under its jurisdiction. Presumably, in the interest of managing
their fiscal affairs efficiently, each court would be left to identify the inef-
ficiencies within their own sub-agencies. Then, for example, when a

lower court's clerk of court agency delays in forwarding the paperwork to the higher courts, officially binding over an offender to the jurisdiction of the higher court, the lower court would pay rental for the jail space during that period of delay. The court in question would, in the interest of saving money, consider that delay a problem and choose to take some management steps to eliminate the delay. Thus, in this scheme, the courts would be considered the overriding body and be charged jail rental for all offenders under its jurisdiction. The court would be left to manage its own sub-agencies — probation department, prosecutor's office, clerk of courts, administrative support systems, as well as its own docket scheduling. In addition, other jurisdictions such as Federal criminal justice organizations, state parole, etc., should be charged per diem jail space rental for the housing of offenders of their jurisdiction.

Perhaps the most difficult question to grapple with is the amount of money that should be allocated to each court for the purpose of renting jail space. Relying upon past patterns of jail use by courts to allocate funds for future use is one approach. However, if funds were allocated based upon 100 percent of past practices, no change would be effected. Even if past practices were used minus some percent based upon an apriori judgment, it could be argued that the systems that were inefficient in the past would be rewarded. Another approach, would be to calculate the average jail days spent for offenders from the lower court systems and allocate funds in proportion to the varying case loads back to the courts. This, of course, would apply to communities that have more than one lower court. The argument against this might be that one court may have a case load with higher risk and higher sentence potential than its counterparts. In short, an objective or systematic method to allocate jail rental funds to courts would be difficult to devise and may be the most difficult programmatic aspect of this approach to implement.

The courts could simply be left to request their jail rental funds through a lump sum or line item budget approach. The budget request would likely be based on past jail use and, as such, no incentive would exist to process cases more efficiently. An incentive such as allowing courts to utilize realized savings — the difference between jail rental funds alloted and expended during a fiscal period — for training or equipment purchase would need to be an explicit part of such an innovation. This, in turn, may give courts the incentive to overstate jail rental budget requests to gain extra operating funds from the difference that will be spent on projected jail use and the amount requested.

Other practical problems may result from the implementation of a jail rental budgeting system:

- District courts (lower court) and circuit courts (higher court) are managed by different branches of local governments. Therefore, budgeting for conceptually the same criminal justice system is controlled by two separate authorities. This could create a myriad of problems.
- Quality of decision making about releasing or incarcerating offenders may be negatively affected. Offenders may be released spuriously just to avoid cost responsibility and system accountability.
- Alternative forms of incarceration may be created by agencies when forced to bear the expense of using the county jail. Lockups may be used with more frequency. Offenders who would ordinarily serve felony sentences in county jails might be sentenced to the State Department of Corrections.
- Political friction between criminal justice components may develop or increase as they attempt to pass jurisdiction, responsibility and/ or accountability for offenders to one another.
- Arresting agencies may inappropriately be pressed to reduce arrest rates.

Before such programmatic problems would come to bear, major political problems would probably preclude even serious consideration of a plan that requires courts to rent jail space for the incarcerated offenders that are within their jurisdiction. To begin with, courts have traditionally been viewed as the dominant power in the formal political criminal justice network and the focal point of the most crucial decision making. At least this view is taken by the courts, and their political influence is usually greater than other criminal justice actors. From the court's point of view the jail's role is to serve the court; and, as such, the court system need not be tampered with or subjected to accountability to serve the jail. In addition, the judiciary would undoubtedly struggle to preserve their power to incarcerate individuals without facing any controls or incumbrances outside of existing legal constraints. The judiciary, which is a powerful political force in county government would most likely successfully oppose such a scheme.

Opposition would probably come from the prosecutor's office and probation department which are accustomed to using the local jail as a filing cabinet for pending work. In fact, having offenders in jail gives the prosecutor a relative advantage in plea bargaining. Probation officers benefit by being able to give low priority attention to those offenders referred for presentence work who remain incarcerated. In short, the actors in the criminal justice system, especially the court system, would not stand still for a system that required greater efficiency of them for the benefit of the jail. All of the programmatic objections alluded to above would be articulated in opposition to the budgeting proposal put forward here. However, the hidden premise for such arguments would probably be the reaction against a system of accountability which focus on jail needs and places constraints on judicial prerogatives (Bolduc, A., 1981).

AN ALTERNATIVE APPROACH: A REALISTIC SCENARIO

The jail rental system proposed does not have much of a chance for implementation. However, there is an alternative approach that can be implemented that is based upon the factors implicit in the jail rental concept of jail use accountability. The logic presenting an accountability system that is not politically feasible was to make a case for the legitimacy of accountability being imposed upon the agencies using the jail as well to argue that accountability can be measured on a per diem cost basis for the use of the jail. The alternative approach to accountability being presented is one of cost recognition that can be deployed as feedback or pressure on those who are inefficient with the use of the jail as opposed to a jail rental scheme.

Those who are familiar with jail operations understand that jail administrators and often other members of the jail staff, have an impression of what criminal justice actors, agencies, or sub-systems use the jail with the most frequency. For example, jail administrators know which judges give long sentences to offenders that are usually handled leniently by other judges, and can identify probation officers who give low priority to presentence investigations on incarcerated referrals, etc. What is suggested is that those impressions be made discrete and interpreted into cost figures so that the agencies, their sub-agencies, and actors can be tracked in their use of the jail. The use of the jail demonstrated in cost figures could show the relative use or misuse of the jail facilities by the agencies, sub-agencies, and actors of the local criminal justice system. This information could be converted into feedback into the criminal justice system and the local governmental system to pressure inefficient agencies into more efficient use of the jail facilities.

Much of the data needed for this system can be found in the inmate files created by the jail facilities. The remainder is to be found in the criminal justice system, especially in the clerk of courts office. Collecting and systematically organizing the data would take some planning and effort on the part of the criminal justice system or jail administrators. In short, the data have always been available but there has been no incentive to use it for jail management purposes. The possibility of distributing the responsibility for overcrowded jails back to the criminal justice system would seem to be ample incentive for jail administrators and other actors in the criminal justice system concerned with efficient processing of offenders to develop a system to collect the necessary information. The more crucial question is how to feed the information back into the system to create inputs that will cause agencies, sub-agencies and their actors to break well established habits that cause misuse of the jail facility.

Feedback represents the influences that an organization's outputs have upon its working environment that shape subsequent inputs (Sharkansky, 72). In the case of a local criminal justice system typically, the working environment includes interested members of the local community, the media (during times of crises), inmates and their relatives, defense attorneys, local governmental bodies, and federal district courts. The output from the jail in the form of information on cost consequences of misuse of the jail facility must have sufficient impact upon some or all of those components of the criminal justice system environment to influence them to the extent that inputs from that environment into the criminal justice system create a demand for more efficient use of jail facilities. In addition, withinputs from the jail to the criminal justice system components should be brought to bear to press for more efficient use of the jail. What needs to be considered are strategies to create sufficient environmental and system-wide static to produce inputs and withinputs from jail use cost information. The inputs and withinputs must be strong enough to create a positive substantive response from the members of the criminal justice system that directly or indirectly contribute to inefficient use of jail space.

Two strategy extremes would be to quietly convey the information to members of the criminal justice system, or, at the other extreme, to use the local media to expose those criminal justice components that are wasteful with jail resources. The failure of the former is self-evident, and the latter strategy would likely gain very short-term public attention and long-term hostility from the "exposed" criminal justice system members. Although, judicious use of the media can create useful static. The strategy developed must be forceful enough to get the attention of policy makers and staff within the criminal justice system and be perceived by them as legitimate. In addition, the strategy selected must create linkages to components of the criminal justice system working environment in order to create both demand and support for change within the criminal justice system that may be required to promote systems wide parsimonious use of the jail facility. A myriad of strategies can be created by the imaginative organizational mind. One in particular that fits the requirements just described will be discussed. That to be discussed is the development of a broad based Jail Advisory Committee to turn the jail use cost output information into inputs and withinputs for the criminal justice system.

The immediate response for practitioners and academics alike is to shudder at the thought of "oh my God, another committee!" However, it makes eminent sense if the committee is structured and functions to place pressure on particular criminal justice system components or members rather than acting as a passive advisory board, as is usually the case. The committee should be formed ostensibly to make recommendations of jail problems, and membership should include individuals from significant components of the criminal justice system working environment, including the media, as well as representatives from the components of the criminal justice system. Bringing information to a committee with this membership that exposes inefficient use of jail space by criminal justice system components and its members measured in monetary terms can create both environmental static and conflict within the criminal justice system. The static can create demands and support for new programs and approaches to processing offenders and utilizing jail alternatives. The conflict within the system can create vulnerability on the part of criminal justice agencies and members who misuse the jail facility; hence, creating conditions for change. In the long run, continued explicit analysis of jail overcrowding in monetary terms as a function or inefficient use of jail space by criminal justice system agencies and its members can force viewing overcrowding as a system problem rather than a jail problem. It is common to hear reference to system-wide planning, but long-term solutions typically focus on seeking additional jail space and not on substantial improvement in efficient use of existing jail space.

The effectiveness of any strategy depends first upon a cost accounting system for jail use that accurately describes the varying case per diem use of jail space by various criminal justice system agencies in dollar terms. Then efficient use of jail space can be questioned in relative terms, i.e., court A costs more than court B, and in absolute terms, i.e., is it worth the dollar cost to take five to seven weeks to produce a presentence report on an incarcerated offender, and can that time be shortened? In addition, the jail committee strategy recommendation requires active members, and the cost information must be presented to such a committee with the intent to create static and conflict — a delicate task for the sheriff, an elected official. However, a passive board will be ineffective, and cost data submitted to even an active committee in a passive format may not get attention.

In the brief outline of working environment components above, the Federal District Court was mentioned. While it is not necessarily recommended that an officer from that court hold membership on a jail advisory committee, it is not unusual for jail problems, especially overcrowding, to be addressed by such courts as a result of civil rights suits. It is routine for a settlement between the District Court and the local jurisdiction to be reached by compromise through a consent decree. Invariably, the focus of the decree is upon the jail and population, and population caps are common. By being able to show that jail overcrowding is partially a function of inefficient use of jail space on the part of some or all of the components of the criminal justice system the jail serves, negotiations toward a consent decree could focus on offender processing practices as well as the jail itself. While federal district courts may be reluctant to reformulate policy for offender processing and use of jail alternatives, going to court with documentation that spreads the responsibility for jail overcrowding across the criminal justice system is a far stronger posture than jail administrators or sheriffs usually assume when federal courts intervene into their affairs.

Jail administrators may view this approach as another prescription that will result in more paperwork and responsibilities and meetings upon which to spend their limited time and energies. They may feel that nothing will bring relief except new facilities and more personnel. And, if one is patient, additional resources will be forthcoming: "someone will have to do something." These are undoubtedly the thoughts of those who see prescriptions for actions as "pie in the sky" as they wait for "someone to do something!" At the risk of sounding simple minded, it seems the recommendations presented here are superior to "sneaking inmates down the alley with their bed rolls."

NOTE

[1]Information from the Michigan Department of Corrections, Bureau of Facility Services, Jail Inspection, 1985.

REFERENCES

Allison, R., "Overcrowding Is Now A National Epidemic." From Crisis In The Jails, *Correction Magazine*, Vol. 7, No. 2, (April 1982):18-34.

Barnes, Harry and Negley K. Teeters. (1959) *New Horizons in Criminology*, 3rd edition. Englewood Cliffs, NJ: Prentice-Hall, Inc.

Blumenthal, M.; J. Neubaum; and A. West. *Jail Overcrowding and Pretrial Detention: A Program Evaluation (May 1979-September 1980)*. LEAA Grant, Denver Research Institute.

Bolduc, A., "Jail Overcrowding Issues and Analysis." *Annual Journal*, Vol. 4, (1981):122-136.

Bureau of Justice Statistics Bulletin. "The 1983 Jail Census." Washington, DC: National Bureau of Justice Statistics. (1983).

Cromwell, Paul F., Ed. (1975) *Jail and Justice*. Springfield, IL: Charles C Thomas, Publisher. See "The Evolution of Judicial Involvement" by Mike Place and David Sands.

Dale, J. H., Jr., "Strategies to Reduce Local Jail Overcrowding." National Institute of Justice.

Finn P., "Judicial Responses to Prison Crowding." *Judicature*, Vol. 6, No. 7, (February 1984):318-325.

Garry, Eileen, "Options to Prison Crowding." Washington, DC: National Criminal Justice Reference Service, U.S. National Institute of Justice (1981).

Hammond, Thomas and Jack Knotts. "A Zero Base Look at Zero-base Budgeting." Transaction Books, (1980).

Hudzik, John and Gary W. Cordner. (1983) *Planning in Criminal Justice Organizations and Systems*. New York, NY: Macmillan Co., Inc.

Kramer, F. (1976) *Contemporary Approaches to Public Budgeting*, Winthrop Publishers.

LaFay, M. "Double-celling in the Prisons—The Shame of the Courts." *New England Journal on Criminal and Civil Confinement*, Vol. 9, No. 1, (Winter 1983):249-278.

New York State Commission of Correction. *Correctional Facilities Populations Across New York State—Final Report*. Albany, NY: National Institute of Justice.

Paulus, P.B. and G. McCain. "Crowding in Jails." *Basic and Applied Social Psychology*, Vol. 4, No. 2, (1983):89-107.

Perlman, E.; A.C. Price and C. Webber. "Judicial Discretion and Jail Overcrowding." *Justice System Journal*, Vol. 18, No. 2 (Summer 1983):222-223.

Sharkansky. (1972) *Public Administration: Policy-Making in Government Agencies*. Markham Publishing Co.

Taft, P.B. Jr. "Backed-up in Jails—County Lock-ups Overflow as Courts Clamp Down on State Prisons." *Corrections Magazine*, Vol. 5, No. 2, (June 1979):26-33. New York, NY: Criminal Justice Publications, Inc.

Wildavsky, Aaron. (1979) *The Politics of Budgeting Process*. Little, Brown and Company, 3rd edition.

CHAPTER 7

PROBLEMS FACING WOMEN
IN LOCAL JAILS*

Ralph A. Weisheit and
Lesley I. Parsons

ABSTRACT

Despite the current interest in women in criminal justice, both as offenders and as employees, the status of women in jail is a largely unexplored area. In particular, we know little about the unique problems facing the female jail inmate and the availability of services to meet these needs. This study begins by summarizing what we know about the processing of female offenders through the criminal justice system, followed by a brief overview of the treatment of special populations within the local jail. Next, data from the 1978 Survey of Jail Inmates are analyzed to determine characteristics of females housed in local jails. Attention is focused on background and individual characteristics which are distinct from male inmates. Finally, the implications of these unique characteristics are considered as they relate to the treatment of female offenders.

INTRODUCTION

IN RECENT YEARS, the number of females in local jails has increased at an alarming rate. Comparing the 1978 and 1983 Census

*The data utilized in this article were made available by the Inter-University Consortium for Political and Social Research. The data were originally collected by the U.S. Department of Justice. Neither the original source or collectors of the data nor the Consortium bear any responsibility for the analyses or interpretations presented here.

of Jail Inmates, for example, shows that in just five years the number of women in jail have increased 73 percent while the number of male inmates have increased by only 41 percent (U.S. Department of Justice, 1984). While, the actual number of women in jail is still relatively small, their numbers are growing. In 1978 women represented 5.8 percent of the jail population, and by 1983 this figure had grown to 7.2 percent. Thus, although women traditionally have been a small group, their growing numbers promise to present major management problems for jail administrators in the near future.

Responding to these management problems has been given a new sense of urgency by recent litigation on behalf of female offenders. It was not until 1979, for example, that the first case granting female offenders equal protection was heard (Leonard, 1983). And, while female offenders have traditionally avoided recourse to litigation to force the implementation of prison programs, their lawsuits have been relatively successful in court (Aylward and Thomas, 1984). Alpert (1982) has noted that women in prison seeking legal remedies have a variety of avenues available for pursuing programs comparable to those for men, including Section 1983 of the Civil Rights Act of 1871, the eighth amendment, and the equal protection clause of the fourteenth amendment. He also notes that possible future avenues, which have not been utilized or available to date, include Title VII of the Civil Rights Act of 1964 and the Equal Rights Amendment.

Prison litigation by women is relatively rare compared to that by men and cases brought by women have, for the most part, focused on conditions in prisons, rather than local jails. There are a variety of likely reasons for this. First, the local jail is much more of a short-term facility. Second, while large jails may give prisoners access to law materials, most offenders are housed in small or medium sized facilities in which law materials are less readily available. Third, offenders awaiting trial are likely to spend much of their jail time preparing for their defense in court, and once convicted, those serving time in jail are not likely to be there for any extended period.

While there are only a few studies of programs available for women in prison (Glick and Neto, 1977; Chapman, 1980; Ryan, 1984), there is almost no information about programs for women in jails. The purpose of the present study is to examine characteristics of female offenders housed in local jails to determine the special program needs of this population.

The study is based on responses to a national survey of jail inmates conducted in 1978 in which a variety of questions were asked about the offender's background, offense, and experiences in the jail setting. Before turning to the data, it is important to describe the local jail and to highlight problems in jail management, particularly as they relate to the provision of programs for offenders.

THE LOCAL JAIL

History and Overview

Most reforms within the criminal justice system have been directed at prisons and long-term incarcerated offenders. In contrast to prisons, jails are primarily pretrial detention facilities which are administered at the county level. They are also holding facilities for short-term misdemeanant offenders and for those not suitable for other facilities or the community. The predominant types of people in jail are the poor, who cannot afford bail, or those charged with a serious offense for which bail has been denied (Goldfarb, 1976:3).

The first jails were established in England around 1100. These jails were usually used for pretrial confinement, but not to house offenders after a conviction (Moynahan and Stewart, 1980:13). Corporal punishment, rather than incarceration was the typical punishment for convicted offenders. These early jails were "located in pre-existing structures such as towers, cellars, dungeons, and under-bridge abutments (Moynahan and Stewart, 1980:15)." These jails were often only a single room and there was no attempt to segregate prisoners by sex, age or offense. "Men and women, children and hardened offenders, murderers and beggars were all confined together (Moynahan and Stewart, 1980:15)."

By the 1700's jail conditions had not improved but the function of the jail had changed. Reformers had shifted the focus from corporal punishment to long-term confinement and convicted offenders were housed with pretrial detainees. As this method of punishment became more popular prisons were designed to hole the long-term offenders and jails were returned to their previous state of holding suspected offenders. The reformers then focused on bettering the conditions of prisons for the convicted offenders. The jails were not touched by the early reform movements and "remained the same deplorable places they had always been (Moynahan and Stewart, 1980:36)."

By the 1900's various steps had been taken to improve the conditions of jails. Most states passed legislation to improve jail conditions, however, the laws were often not enforced (Moynahan and Stewart,

1980:69). Most jail legislation has been concerned with separating offenders and improving the sanitary conditions of jails. Ironically, reforms may have actually made conditions in jails worse. Briar, for example, notes that early jails were utilized as and modeled after shelters for the mentally ill, the handicapped, and the poor, while "Jails today are modeled after prisons and, as a result, they are more dangerous, punitive, and personally damaging than those of colonial times (Briar, 1983:388)." While the local grand jury is generally charged with monitoring jail conditions, their impact on conditions seems minimal at best. For the most part, jails have not been under the kind of close scrutiny common with prisons.

Special Populations

Adverse conditions in local jails particularly impinge upon some special populations. The term "special" refers to the fact that these groups pose unusual behavioral problems or for other reasons require special treatment. Among these groups are children, the mentally ill, and women. Our discussion will focus more directly on women in the next section, for now we will note the problems of children and the mentally ill.

The history of jails shows that children were given no special treatment. Children were placed in the same cells with men and women with no regard for offenses committed (Moynahan and Stewart, 1980:44). Not surprisingly, such young people were particularly susceptible to physical and sexual abuse. In recent years there has been a trend to physically separate juvenile offenders from adults (Moynahan and Stewart, 1980:44).

In 1974, the Juvenile Justice and Delinquency Prevention Act said that juveniles had to be separated from adults by sight and sound (U.S. Department of Justice, 1983:5). Although the idea behind this act was good, it created further problems concerning juveniles in jails. In many jails the only area that would provide sight and sound separation is solitary confinement (Community Research Forum, 1980:1). Being placed in solitary confinement may, in the long run, be much more damaging than being in contact with adult offenders. Children have a difficult time adjusting to incarceration and may develop deep psychological problems from even a short stay in an institution. Phobias and nightmares are common symptoms of the psychological stress placed on youthful inmates (Cottle, 1979:332) and the suicide rate among these youth is particularly high (Flaherty, 1980).

Even if juveniles are not placed in solitary confinement, they will be left in virtual idleness. Most jails have no recreational or educational programs. If recreation is provided it is usually for about an hour a day, leaving 23 hours of idleness (Goldfarb, 1976:313).

The mentally ill in jail also pose problems. Since jails are only intended for short-term incarceration, few have the facilities available to care for and treat mentally ill inmates. The concern of most administrators in county jails is that of apprehending offenders and holding them for the court. "Treatment of any sort is not included in this mission either by mandate or by orientation (McCarty, Steadman and Morrissey, 1982:62)."

The mentally ill in jail also pose security risks. These individuals "must be protected from themselves and other inmates, and prevented from endangering others or disrupting the tense, delicate balance of the jail environment (Goldfarb, 1976:94)." The mentally ill require additional supervision to prevent harm to themselves or to other inmates.

In many instances mentally ill inmates will be untreated or unsupervised because they are not identified as mentally ill. Inmates who are confined while awaiting competency hearings or those waiting for placement in a medical facility are obviously identified and given special consideration. However, there are many inmates who have not been formally recognized as mentally ill but suffer from a wide range of mental illnesses. These are the inmates who create the "serious suicide risks, the preponderance of their aggressive-assaultive prisoners, and no doubt many of the inmates who create serious disciplinary problems (Goldfarb, 1976:100)." Most of the problems will be dealt with through disciplinary measures rather than through treatment. "The results, whether they take the form of a reprimand, a deprivation of privledges, or a spell in solitary confinement, merely serve to exacerbate the prisoner's mental condition (Goldfarb, 1976:111)."

WOMEN IN JAIL

Women who are placed in jail also create special problems for administrators due to their special problems and needs. Because of their limited numbers, and a greater willingness to view them as members of a "dependent" class, women share many of the problems faced by children and the mentally ill in jail. The U.S. Department of Justice estimates that only about 7 percent of jail inmates are female (U.S.

Dept. of Justice, 1984). Their relatively small numbers make the provision of special programs difficult and expensive, reducing the likelihood that mechanisms will be in place to identify and deal with special needs.

A variety of problems may be faced by the female offender in jail, including those related to health, family problems, financial problems, and alcohol/drug use. In addition, we might also expect women in jail to be without many basic skills which would enable them to be financially independent upon release. The extent to which female inmates experience these problems may be examined utilizing data from the 1978 national survey of over 5,000 jail inmates. First, our attention turns to a brief description of the data.

THE DATA

Jail data were gathered from 5,247 individuals in a national sample of 421 jails during 1978. The survey was conducted by the U.S. Census Bureau for the Law Enforcement Assistance Administration, utilizing personal interviews and including more than 500 variables. The data are particularly useful for this study since a self-weighted sample was collected to obtain a sufficiently large number of females (n = 1500). The sample included individuals from all stages of the judicial process in which local detention (i.e., jail) is an option, from those not yet arraigned to those sentenced and serving time. Before discussing specific problems facing women in jail, our attention turns to a general description of the criminal histories of inmates in the sample. Readers interested in a more detailed description of sampling and measurement issues should refer to the **Profile of Jail Inmates** (U.S. Department of Justice, 1980).

OFFENSE PATTERNS AND CRIMINAL HISTORY[1]

To simplify the analysis, the original 66 categories of crime were collapsed to form 5 major offense categories: (1) violent crime, (2) property crime, (3) drug trafficking, (4) drug use, and (5) other miscellaneous categories (e.g., invasion of privacy, morals, prostitution, drunkenness, court offenses, etc.). Table 1 shows the distribution of these offense categories throughout the sample by sex.

TABLE 1

Percent of Offenders in Each Offense Category by Sex

OFFENSE CATEGORY	MALE	FEMALE
VIOLENT	28.2%	21.3%
PROPERTY	42.6	45.4
DRUG TRAFFICKING	3.6	5.1
DRUG USE	4.4	9.4
OTHER OFFENSES	21.2	18.8
TOTAL %	100.0	100.0
TOTAL N OF CASES	3551	1518

Table 1 shows that most offenders are in jail for property offenses, and consistent with studies based on self-reported criminality (Canter, 1982; Hindelang, 1971; Mawby, 1980; Richards, 1981), males and females tend to show similar patterns of offending. A closer examination of observed and expected frequencies in Table 1 shows that the greatest sex difference is in the category of drug use; females are more than twice as likely as males to be in jail for using drugs.

The survey also inquired about prior incarcerations both as juveniles and as adults. Table 2 shows that males of both races were more likely than females to have served time before, and both sexes were more likely

TABLE 2

Prior Incarcerations as Juveniles and as Adults for
Public Order Offenses and for Other Offenses

PRIOR INCARCERATIONS	MALES	FEMALES
Drunkenness, Vagrancy, or Traffic Offenses		
Percent Having Been Incarcerated	24.0%	10.7%
Mean Number of Times as Juvenile	3.8	9.1
Mean Number of Times as an Adult	8.0	8.3
Other Types of Offenses		
Percent Having Been Incarcerated	54.1%	42.1%
Mean Number of Times as Juvenile	3.7	3.7
Mean Number of Times as an Adult	2.6	2.2
TOTAL NUMBER OF OFFENDERS	3598	1510

to have served that time for offenses other than vagrancy, drunkenness, or traffic violations. Among those who had previously served time, females had a greater number of prior institutionalizations than males for drunkenness, vagrancy, and traffic offenses, and this difference was particularly marked for juveniles. What is particularly noteworthy is the high percentage of both sexes with prior institutional stays for other than public order offenses (53 % of the males and 41 % of the females).

Thus, although there are some minor differences by sex, males and females are likely to find themselves in jail for similar types of offenses. Further, although females were less likely to have had prior institutional experience, members of neither sex could be considered complete neophytes to the jail setting. This suggests that institutional programs to meet jail inmate needs should be designed to allow inmates to participate on more than one occasion (i.e., during more than one stay). Programs which are set up in distinct modules or units, for example, may be particularly appropriate for the jail setting.

PROBLEM AREAS

The discussion of problems faced by women in jail will focus on three related problem areas: financial, health, and alcohol/drug use. For each of these areas, data from the survey of jail inmates will be used to determine the extent to which women in jail face these problems and will also allow for a comparison between male and female inmates.

Financial

As a group, females enter the jail with an annual income nearly $1,000 less than that of males. Sixty-four percent of males and 79 percent of females reported an annual income of less than $5,000. Part of this difference is probably due to the fact that females were far less likely than males to have had a job at the time of their arrest. Seventy percent of males but only 35 percent of females reported their main source of income as "wages and salaries." Further, only about four percent of males but over 25 percent of females cited "welfare" as their main source of income. It is clear from these data that females in jail are less likely to be financially independent at the time of their arrest. These data are particularly interesting in light of the observation that males are as likely as females to report being married, both sexes report a similar number of dependents, and their educational levels are similar.

One clue to explaining why females have lower annual incomes and are more likely to be dependent on welfare comes from asking those unemployed inmates if they had been looking for work at the time of their arrest. Sixty-four percent of the males but only 45 percent of the unemployed females said they were looking for work. When asked why they were not looking for work, 24 percent of the females and **none** of the males cited "home responsibilities." The most cited reason for males (31 %) and the second most cited reason for females (22 %) was having a "physical disability." Of particular interest to those preparing job programs for offenders, only a handful of males or females cited lack of training or lack of available jobs as their main reason for not seeking employment.

Clearly jail inmates are drawn from the lowest socioeconomic classes, those Irwin (1985) refers to as the "rabble." It is clear that female inmates fall even lower on the socioeconomic ladder than males. While unemployed members of both sexes report physical disabilities as major reasons for not seeking employment, females even more frequently stay out of the labor market because of family responsibilities. Programs aimed at improving the employability of male offenders are likely to prove ineffective for females if problems relating to child care are not also addressed. Further, programs for both sexes must take into account the prevalence of physical handicaps in the jail population.

Health

The jail survey also asked about health-related problems of inmates and services provided to deal with those problems. These data support the contentions of Resnik and Shaw (1981) that female inmates are particularly likely to enter the jail with health-related problems. Half of the women but only one-third of the men reported having had a health or medical problem which would require them to see a doctor on a regular basis, with the majority of both males and females (87 and 90 %, respectively) reporting that these problems existed before their admission to jail.

Table 3 shows the frequency with which ten health-related problems were reported by the jail population. It is clear that no single problem best characterizes male or female inmates and that the pattern for both sexes is generally similar (Spearman's rho = .68). Several points are worth noting about these problem areas. First, across these ten problem areas a greater percentage of females than males is likely to report problems. Second, females are likely to report a slightly higher average number of problems than males. Third, depression is ranked near the bottom of problems listed by female inmates, a surprising finding given that depression is sometimes characterized as a malady to which women are particularly prone. Similarly, among these ten problems mental and emotional problems are ranked higher among males than among females.

TABLE 3

Types of Health Problems Reported by Offenders.

TYPE OF PROBLEM*	MALE	FEMALE
HEART CONDITION	6.9%	10.1%
RESPIRATORY, LUNGS	12.9	12.7
NERVOUS SYSTEM	12.0	13.0
MUSCLE OR BONE	13.9	11.4
URINARY PROBLEMS	2.8	8.5
BLOOD PROBLEMS	4.2	9.0
SKIN PROBLEMS	5.8	6.1
EMOTIONAL PROBLEMS	5.7	7.6
DEPRESSION	3.1	4.8
TOTAL N OF CASES	1262	754
MEAN PERCENT REPORTED	7.2%	8.7%

More than two-thirds of the inmates report that their jail was equipped with an infirmary with beds for overnight stays, and of these, females were nearly twice as likely as males to have spent a night there (25 versus 14%). There were no significant differences between males and females in the reported number of times they asked to see a doctor or in the likelihood that their request would be granted. Females report having been given a slightly greater number of medical tests upon admission to the jail.

These findings suggest that females are more likely than males to enter the jail with health problems, and are more likely than males to use an infirmary. Spradley (1970) has detailed how the jail may serve as a source of free health care for males on skid row. It is likely that a similar function may be served for women who, as noted earlier, may come to the jail in an even more desperate economic situation than males.

---

*Percents do not total 100 due to multiple responses and because some problems may not be among those listed; total N represents only those inmates who reported some health problem.

Alcohol/Drug Use

Alcohol and drugs were used frequently by these jail inmates. About three fourths of the males but less than one half of females reported drinking either beer, wine, or liquor in the year prior to their arrest. Not only were females less likely to drink, but they were likely to drink less on a typical drinking occasion. Among those inmates already convicted, more than half of the males and about a third of the females reported having been drinking at the time of the offense.

While there were sharp and consistent sex differences across several measures of alcohol use, drug use followed a less recognizable pattern. There were some respects in which males and females had similar patterns of drug use. First, about one third of both males and females (32 percent and 35 percent) were under the influence of drugs at the time of their offense. Second, both sexes reported using the same number of different drugs, an average of 2.3 types each. Third, across eight types of drugs, the reported age of first use was nearly identical for both sexes, ranging from 16 to 21 years old, depending on the drug involved.

There were also several regards in which the sexes differed in drug use. As Table 4 shows, females were far more likely to have used heroin (39% versus 26%). Further, females were nearly twice as likely as males to have been in a drug treatment program at the time of their arrest (11% versus 6%). It is also worth noting that while males were more than twice as likely to have been using alcohol rather than drugs at the

TABLE 4

Percent of Jail Inmates Who Have Ever Used Various Types of Drugs

TYPE OF DRUG*	MALE	FEMALE
HEROIN	25.6%	39.0%
METHADONE	7.1	8.9
COCAINE	29.2	32.5
MARIJUANA	67.1	61.0
AMPHETAMINES	31.1	29.1
BARBITURATES	29.9	30.1
LSD	21.3	18.4
PCP	16.5	12.7
TOTAL N OF CASES	3689	1558

*Percents do not total 100 due to multiple responses.

time of the offense, females were somewhat more likely to have been using drugs rather than alcohol.

Thus, it appears that females are less likely than males to enter the
jail with alcohol-related problems. They are, however, just as likely to
experience problems with drugs, and even more likely to have been using drugs at the time of their offense. At the same time, females were
more often participating in some type of drug treatment program at the
time of their arrest. Regarding implications for programs, these findings
suggest that females may be more receptive to drug-related programs
and may have a less pressing need (than males) for programs to deal
with alcohol problems.

SUMMARY AND DISCUSSION

The absolute and relative number of females in jail are growing rapidly.
Further, if current trends in prisons for women are followed by jail inmates, we can expect growing legal and social pressures to provide services
and programs for female offenders comparable to those for males. Doing
this, however, first requires a more thorough understanding of how the
needs of male and female jail inmates differ. Data from a national survey of
jail inmates were examined to provide information about financial, health
and alcohol/drug problems of female inmates. In all of these areas female
offenders pose problems distinct from those of males.

Females enter the jail with a lower annual income than males and
with a smaller likelihood of holding full-time employment. Like males,
many are kept out of the job market by physical disabilities, but an even
greater number cite responsibilities at home as their main reason for not
working. Successful vocational programs for women in jail must take
these home responsibilities into account.

Females also enter the jail with a greater number of medical problems than male inmates. It is difficult to argue, however, that women are
denied medical care because of their sex. They tend to be given a greater
number of medical tests upon admission, not including those tests
unique to women (e.g., a PAP smear). Further, they are no more likely
to be denied requests for a doctor's care and are even more likely than
males to have had an overnight stay in the jail infirmary.

Although women in the study were less involved with alcohol than
males, their overall use of drugs was similar to that of males. A notable
exception to this was the surprisingly high use of heroin among females

compared with males. Female inmates were nearly twice as likely as males to have been participating in a treatment program at the time of their arrest, but were also more likely to be using drugs at that time. This suggests that drug programs in the jail may be of particular interest to female inmates, while there might be less demand for alcohol-related programs.

Overall, these data suggest that programs for female inmates may be inadequate if they are modeled too closely after programs for males. A variety of social and physical factors associated with the female role interact to produce a jail population whose needs are unique.

NOTES

[1]For ease of presentation most tests of significance are not reported in the discussion that follows. However, where differences are noted these are statistically significant at the .05 level or less.

REFERENCES

Alpert, G.P., 1982. "Women prisoners and the law: which way will the pendulum swing?" Journal of Criminal Justice. 10:1:37-44.

Aylward, A. and J. Thomas, 1984. "Quiescence in women's prisons litigation: some exploratory issues." Justice Quarterly. 1:2:253-276.

Briar, K., 1983. "Jails: Neglected asylums." Social Casework. 64:7:387-393.

Canter, R., 1982. "Sex differences in self-report delinquency." Criminology. 20:3-4:373-393.

Chapman, J.R., 1980. Economic Realities and the Female Offender. Lexington, MA: Lexington Books.

Community Research Forum, 1980. Removing Children from Adult Jails: A Guide to Action. Champaign, IL: University of Illinois.

Cottle, T.J., 1977. Children in Jail. Boston: Beacon Press.

Flaherty, M.G., 1980. An Assessment of the National Incidence of Juvenile Suicide in Adult Jails, Lockups, and Juvenile Detention Centers. Washington, DC: U.S. Government Printing Office.

Glick, R.M. and V. Neto, 1977. National Study of Women's Correctional Programs. Washington, DC: U.S. Department of Justice.

Goldfarb, R., 1976. Jails: The Ultimate Ghetto of the Criminal Justice System. Garden City, New York: Anchor Books.

Hindelang, M.J., 1971. "Age, sex, and the versatility of delinquent involvements." Social Problems. 18:4:522-535.

Irwin, J., 1985. The Jail: Managing the Underclass in American Society. Berkely, CA: University of California Press.

Leonard, E.B., 1983. "Judicial decisions and prison reform: the impact of litigation on women prisoners." Social Problems. 31:1:45-58.

Mawby, R., 1980. "Sex and crime: the results of a self-report study." British Journal of Sociology. 31:4:525-543.

McCarty, D., H.J. Steadman, and J.P. Morrissey, 1982. "Issues in planning jail mental health services." Federal Probation. 46:4:56-63.

Moynahan, J.M. and E.K. Stewart, 1980. The American Jail: Its Development and Growth. Chicago: Nelson-Hall.

Resnik, J. and N. Shaw, 1981. "Prisoners of their sex: health problems of incarcerated women." Prison Law Monitor. 3:3:57, 68-83.

Richards, P., 1981. "Quantitative and qualitative sex differences in middle-class delinquency." Criminology. 18:4:453-470.

Ryan, T.A., 1984. Adult Female Offenders and Institutional Programs. Washington, DC: U.S. Government.

Spradley, J.P., 1970. You Owe Yourself A Drunk. Boston: Little, Brown.

U.S. Department of Justice, 1980. Profile of Jail Inmates: Sociodemographic Findings from the 1978 Survey of Inmates of Local Jails. Bureau of Justice Statistics. Washington, DC: U.S. Government.

U.S. Department of Justice, 1984. The 1983 Jail Census. (Bulletin NCJ-95536). Bureau of Justice Statistics. Washington, DC: U.S. Government.

CHAPTER 8

JAILS: AN INVISIBLE POLITICAL ISSUE

Carl F. Pinkele

IT IS NATURAL for essayists to believe their efforts are directed at important topics. What follows is no exception. The contention of this essay is that focusing on the politics of jail reform is telling not only about the specific topic but also speaks to broader concerns on the American political landscape. The central presumption is: change is far more difficult to arrange than the status quo is to sustain. The primary conclusion is: exempting or excluding governmental institutions — jails — from the public's purview serves antidemocratic ends, and presents those who would pursue democracy with a series of interactive difficulties. The general prescription is: notwithstanding the difficulties involved in initiating jail reform, it must be pursued, even if one ends up being more Sisyphus than victor.

To date much has been written about jails and jail life. The tales told and the descriptions rendered are not the stuff of enjoyable or pleasant reading. Jails, by and large, are hellholes where people live in overcrowded, squalid conditions. They are places where boredom mixes with anger and frustration to produce festering social and human sores. Indeed, as many have said and witnessed, if you want to make a person worse in terms of their antisocial attitudes, then send them to jail.

However, as bad and counterproductive as they are, the conditions of jails are ultimately not their worst dimension. Of greater consequence, is the degree to which jails, and those who are the beneficiaries of the present institutional arrangements, continue to function without meaningful constraints being placed upon them by an engaged public and competing elites. In this sense the crises reflected by our jails is a symptom of a deeper crisis in the American polity. What we find existing in

115

the political context of jails warrants our closest attention because there we can see clearly the penalties and costs of having institutions and practitioners insulated from public scrutiny and immunized against meaningful change. This chapter is about the politics of jail reform but its meaning goes farther to embrace issues of central concern for a working democracy.

As a result of their belief patterns, for most Americans jails are invisible public policy arenas (see Bennett, 1980). For those who do not and conceivably would not want to engage in jail reform, given other attitude patterns, jails are simply something not to worry about and to leave for others to handle. The test for these folks is that the success or not of jail policy is roughly: "do what you have to, but don't bother me with that matter." For those who do or might care about jail reform a variety of obstacles act to constrain their ability to influence positively either the institution or the conditions prevalent therein. When these reforming-folk ask: "what can we do?" and, "nothing that we do seems to make any difference?" by and large they are reflecting the kind of frustration associated with trying to have an enduring, measurable effect on an ill-defined and virtually invisible target. And, as this presentation will argue, that is precisely what jails are — an invisible target for reformers.

Efforts to achieve meaningful jail reform have to begin with a firm acknowledgement that both the institution and those associated with it from a public policy making perspective are invisible political-governmental institutions. Jails, of course, are real enough in several senses: they occupy space, need funding, employ people and house people who have been detained, and jails are a part of the local governmental structure, apparatus, and bureaucracy. Usually, however, jails are not considered to be features of the everyday political process and landscape. This special characteristic — the depoliticized, indeed, virtually denatured perception of jails — contributes to their being hidden from public view and invisible. And the invisibility of jails as part of the political world is a significant problem for reformers at both a theoretical and practical level. It should be noted that the invisibility of jails as a public policy arena is a tremendous asset for those who care to blunt rather than initiate jail reforms.

The heart of the argument presented here is that the invisibility of jails as policy making targets for one side is a burden while, for the other side, it is an ally. The former need to make jails visible policy targets, galvanize support for their proposals, and secure pressure for changes. Those who either resist all or anything beyond the most marginal of changes need only to keep jails invisible; they have the easier of the two tasks.

As the term is employed here, invisibility is borrowed from Ralph Ellison's masterful work, **The Invisible Man** (1952). It denotes a state of mind wherein things which exist in a physical sense are systematically overlooked, not counted, or looked through for ideological and self-interested reasons. By rendering something (or someone) invisible, the necessity to attend and to deal with it on its own terms or merits is avoided. In the dynamics of public policy making, invisibility shifts the burden of proof to those who would make an issue viable and place it on the agenda and away from those who deny its salience and worthiness as a topic for public debate. And, as we shall explore below, insofar as jails are concerned, such a manipulation as that involving the making of an heretofore invisible institution visible proves to be a difficult yet necessary political symbolism maneuver (see Edelman, 1964).

The politics of establishing the visibility of an issue is far more difficult than keeping it invisible; a strategic rule of thumb made all the more important when one is dealing with an arena and arrangements which have dominated the dialog in a particular manner for so long. People grow accustomed to understanding matters in one way, and, to institute a change, almost always proves to be a far more difficult feat than to arrange to have the picture remain the same. Furthermore, it is easier to veto change than to sponsor and negotiate it (Bachrach and Baratz, 1986).

Invisibility contains theoretical and practical challenges and problems for democratic polities. It is the midwife of several untoward effects, and little good whatsoever. Democratic polities rely upon inputs from their citizens for public policy directions. These inputs come in a variety of looks, temperaments, and modes, but come they must or there is "trouble in paradise."

To assist in the explanation of how jails are invisible and what might be done to make them visible, a brief excursion into the theory of agenda formation is in order. Agendas are the keystone ingredient in moving jails from the present state of invisibility to one of visibility. Cobb and Elder provide us with a succinct definition of agendas: "a general set of political controversies that will be viewed at any point in time as falling within the range of legitimate concerns meriting the attention of the polity" (Cobb and Elder, 1983:14). They point out that there are two types of agendas — "systemic" and "institutional." The former has to do with issues (items about which there is controversy and conflict) (Anderson,

1975) in the general public and the latter pertains to those items on the table for decision by those in positions of authority.

What we are talking about here is a multistep process. The first step involves the consolidation and the mobilization of opinions in the general public. This vital step can be initiated either from forces and individuals (or groups) within the public itself or it can be the result of efforts of some persons or segments of the institutional elite who are for whatever reasons dissatisfied with the current state of affairs. The second step involves the transfer of an issue from the systemic agenda onto the institutional agenda where the decisions about what to do and how to do it are made. The transmission modes vary — they may involve political parties, pressure groups, intra-elite connections or a personal or patron-client variety, or a host of other methods. Those involved at this stage of the process act as gatekeepers. They regulate the flow of items from one agenda level to the next. They also rearrange and even reorient or reshape the items to fit, according to a number of criteria, the prefiguring institutional, ideological, and partisan constraints which dominate the decision making arena at the time. What emerges as policy is not necessarily what was requested; and while it is of interest to us, policy outputs must await another essay. Our concern is primarily with the process of agenda building and the necessity for jail reform to be made visible for it to have any chance at all of being successful.

What we have just described is a political process. The entire agenda building process is highly political, no matter whose definition of politics is selected. It involves a series of decisions about the allocation and distribution of resources as well as the mode of implementation and the goals of the policy. From Plato through Marx, Lasswell and Easton, from A-to-Z, this is political stuff. To view it otherwise is either a fundamental error or a diversion for political gain.

What we are now going to describe with respect to the politics of jail reform is a classic political confrontation. Those presently ascendant profit from keeping jails invisible, or at most opaque, and thereby off the systemic and axiomatically the institutional agendas. This side depoliticizes and denatures the political nature of jails, and, by so doing, reaps policy and personal benefits. Their opponents, the jail-reforming folk, must tactically as well as theoretically, undertake to politicize jails by first making them visible and then seeking to correct past mistakes.

The political cultures of the criminal justice system and of jails differ across the United States. The nationalization of the Bill of Rights revolution associated with the Warren Court and developments such as television have functioned to expand considerably the theretofore narrowing localism of criminal justice issues. But geographical-political isolation and insulation remains today the prevalent pattern.

Two brief examples make the point: in the South, jails for many decades have been an obvious mechanism for the social control of non-whites and poor whites. There, jails were and are both a symbol and a reality of the control of some by others. In the southern political environment most people knew who the sheriff was, where the jail was, frequently who was in jail and for what. Jails were not at the margins but at the center of daily life for many southerners, especially if they fit into one of the two aforementioned sociological categories. Circumstances were quite different across the Ohio River, and, as one moved north into the urban areas, more markedly so. In urban areas the sheriff has been known to a comparative few; what the sheriff did was and is either an unknown or puzzling feature of the landscape, and most items about jails exist beyond the normal obit of knowledge or concern. For the most part, jails and sheriffs outside the South, and probably the Southwest (anywhere that there was a significant mix of cultures and skin colors), were noticeable only at election time.

We must begin our political understanding of jails and jail reform by acknowledging the formidable challenges ensconced within the variegated pattern of sub-national cultural settings. However, there are sufficient common denominators to allow us to make the following general observations; while at the same time remaining alerted to the likelihood of at least regional nuances.

The perceptual obstacles leading to invisibility and standing in the way of reforming jails originates in an inextricably interwoven pattern of feelings involving three key briefs against jails: irrelevance, antagonism and confusion. Efforts to reform, readjust or reallocate people, funds, perceptions, or materials having to do with jails initially must confront this bastion of attitudinal opposition to such policies.

Jails are considered irrelevant as issues for public policy because most people suppose they will never have either to endure them personally or know anyone who will have to do so. This feeling buttresses the additional perception that jails are not considered the ordinary business of citizens but of governmental officials—sheriffs—and the legal system.

Related to their irrelevance is that in the minds of many citizens (probably most) jails are places which house people who are, in one significant manner or other, disreputable. There is a prevalent feeling, the presumption of innocence myth notwithstanding, that those who are in jail deserve to be there. In point of fact, today a commonly heard opinion holds that not only do those inside "deserve it" but, furthermore, those outside are far better off whenever the stay of those incarcerated is prolonged indefinitely. These antagonistic attitudes are accompanied by the notion that those inside should not be treated well because of who they are and what they are; a feeling enhanced during insecure times such as those wrapping today's choices.

A characteristic feature of today's (mid-1980's) political opinions, associated in the popular press with a "Prop 13" mentality, is a turning inward—what in other, more general contexts, Christopher Lasch (1979) refers to as the "culture of narcissism." The general citizenry does not care to hear about the supposed problems of those who they already believe have done, or will do, wrong. This is particularly true when life for most "decent folk" is enough of a budgetary scramble and the strain on scarce resources forces people to make hard choices in other areas more central to their lives than the criminal justice system. Whenever they hear about jails—presuming that "they" do not include inmates, lawyers, the constabulary, social workers, or ministers, rabbis or priests—it is normally the case more money is wanted to build a new jail, there are problems with prisoners rioting or protesting about one thing or another, someone is let out who "should be kept in," or, any variety of items that are condensed into the perceptions of "pampering criminals."

Antagonism toward jails was vented recently in a Central Ohio instance; one which, by the time it subsided, became a rough knock against jail reform. A new jail had been built to accommodate the inmates; a situation which in and of itself was of no mean achievement. However, the funding allocated for the facility was found to be short of what was needed, both by jailers and inmates. Among the additional things which were requested to bring the jail up-to-speed was a television satellite dish. This item on the proposed new spending schedule caught the attention of the local television newspeople. Needless to say, the request for supplementary funding unleashed a torrent of opposition spearheaded by those who openly wondered about the necessity to have persons incarcerated in jails receive luxuries which the citizen with an average, or even above-average, income did not enjoy. This episode rekindled the significantly large reservoir of anger and frustration targeted at the broader criminal justice system and, to say the least, put a damper for quite some time on increased spending for jails in the area.

There is also confusion about what jails are and what they are supposed to accomplish. The most common confusion occurs between jails and prison. That jails are designed primarily to house those awaiting trial, and who cannot for whatever reason make bail, is an institutional feature of no perceptual consequence. Again, for most, the presumption of innocence is an artifact of the adversarial criminal justice system that is both generally little recognized and even less appreciated. Ignorance of what jails are for thereby adds fuel to the prefiguring atmosphere against reform.

And overlaying of all those and other attitudes is the combined baggage of racism and class prejudice. Those who are in jail either cannot or should not make bail or have a good attorney. To middle class and to working class Americans—the solid core of public opinions—this symbolically signals shiftlessness, unworthiness, and a host of other "failings" on the part of those incarcerated. The bottom line is therefore a strategically satisfying invisibility (see, Edelman, 1977).

The general perceptual obstacles are only a part of the total package which stands between the situation as it exists today and meaningful jail reform tomorrow. Surely as consequential, and perhaps even more so, are the propositions and perceptions which hold that jails, as a part of the criminal justice system, are not a legitimate part of the political system. These maintain that although jails and jailors are public institutions in a narrow sense they are not to be confused with the political process or political affairs. Jails are in something of a state of limbo existing outside the boundaries of politics and yet within the broader reaches of governmental concern. This configuration is a source of tremendous problems for any jail reform movement.

The problems begin with the fact that the entire criminal justice system, to a considerable and unhealthy extent, has been characterized as being inherently nonpolitical (Pinkele, 1985). By prefiguring the criminal justice system as being outside the parameters of political concern, the attention of the citizenry becomes sporadic and episodic; and thereby easily manipulatable by reform opponents. The picture resembles closely that developed by Ellison as a reaction to the actions of "invisible" actors—ignorance and fear.

Depoliticization of jails makes them invisible. On the one hand, this means blindness toward jail conditions. On the others, and acting in a manner that reinforces jail invisibility, in addition to being fearful when citizens are systematically excluded from being concerned about jails prior to a crisis of one form or another, they rather easily fall prey to the notion that one should let the professionals, or at least those in charge like sheriffs and deputies, do "whatever is best and called for" (Edelman, 1977). In some ways this is potentially an even more devastating perspective than that of unconcern.

Like other public officials, sheriffs and other jailors have agendas which are quite their own. Sheriffs — the principal managers and operators of jails in the United States — have a vested interest in a number of things about jails. They desire to be left alone to do things as they themselves see fit. They also posture themselves, rightly or wrongly, as being able to handle their jobs without outside interference. Frequently, sheriffs make announcements to the effect that they are "experts" and like other experts should be allowed to do what they are best able to do. And, ultimately, unless they are that very strange one indeed, sheriffs, want to be re-elected as sheriff or elected to another position — like other politicos, sheriffs are upwardly mobile.

What happens far more frequently than not is that jails become in fact duchies wherein whatever the sheriff wants, and for whatever reasons, goes. While the sheriff might be marginally politically visible, jails are not. The jail is considered part of his (by far most sheriffs are male) domain, and like the routes of patrol cars for the most part, they are his business. And, like the maintenance of patrol cars, what happens in jails goes unnoticed because it is the sheriff's job to take care of such routine items. Who would want a sheriff who asked when and how he should do his routine jobs?

From the theoretical standpoint whenever citizens turn over their final judgment on policy matters to someone else, they are surrendering their sovereignty. From a practical point of view, by first allowing that sheriffs know best and second that they should make the overwhelming majority of decisions pertaining to jails and jail life, citizens are setting themselves up or have been set up to be virtual victims of those who make decisions. In an ironical way, therefore, a citizenry which relinquishes its decision-making power to a sheriff is held hostage to the sheriff's agendas. The result again is the invisibility of jails.

Overcoming invisibility ultimately is both the most enduring and significantly democratic of jail reforms. The task for jail reformers interested in achieving their goal, assuming they are also interested in being democratic, is to politicize jails in all respects. Liberating jails from the layer-upon-layer of beliefs and depoliticized bureaucratic structures is a formidable undertaking. It is not a task for the timid, the restless and impatient, or those who are afraid of the greater odds being against them.

The initial step to take is a recognition of the fact that, in the terminology of E.E. Schattschneider, some benefit from contracting the scope of conflict while others produce gains by expanding it. The key is the audience (see, Schattschneider, 1975).

Insofar as jails are concerned, those benefiting from the present arrangements — sheriffs and other institutional players within the criminal justice system — are most likely to support either keeping the scope of conflict within its present boundaries or even contracting it further. This is to be expected and what it means is keeping jails invisible from public eyes and off of the systemic agenda. Making jails, or anything else for that matter, the business of only a few means that no significant, enduring changes will occur; or, at most the changes will be such as to not disrupt how things are done and who does them.

Special note needs to be taken of how **not expanding the scope of conflict** limits the likelihood of meaningful change. If it is the case that we are considering those wishing not to alter the structural context of events, or at least not by much, then an interesting package of strategic retreats will be initiated to restrain the scope of conflict. While the variety of symbolic, choreographed diversions is too long to list here, three favorites require mention: (1) an elite commission is established to study the problems; (2) several administrators gather with some of those proposing a change (undoubtedly those who are "reasonable" and not those who are most active in pursuing their beliefs) and work out a relatively silent compromise package, "to everyone's satisfaction"; and, (3) minimum level changes and perhaps even a sacrificial lamb are announced as new policies (see, Chafe, 1981). These actions purchase time with little cost or altering of the environment. Depending upon the circumstances of a given situation, one of these or another mode of operation will be utilized to keep an issue off from the public's systemic agenda.

Ironically, those who are or seem desirous of changing how things are done and who does them often agree to adopt or go along with one of the above three strategies. How can it be that there will be this sort of agreement between opponents? One significant answer is found in the fear and puzzlement present on the part of both sides surrounding efforts to expand the boundaries and audience. Both sides, for different reasons, see an expansion of the conflict to be fraught with many problems and dangers.

Therefore, the contraction of or as Schattschneider (1975) would say the "privatization" of conflicts over jails is appealing to people with different goals in mind. Numerous professional criminal justice people, from either the status quo, status quo ante, or reform orientations, find privatization and invisibility convenient solutions to varying fears; but the results are likely to be roughly the same—little or no meaningful changes will occur with intra-elite skirmishing within established rules demarcating and regulating the arena of conflict.

The soundest reform strategy, and coincidentally the one which squares with democratic precepts, is to expand the scope of conflict over jails and jail reform to include a wider audience. As indicated before, this is no place for the timid or someone in a hurry. There are many problems: the attitudes of irrelevance, antagonism, and confusion surrounding jails obtains the opposition of those presently benefiting from the ways things are presently done and will intensify the hesitations of potential allies who will balk at working with nonprofessionals, and, as solutions are delayed, the problems will grow. This partial list of difficulties is a legitimate reason for pausing, but not for turning back or selecting a nonpolitical route to shadow reform.

A host of people across the ages have testified to the difficulties associated with making democracy work. Democracy means the socialization of conflict, again borrowing from Schattschneider (1975), and it means making issues visible. The place to begin is talking, educating, and mobilizing within the general public so as to create the item of jail reform as a fixture on the systemic political agenda. Undoubtedly this step will have to be accomplished outside preexisting party and pressure group channels. The established mechanisms are too encumbered by personal and partisan constraints to be useful. The route to reform is, and probably must be, initially through a grass roots movement. From there pressures can be brought to bear on those in authority to move it onto and through the institutional agenda (Boyte, 1980). It seems so simple that there must be some inherent reasons why invisibility is so attractive and visibility so unappealing.

REFERENCES

Anderson, J. (1975) *Public Policy Making*. New York: Praeger.
Bachrach, P. & Baratz, M.S. (1986) Two faces of power, in Nivola and Rosenbloom (eds.), *Classic Readings in American Politics*. New York: St. Martens.
Bennett, W.L. (1980) *Public Opinion in American Politics*. New York: Harcourt Brace Jovanovich.
Boyte, H. (1980) *The Backyard Revolution*. Philadelphia: Temple University Press.
Chafe, W.H. (1981) *Civiliberties and Civil Rights*. Oxford: Oxford University Press.

Cobb, R.W. & Elder, C.D. (1983) *Participation in American Politics*. Baltimore: Johns Hopkins Univ. Press.

Edelman, M. (1964) *The Symbolic Uses of Politics*. Urbana: Univ. of Illinois Press.

Edelman, M. (1977) *Political Language*. New York: Academic Press.

Ellison, R. (1952) *The Invisible Man*. New York: Random House.

Lasch, C. (1979) *The Culture of Narcissism*. New York: Norton.

Pinkele, C.F. (1985) Discretion fits democracy: an advocates argument, in Louthan W.C. (ed.) *Discretion, Justice and Democracy*. Ames: Iowa State University Press.

Schattschneider, E.E. (1975) *The Semisovereign People*. Hopdale, Illinois: The Dryden Press.

CHAPTER 9

JAILS AND JUDICIAL REVIEW
Special Problems for Local Facilities

N.E. Schafer

ABSTRACT

The local character of county jails leaves them more susceptible to court intervention than state prisons, yet less prepared to respond. Their participation in remedy formulation tends to be reactive rather than proactive and their compliance with court orders is often marked by delay and confusion. A case study of one jail suit illustrates the problems caused by the jail's local perspective and isolation from other corrections systems. Judges must recognize and accommodate the jail's local character by assessing the jail's ability to respond and choosing remedy formulations based upon this assessment.

COUNTY JAILS are unique institutions bound by their own histories to a local perspective and limited by local control and local budgets to traditional methods of operation. They are short term facilities which house both pre-trial and sentenced prisoners and thus differ from state and federal prisons in both function and orientation. When in the 1970's federal courts began to intervene in jail and prison management, many jail administrators reacted with anger and hostility to what they viewed as the court's interference in a purely local matter. Although in applying constitutional standards the courts recognized differences in the functions of jails and prisons. Most correctional case law arose from prison cases and many of these were applied equally to jails. Remedy formulations in jail suits should have differed from those arranged in prison suits because most defendant jails were not only unwilling but **unable** to respond to judicial review.

The jail's inability to deal with judicial intervention is the subject of this paper. Differences in jail and prison law suits are noted, and jails and prisons are contrasted for their preparation for, and response to, court review. A case study of one jail's response to a class action suit filed in federal court serves to underscore the inability of jails to deal in a timely fashion with court orders.

The federal courts had traditionally been loath to intervene in the internal operation of jails and prisons. They had preferred to rely on the professional expertise of correctional administrators and entertained few suits from jail and prison inmates until the mid 1960's. However, following passage of the 1964 Civil Rights Act the courts increasingly responded to suits from all classes of prisoners for relief of the conditions of their confinement. The majority of these suits relied on Section 1983 of the Civil Rights Act:

> Every person who, under color of any statute, ordinance, regulation, custom, or usage of any State or Territory, subjects or causes to be subjected, any citizenry of the United States or other persons within the jurisdiction thereof to the deprivation of any rights, privileges or immunities secured by the Constitution of laws, shall be liable to the party injured at an action at law, suit in equity, or other proper proceeding for redress. (42 USC 1983, 1964)

This law had a role in changing the "hands off" policy of the federal courts whose reluctance to interfere in jail and prison management was overcome by their unwillingness to allow deprivations of federal rights.

The courts seem to have been especially solicitous of the status of pretrial detainees because of the presumption of innocence. Indeed, Eighth Amendment standards were sometimes more strictly applied for pretrial detainees than for convicted prisoners and the equal protection clause of the Fourteenth Amendment was invoked to compare their rights with the rights of those admitted to bail (e.g., Inmates of Milwaukee County Jail v. Peterson, 353 F. Supp. 1157, 1160, E.D. WIS, 1973). These higher standards changed in 1979 when the Supreme Court established that the prohibition of punishment for the legally innocent should be balanced against necessary jail security (Bell v. Wolfish, 441 U.S. 520, 995C 1979). Presumption of innocence does, however, require that the equal protection clause of the Fourteenth Amendment be strictly applied to detainees in relation to those convicted of crimes. Pre-trial prisoners must not be confined under conditions worse than those of convicted prisoners (Rhem v. Malcolm, 371 F. Supp. 594 (S.D.N.Y., 1974); Hamilton v. Love, 328 F. Supp. 1182 (E.D. ARK, 1971) and others). The special attention given to the presumption of innocence reveals that judges recognized differences in function between jails and prisons but, in ordering relief, the courts did not seem to recognize the limitations implied by other differences.

Jails are defined as local institutions (U.S. Dept. of Justice, 1978 et al.) while prisons are defined as state or federal facilities housing prisoners with sentences of more than one year. Most state prisons are part of a larger state corrections system and, of course, the Federal Bureau of Prisons constitutes a federal prison system. Prison officials have access to a larger network of information and assistance as well as to a larger tax base than do jails which are county funded and often operate in isolation from similar institutions.

Prisons have long been defined as correctional institutions and the officials who operate them have professional affiliations with correctional associations. Jails have only recently been included under the corrections label. History and tradition have placed pre-trial facilities outside the corrections category. The National Advisory Commission on Criminal Justice Standards and Goals found it necessary to justify the inclusion of jails in their volume **Corrections** (1973, p. 98) and suggested that the "stepchild" status of jails reflected an abdication of responsibility for pre-trial detainees.

The chief administrator of the county jail is usually a locally elected official, the county sheriff, who has, among other duties, a centuries old responsibility to assure the appearance at trial of persons who could not post bond. Except for this custodial function the sheriff's is primarily a law enforcement department and, unlike prison administrators, the sheriff and his deputies are more likely to be professionally affiliated with the police than with corrections.

The difference in professional orientation is an important one. Professional affiliations permitted prison personnel to participate in a dialogue on judicial review at national conferences and in professional publications. The American Correctional Association (ACA) frequently reviewed court suits in its member journal between 1969 and 1980, and the topic of judicial review was regularly on the program at the annual conference. The ACA developed a proactive response to litigation which served to defuse some of the charges and to persuade judges to rely again

on their professional expertise in prison management. The movement
for accreditation of correctional facilities and agencies accelerated while
court suits proliferated. A Self-Evaluation and Accreditation Project
was conducted by ACA between 1968 and 1970 and in 1974 a Commission on Accreditation for Corrections was funded by LEAA to develop
and apply operational standards for correctional agencies. Accreditation
standards were published in 1977 (ACA, 1977). Judges welcomed this
trend and some prison suits were settled pending accreditation by the
national association (Jones, 1982). In contrast, jail administrators remained outside the corrections network until fairly late in the decade
and many remained unaware of judicial review in other parts of the
country. Their isolation locked them into reactive responses as defendant institutions.

Articles in scholarly journals assessing responses to judicial review
appeared in the late 1960's. Kimball and Newman (1968) addressed only
suits filed against state and federal prison authorities and identified
three postures taken by defendant agencies. The "defensive response"
was tied to the prison officials' belief in their own expertise and in their
legislatively delegated authority. This response was based upon the im-
propriety of any judicial review of the activities of corrections professionals. A second reaction, "apathy/acquiescence," was a passive
response that denied any role for corrections in the review outcome and
was, in effect, a denial of professionalism. The third and most desirable
response was "prevention" or "rational persuasion," an active response
which involved persuading the court that review was unnecessary by improving procedures, encouraging professionalization of staff, etc.

Rubin (1969) suggested a reaction beyond defensive which he called
"provocative." This reaction was based on illegality or actual defiance of
the law. He cited as an example Jordan v. Fitzharris (257 F. Supp. 674
(1966)) in which the court required a prison to maintain certain conditions of "elemental decency" in its strip cells. The prison administration
fought for its right to impose whatever treatment it deemed best under
whatever conditions. Rubin's characterization of the "defensive response" fits that described by Kimball and Newman though he also appears to assimilate within it the "apathy/acquiescence" posture they
discussed. In a later article he calls this a "sit-tight" response (1974). Rubin's third "positive" response is characterized by anticipating court requirements and/or providing more than the minimum. Such a response
includes "rational persuasion," i.e., convincing federal judges that their
professionalism makes review unnecessary.

The courts had never fully abandoned their reliance on the professional expertise of defendant administrators. They maintained that judges were qualified only to assess the constitutionality of prison conditions not to manage the institution. Usually they left the means of correcting conditions to the defendant facility. Such language as "make a prompt and reasonable start toward eliminating the unconstitutionalities. . ." (Holt v. Sarver, 309 F. Supp. 362 (E.D. ARK, 1970)) implies continued reliance on the experience and expertise of prison or jail officials.

Isolated from networks of information and expertise and bound by local tradition and history, jails were unable to respond professionally to such language and were locked for a much longer period of time into defensive or even hostile, postures when suits were filed against them. Judge Young, in Jones v. Wittenburg (330 F. Supp. 707, W.D. Ohio 1971) noted some of the problems he found more common in local than in state compliance: local appropriations, archaic laws and customs and the actions and attitudes of responsible public officials. Two years after this opinion the court found no changes in the jail and faulted the sheriff for deliberate delay based on a desire for revenge against the court. (Jones v. Wittenburg, 357 F. Supp. 696, N.D. Ohio, 1973.)

Four case studies of implementation of court orders by Harris and Spiller (1977) illustrate some of the problems of responding in isolation. The only prison case reviewed was Holt v. Sarver, in which an entire state prison system was found to be operating unconstitutionally. The quality of Arkansas prison personnel and the nature of administrative appointments suggest that there was little, if any, tie to professional networks and the conditions revealed in the court suits and reported by Murton (1976) describe a system so bound by its antiquated traditions and so thoroughly directed inward that it could only be impacted by the very drastic measures required by the court.

The three remaining cases involved jails. Like most jails they were locally funded, locally operated, locally staffed. All were old and all were designed for short-term confinement and strict custody. Crowding, poor conditions and unconstitutional processes and procedures were cited in all three suits. In only one case was assistance sought from outside. One year after the Baltimore City Jail (Collins v. Schoonfield, 344 F. Supp. 257 (1972)) suit was filed, the mayor of the city requested an inspection of the jail by the Federal Bureau of Prisons.[1] Problems with compliance noted by Harris included lack of funds, inadequate staff, and inadequate facilities (1977:386).

The other jails studied were Louisiana Parish jails. In Holland v. Donelon the initial complaint was filed in 1971 and court orders were handed down in 1972, 1973 and 1974. When Harris conducted the study in 1975 the jail was still not in full compliance. Reasons cited included budget, physical limitations and "lack of clarity as to who was responsible and for what. . ." (1977:165).

In Hamilton v. Schiro, Spiller noted that "divided administrative responsibility" (between city and sheriff) was a special problem in compliance (1977:296) and also noted animosity between sheriff and city government. At the time the field work was completed this jail, too, was still not in compliance.

In each of these cases anger and disbelief were the initial responses to the filing of the suits and to the courts' willingness to hear the plaintiffs. There was also an attempt to place blame upon Legal Aid lawyers, "radicals," and on co-defendants.

While responses to the court's review are part of these implementation studies, the emphasis in the studies is on assessing compliance rather than on assessing responses. In the following case study the focus is on the reaction of public officials to judicial intervention, and note is made of the court's contribution to the delay and confusion which marked compliance.

Marion County Jail Suit

The Marion County Jail serves as the detention facility for the county, the city of Indianapolis, and the cities of Beech Grove, Lawrence, Southport and Speedway—a total population of approximately 800,000. The four-story jail, completed in 1965, had an official capacity of 776. It was built with security and control as the primary concerns and was, according to one observer, obsolete before it opened.

SEQUENCE OF EVENTS (Partial)

DATE	COURT ACTION	COMPLIANCE ACTIVITY
Sept. 1972	suit filed	
Nov. 1972	amended complaint	
March 1973	order to proceed as class action suit	
1974-75		new jail rules formulated for submission to court resulting in consent decree and partial judgment

DATE	COURT ACTION	COMPLIANCE ACTIVITY
June 1975	*Consent Decree and Partial Judgment* contact visiting out of cell block recreation over crowding	
March 1976	*Court Order*	
April 1976		Steering Committee appointed to select consultants
June 1977		consultants' report submitted
Jan. 1978	mayor's memorandum re. compliance	
Feb. 1978	Sheriff's memorandum re. compliance	
Aug. 1978	plaintiffs interrogatories to Sheriff	
Sept. 1978	Sheriff's response to interrogatories	
April 1979		Consolidation of Jail & City-County lockup
Autumn 1979		Jail sends letters to facilities around the country seeking assistance and advice
Dec. 1979	-motion for order to show cause -motion to appoint special master -motion to restrain further incarceration	
Jan. 1980		Ad Hoc Jail Committee recruited
Feb. 1980		new classification system in operation
May 1980	Stipulation and order programs ordered Commission appointed Commissioners appointed	GIPC begins to monitor compliance
July 1980		Contact visits begin
Aug. 1980		Indoor recreation area opened Outdoor exercise begins T.V.'s installed cubicles for attorney/client conferences
April 1981		City-County Special Resolution to commence expansion of jail
March 1982	Stipulation and order 1979 motions held in obeyance until July 1982	
June 1982		architect's drawings

DATE	COURT ACTION	COMPLIANCE ACTIVITY
July 1982	Report of Commission filed	
Dec. 1982		jail addition construction contracts signed
April 1983		construction begins

Figure 1.

Just a few years after the jail opened it was the subject of a lawsuit which was not fully settled until a new jail addition wing was completed. Figure 1 lists sequentially the events related to the suit and the resulting actions of the defendants. Some of these will be discussed in detail. Briefly, the events and charges are as follows: In September, 1972, a suit was filed by the Legal Services Organization (LSO) on behalf of pre-trial detainees at the Marion County jail. Named as defendants in the suit were the Sheriff of the County, the jail commander, the Commissioner of the State of Indiana Department of Corrections, the Mayor of Indianapolis and specific members of the Board of County Commissioners. The complaint, brought under Section 1983 of the Civil Rights Act (42 U.S.C. 1983), alleged violations of the pre-trial detainees' rights under the First, Fourth, Fifth, Sixth, Eighth, Ninth, Thirteenth, and Fourteenth Amendments to the United States Constitution. At issue were overcrowding, physical and sanitary conditions, failure to classify prisoners for housing assignments, inadequate medical and dental care, lack of recreation, of contact visits, and of access to telephone and mail services.

Because of crowding, detainees were sometimes required to sleep on the floor in the shower rooms. Although mattresses were provided, mattress covers often were not. Jail issue clothing consisted of dresses for females and trousers for males. The prisoners wore the underwear they had on when admitted. Although they could purchase more underwear, as well as towels and pillows, or receive them from a visitor, indigent prisoners often had to do without. No provision was made to launder clothing or towels. Though these could be washed in the cell block basins, it was against regulations to hang them up to dry.

All detainees could purchase postage and writing materials. They were allowed to mail only one letter per day containing no more than one piece of paper. Jail officials read all correspondence to and from family and friends. Telephone calls were not permitted except by special arrangement.

There was no recreation program or exercise area. Playing cards could be purchased and there was a meager library. Detainees could exercise only in the open area of the cell block. No televisions or radios were available.

There was no regular dental program, no provision for medical examinations, no law library. Visits were "closed." The detainee visited from inside the cell block looking through a small plexiglass window and talking through a metal grating. Only two visitors were allowed per week. Children were never permitted.

In 1975 a consent decree and partial judgment corrected many of the physical and sanitary problems. New jail rules were formulated and submitted to the court. These covered the sanitizing of mattresses, issuance of jail clothing and provisions for laundering these, improvements in medical and dental care, counseling services, and more liberal correspondence rules. However, many of these were "paper" changes only.

A 1976 court order required attention to all areas left unresolved by the consent decree. The judge ordered that clothing be issued and laundered weekly; that a bed above floor level be provided for each detainee along with sheets, pillow, blanket and mattress cover. He ordered that telephone calls be permitted "in reasonable number and for a reasonable length of time without censorship," and that correspondence opportunities be greatly expanded.

Contact visiting was ordered with the visitation schedule to be equal to that provided by the state for the convicted. Reasonable facilities for both indoor and outdoor recreation were also ordered. The court recognized that many deficiencies resulted from lack of funds but ordered that appropriations be made in order to correct them.

Defendants' official response was the appointment of a Steering Committee, with representatives of the Mayor, the county commissioners and the Sheriff as members, to select consultants who would propose solutions. The contract to the consultants was let by the Department of Metropolitan Development, an arm of city government attached to the Mayor's office.

The Consultants' Report was submitted fourteen months later in June of 1977. In January and February, 1978 the Mayor's office and the Sheriff's office submitted memoranda based on the report to the court advocating certain of the compliance options which particularly addressed the problem of overcrowding. These memoranda were followed by the plaintiffs' memorandum in opposition to some of the proposed solutions.

In August, 1978, interrogatories to the Sheriff were propounded by attorneys for the plaintiffs and were answered in the required 30 days by the Sheriff. There were 87 questions and it was clear from the responses that no major concerted effort had been made to implement the judgment of the court. Neither the 1977 nor the 1978 Sheriff's budgets had allocated funds for compliance, nor had the sheriff requested special funds. Whatever improvements had been made had come from the jail's normal operating budget. The 1979 budget request included $12 million for an addition to the jail but it was denied by the County Commissioners.

In 1979, seven years after the suit was initiated, the jail commander sent letters to jail officials throughout the country seeking advice and assistance in achieving compliance. During this year also, the Sheriff's Department assumed command of the city lockup. All prisoners were then booked at the lockup and transient prisoners (held for up to 3 days) were not transferred to the jail. This had the immediate effect of reducing the population. But on December 28 lawyers for the plaintiffs filed three motions: an order to show cause why defendants should not be held in contempt of court and assessed fines and damages of over $300,000; a motion to appoint a Special Master to oversee compliance with the order issued three years earlier; and a motion to restrain further incarceration of detainees at the Marion County Jail.

These motions produced immediate action. By January 14, 1980, an Ad Hoc Jail Committee had been appointed which included criminal court judges, City-County Councilmen, representatives of the Mayor's office, the Sheriff's office, the Prosecutor's office, the Auditor's office, and the Greater Indianapolis Progress Committee (GIPC), a privately funded citizens group advisory to the Mayor.

In the Court's Stipulation and Order of May, 1980, GIPC was appointed jail commission and two commissioners were named. The Court held in abeyance the show cause order and the motion to restrain incarceration but ordered further progress toward compliance within six months and recreation, televisions, and radios and private attorney-client conference booths by July 1, 1980. Threatened with a contempt of court citation, the defendants began to engage seriously in compliance attempts. A new classification system went into effect in March, 1980; in July, both contact visits and outdoor exercise were begun; by August, private attorney-client cubicles were in use; and by the end of the summer there was a television set for each cell block.

The Ad Hoc Jail Committee met regularly throughout the year and ordered an update of the 1977 consultants' study which was submitted in December. In December the City-County Council passed a resolution to undertake a survey of jail renovations and additions. The federal court judge cooperated in this progress by accepting improvements and postponing action on the 1979 motions.

In April, 1981, expansion of the jail and a necessary bond issue were approved by the City-County Council. Architects' drawings were approved in June of 1982, construction bids were accepted in the fall and contracts signed in December. Construction began in April, 1983. This new addition would bring the jail into full compliance in all areas requiring additional space and structural change.

By March, 1983, compromises had been made on the larger issues: outdoor recreation was available once per week rather than daily; holding cages had been converted for contact visitation by setting up folding chairs on each side of the bars; cubicles were made available for attorney-client conferences; telephones had been installed in each cell block with 16-24 hours of access per day (collect calls only); and a law library was in operation. Compliance was lax in other areas: mattresses were not hygienically treated on a regular basis; clean clothing was not regularly issued; the promised counselors were interns from a nearby university's School of Social Work; and often there were not quite enough blankets, pillows or towels for every inmate.

The Response: Problems and Issues

Resentment is a natural response to what was perceived as unnecessary interference in a local matter. While state and federal prison officials had already begun to discuss the "threat" of judicial intervention (Kimball and Newman, 1968), officials of local jails were not engaged in the late 1960's and early 1970's in dialogues with one another. Each jail decision was a surprise to the defendants in it and sheriffs in other states and counties remained unaware of the growing willingness of the federal courts to entertain suits from jail inmates.

Their ignorance of this trend was compounded by local laws and local traditions. Jails are, in the main, locally funded and operated facilities. Pre-trial detention is their **raison d'etre** and the statutory responsibility of the sheriff to assure the appearance at trial of those who do not post surety leads to an emphasis on custody and security. Since detention is usually a matter of days or weeks rather than years the conditions of such short-term confinement had been typically overlooked and traditional means of maintaining secure custody were perpetuated. The uniqueness of each jail in terms of local customs and local context results in a local perspective that courts should not intervene in what are perceived of as purely local matters and often results in anger and resentment among defendants in a jail law suit.

Indiana is a conservative, even insular, state which has traditionally viewed federal intervention in local matters with suspicion and resentment. The state, as well as various local governments, had avoided the use of federal funds for a variety of programs out of a fear that accepting federal funds would invite federal control. In this political climate the federally funded Legal Services Organization (LSO) filed a class action suit against the Marion County Jail inviting the intervention of the Federal Court. The defendants named in the suit were unaware that the suit was being considered and were thus taken by surprise when it was filed. To add insult to injury their first knowledge of the suit came from stories in the local news media. The press was apparently notified by representatives of LSO. This "leak" raised the level of anger and resentment among the defendants. The sheriff, in an immediate though irrelevant gesture of defiance, called the U.S. Marshal's office to insist on the removal of all federal and military prisoners and terminated all agreements to detain them in the future.

The initial response was in line with the one Rubin (1969) characterized as "provocative" rather than "defensive" but the "sit tight" response soon followed. In many ways the defendants treated the suit as if it had no real meaning and did not require any serious response. It was eight years before serious attempts were made to correct the problems identified in the suit filed in 1972.

One factor in the delay was an especially serious problem in jail administration known as "discontinuity of management" which is a result of the political nature of the Sheriff's office (Pappas, 1970). In Indiana the Sheriff, by law, cannot serve more than two terms. In the case of the Marion County Jail this fact, coupled with some unexpected events, led to considerable "discontinuity of management." In the 12 years between the filing of the suit and the achievement of full compliance there had been four Marion County Sheriffs.

Sheriff Eads was named in the initial suit in 1972. While his initial negative reaction to the suit suggests that he would not have become a willing participant in the formulation of remedies, it is also true that he was in the final two years of his second term and could not run again. He may have decided to let his successor assume the responsibility of compliance. In any event, no action other than his angry refusal to house federal prisoners was taken during the remainder of his term.

Sheriff Broderick, elected in November, 1974, had formulated by June, 1975 a new set of jail rules based on the facts of the case. These were submitted to the Court and resulted, in 1975, in a consent decree and partial judgment in which the court noted that with these rules some issues were fully resolved, some were partially resolved, and some were still awaiting resolution. This Sheriff was clearly concerned about the suit and anxious to settle the issue. Since he had ahead of him a possible seven years of responsibility for the administration of the jail, it was in his best interest to seek solutions early in his tenure and move on to other concerns. It should be noted, however, that no means of implementing many of the new rules were sought. This sheriff was involved in the Jail Task Force, formed in response to the 1976 court order. Less than a year later he was killed in a traffic accident and his political party appointed a replacement, Gilman.

Under Gilman, the Sheriff's department showed little interest in achieving compliance and the problem of management discontinuity increased. He replaced the Jail Commander who had served under both Eads and Broderick with a Sergeant who had been on road patrol. Both the Sheriff and the new major needed time to learn jail operations and to study the problems associated with the court order. There was, in effect, a two-year lull in the jail's efforts at compliance.

In 1978 the appointed Sheriff was defeated in an election and a fourth Sheriff became a defendant in the case. Sheriff Wells recalled the previous jail commander and began seriously to consider compliance alternatives. One of his early actions (1979) was to hire a number of new deputies and stipulate that they would serve five years' jail duty. Prior to this the jail deputies had been new hires on six months' probation who were promoted to road duty after completing the probationary period. The move to create a staff of career jail deputies was a step toward professionalization of jail personnel.

In the autumn, 1979 he sought advice and assistance from sheriffs throughout the nation who had been involved in court actions. Defendants had only recently become aware that jail suits were common and that theirs was not a singular event arising out of political differences with the federal judge. By 1979, however, eight years had passed since the suit was filed, more than four years since the 1975 consent decree, and more than three since the court order. Counsel for the plaintiffs had become understandably impatient.

Three motions filed in December, 1979 led to immediate action; one was an order to show cause why the defendants should not be held in contempt of court. Although the Sheriff has statutory responsibility for the jail the plaintiffs must take care to name as defendants all those who might reasonably be involved in relief since the court cannot enforce a decree against those who are not named (Buckholz et al., 1978). The Sheriff, the jail commander, the Mayor of Indianapolis, the County Auditor and others were, therefore, threatened with a contemp of court citation. Another of the motions was to enjoin further incarceration of pre-trial detainees at the Marion County Jail. This would have created extraordinary political problems for the county. These two motions were held in abeyance, but the third was approved—the appointment of a Special Master to oversee compliance. In addition LSO (counsel for plaintiffs) were to be included in plans and negotiations. While the new Sheriff, facing a possible eight years of responsibility for the jail, might have continued his efforts to comply, these motions certainly had an impact on the speed of the responses.

It should be noted that none of the four defendant sheriffs requested additional funds for compliance, except for Sheriff Wells' request for funds to enclose an outside recreation area. (The City-County Council denied this request.) All compliance activities had been funded through the Sheriff's normal operating budget or from special jail funds.

Still at issue in December, 1979 were outdoor recreation, contact visiting, a classification system, a basic law library, private attorney-client cubicles, and access to telephones, radios and television. The county officials in charge of appropriations were not in sympathy with these requirements, nor, they were sure, were their constituents. Funds were appropriated for enclosing a small outdoor exercise area and ultimately (1981) the City-County Council did approve, "with reluctance, but with a sense of reality," (Proposal 103, 1981) construction of an addition to the jail. The other issues were negotiated and went into effect in one form or another in the eight months after the three motions were filed.

The new classification system went into effect in February, 1980. No budget appropriations were necessary. Contact visiting was begun in July. The jail purchased used folding chairs which could be set up on either side of the bars of a holding cage in which prisoners had lined up to await sick call, counseling appointments, etc. Kisses and handshakes could be made through the bars while standing, but once seated a clear plastic barricade prevented continued contact. Visits were considerably less frequent than had been promised in the 1975 consent decree.

The same source for the folding chairs also provided materials for the construction of booths for private attorney-client conferences. The materials had been left behind after the closing of a local elementary school, were then used in the building by a neighborhood organization, and were at last given to the Marion County Jail. Jail carpentry staff constructed the cubicles. Books to complete the law library, equipment for the recreation area, and televisions (one for each cell block) were purchased from the jail's commissary fund.[2]

The telephone company installed special telephones on the cell blocks which could be used only for collect calls. This is one area which exceeded the "reasonable access" requirement of the court order. The prisoners have unlimited access to the telephones 14-18 hours per day.

Negotiations led to compromise on many of the other issues, particularly the scheduling of visits and recreation. It was understood that full compliance could not be achieved until the new jail addition was completed, and good faith attempts at partial compliance were accepted by attorneys for the plaintiffs.

Discussion

Remedy formulation in judicial orders vis-a-vis prisons and jails includes: remedial abstention, court imposition, court selection, master-supervised formulation and negotiation (Buckholz, et al 1978). The first of these is the most common and reflects the judge's willingness to rely on the defendant institution to formulate remedies to correct the problems established in the suit. In effect the Court retains jurisdiction and orders responsible officials to submit plans which address the facts of the suit.

In the Marion County suit remedial abstention was the first of three methods of remedy formulation attempted by the Court. The only response by jail officials was a new set of jail rules based specifically on the facts of the case which they submitted to the court in 1975. No plan for implementation of the rules was included. Personnel involved in the submission state that the intent was to mollify the court and convince the judge to terminate the case. The process of putting the new rules into practice was never considered. Though the submission of new rules resulted in a consent decree and partial judgment, the court retained jurisdiction. By 1979, so little had been done by way of implementation that the Court turned to two other judicial prerogatives: a special master was appointed and negotiations between defendants' and plaintiffs' counsel were ordered. These methods of remedy formulation began to produce results. Probably one or the other should have been tried much earlier in the process.

While defendants in all jail or prison lawsuits may be unwilling to cooperate in remedy formulation, defendants in jail suits may not only be unwilling, but also **unable.** Lawsuits arise, after all, out of conditions in the defendant jail, and defendant officials' expertise in jail management is usually based on experience in that jail alone. Participation in the formulation of remedies requires the defendant sheriff to criticize his own prior performance and to do so in isolation since he has seldom had an opportunity to compare his facility with others. Prison officials on the other hand have traditionally had access to a network of information and expertise which has enabled them to respond rapidly and rationally to court orders and to participate knowledgeably in remedy formulation.

In jail suits the Court should consider, very soon after the plaintiff's need for relief has been established, appointment of a special master to assist jail officials in remedy formulation. In the suit studied here there was confusion about what was expected. For example, the court ordered contact visiting at least equal in quality and frequency to that provided for convicted felons in a nearby state prison. Jail personnel were unfamiliar with these visiting facilities and some were unaware that contact visitation was not a euphemism for conjugal visitation. The search for advice from other defendant jails which was undertaken in 1979 illustrated the sheriff's uncertainty about how to deal with judicial review. It also reflected the new realization that this suit was not a local quarrel with the federal court, but part of a national trend.

In the case of Marion County the initial resentment and outright antagonism engendered by the suit made negotiation an unacceptable early method of remedy formulation. However a special master could have been ordered to negotiate remedies between counsel for the plaintiffs and defendant officials. Early appointment of such a master might have kept the attention of jail personnel focused on the suit even during the transition between changing administrations.

The master finally appointed in 1980 was a person of such prestige in the community that he might have been able to influence the local governing body to appropriate funds for at least partial compliance. No requests for compliance funds were included in the sheriffs' budgets until 1979. Earlier budget requests, even though denied, might ultimately have underscored the need for compliance and resulted in earlier acquiescence by the Council. This is, of course, speculation. Since the City-County Council officially inserted the word "reluctantly" into its approval of new jail construction in 1981, they were clearly resistant to the idea of allocating funds for improvement of the jail. It is possible that they would have been moved to action only by the threat of contempt of court citations and of an imposed moratorium on acceptance of prisoners at the jail.

Judicial intervention on behalf of pre-trial prisoners has helped to focus national attention on county jails. The result has been a growing professionalism among jail administrators and increasing interest, among local sheriffs, in quality jail management. The National Sheriffs Association published a jail administration manual in 1974. The American Correctional Association and the National Institute of Corrections offer assistance and training to local facilities and more and more jails have taken advantage of these opportunities.

The jail studied here remained outside this opportunity network for many years after the suit was filed. Some jails continue to operate in isolation, and if they fall under judicial review will be unable to formulate remedies. Courts should consider defendant jails' involvement in professional networks before deciding on a method of remedy formulation.

In Marion County defendants were plagued with all the handicaps to compliance which isolation breeds and were, in large measure, unable to find ways to comply with the orders of the court. For some of the defendants the compliance process was a learning experience. They moved through several responses: defiance and anger, "sit-tight," and, at the last, active involvement. According to one of the originally named defendants the hardest part about responding to the court order was changing attitudes, "including my own." Pleased with the new professionalism among jail personnel and anticipating completion of the new jail extension, he acknowledged that the court order "may have been the best thing that ever happened to us."

NOTES

[1]Baltimore's proximity to the nation's capital was an advantage in knowing that other agencies might play a role. It is unclear from the study if this was a request for assistance or for confirmation that the jail was fine and the court in error.

[2]All of the money each prisoner has when arrested is placed in an account from which he may draw to purchase commissary items (candies, cookies, cigarettes, items

of personal hygiene, etc.). Visitors may deposit additional money in the prisoner's account. Profits from the sale of these items are spent on jail improvements. This was a fairly new source of funds since, until 1977, commissary profits had gone to the Sheriff and were considered one of the perquisites of the office.

TABLE OF CASES

Bell v. Wolfish—441 U.S. 520, 995C 1979.
Collins v. Schoonfield—344 F. Supp. 257 (D.M.D. 1972).
Hamilton v. Love—328 F. Supp. 1182 (E.D. ARK, 1971).
Hamilton v. Schiro—338 F. Supp. 1016 (E.D. LA, 1970).
Holland v. Donelon—Civil Action No. 71-1442 Sec. C (E.D., LA 1973).
Holt v. Sarver—309 F. Supp. 362 (E.D. ARK, 1970); Aff'd 442 F.2d 304 (8th Cir. 1971).
Inmates of Milwaukee County Jail v. Peterson—353 F. Supp. 1157, 1160 (E.D. WIS, 1973).
Jones v. Wittenberg—330 F. Supp. 707 (W.D. OHIO, 1971).
Jordan v. Fitzharris—257 F. Supp. 674 (N.D. CAL, 1966).
Rhem v. Malcolm—371 F. Supp. 594 (S.D. NY, 1974).

REFERENCES

BUCKHOLZ, R.E. JR.; COOPER, D.J.; GETTNER, A.; GUGGEHEIMER, J.; ROSENTHAL, E.S.; and ROTENBERG, M.B., 1978. "The Remedial Process in Institutional Reform Legislation," *Columbia Law Review* 78:784-929.
CIVIL RIGHTS ACT OF 1964, Public Law No. 88-352, 78 STAT. 241 (July 2, 1964).
HARRIS, M.K.; and SPILLER, D.P., 1977. *After Decision: Implementation of Judicial Decrees in Correctional Settings,* Washington D.C.: U.S. Government Printing Office.
JONES, B., 1982. "Impact of Courts on Correctional Management," paper presented at the regional conference of ASPA, Louisville, KY: November, 1982.
KIMBALL, E.L.; and NEWMAN, D.J., 1968. "Judicial Intervention in Correctional Decisions: Threat and Response," *Crime and Delinquency* 14:1-14.
MURTON, T.O., 1976. *The Dilemma of Prison Reform,* New York: Holt, Rinehart & Winston.
NATIONAL ADVISORY COMMISSION ON CRIMINAL JUSTICE STANDARDS AND GOALS, 1973. *Corrections,* Washington, D.C.: U.S. Government Printing Office.
PRESIDENT'S COMMISSION ON LAW ENFORCEMENT AND ADMINISTRATION OF JUSTICE, 1967. "Task Force Reports," *Police, Courts, Corrections, Washington, D.C.: U.S. Government Printing Office.*

RUBIN, S., 1969. *"The Administrative Response to Court Decisions,"* Crime and Delinquency 15:377-386.

———— 1974. "The Impact of Court Decisions on the Correctional Process," *Crime and Delinquency* 20:129-34.

U.S. DEPARTMENT OF JUSTICE, BUREAU OF STATISTICS, 1978. *Census of Jails,* Washington, D.C.: U.S. Government Printing Office.

PART III

RETHINKING JAIL MANAGEMENT

COURT INTERVENTION into local jails suggests a particular diagnosis of the jail problem. Under it, the non-responsiveness of jails is attributed to ignorance, calloused indifference or an inability to compete against other local interests. To address these problems the brute force of judicial decree is required. A different understanding of the jail problem, however, may suggest the utility of alternative change strategies. In this section we will examine the traditional management topics of training, jails design, and planning, but our approach will be based on a different assessment of the cause of some jail problems.

The approach draws on a tradition in the planned change literature with its roots in the studies of Kurt Lewin during World War II. Lewin experimented with the involvement of change targets in the diagnosis and solution of change problems. Under this model staff represent resources rather than obstacles to bringing about change. A wide variety of collaborative change strategies have emerged from the original research. The tradition is seen in industrial settings, with the involvement of management, union officials and assemblyline workers in addressing non-contractual work related problems in Quality of Work-Life Programs. In the human services, and particularly in criminal justice, Hans Toch and J. Douglas Grant have developed and refined the approach. Their work has directly influenced most of the reform efforts discussed in this section.

The unlikely title of Chapter 10, "When Donkeys Fly," refers to the futility of defining mental health problems in jail as simply a problem of sick people. This definition immobilizes staff and suggests improvement will come only when police and courts stop sending people to jail. John Gibbs suggests a more productive view in which the contributions of jails to inmate mental health problems as well as the staff resources for

147

mitigating these problems are recognized. Drawing on a strategy of action research, Gibbs suggests that custodial and mental health staff can study and address the contributions of the jail environment to inmate coping problems.

In "Changing Concepts of Jail Design and Management," Ray Nelson also suggests changes in the traditional management of local jails. While Gibbs based his program on change theory, Nelson describes new roles for jail staff from an historical perspective as well as from the observation of existing facilities. Developments in architecture merge with new management concepts in jails designed for ongoing interaction between staff and inmates. Research suggests that this normalized environment can enhance inmate safety and adjustment as well as improve working conditions for staff.

Lucien Lombardo also acknowledges that jail officers represent an untapped resource in local facilities. The training model he developed and implemented in New Jersey jails takes a unique approach to utilizing those resources. The model merges research and training in a program in which officers study successful and unsuccessful techniques for doing their jobs. Such a collaborative learning process can contribute to reductions in stress for staff and for inmates and create a humane correctional environment.

In the final chapter, Klofas, Smith and Meister provide a description of a planning program at the new Peoria County jail in Illinois. The participatory program drew on indigenous staff resources in planning the operation of the new facility. Participants went well beyond their experiences in collecting and studying data. They developed links between the jail and the local community and even involved inmates in their efforts. The program is presented as a model of participation in human service organizations through its combination of individual and organizational development strategies.

CHAPTER 10

WHEN DONKEYS FLY

A Zen Perspective on Dealing with the Problem of the Mentally Disturbed Jail Inmate

John J. Gibbs

The Problem and Current Perspective

THERE IS a body of evidence which indicates that psychologically disturbed prisoners are a major and growing problem in jails. Some of the research conducted in jails suggests that a substantial proportion of prisoners are psychologically disturbed when they enter jail, and presumably before they enter jail, and many have a history of psychiatric treatment (see Gibbs, 1982 and Gibbs et al., 1983 for a review of the evidence).

A popular explanation of the problem links the growing number of psychologically disturbed in jail with the decarceration of mental institutions and reduction of resources for dealing with the chronically mentally ill in the community. The theory is that some of the mentally ill who have been released to the community cause problems which require their removal from the community. The police who dutifully remove them from the streets find the only timely placement for their charges is jail.

It is on the basis of this theory and similar notions that jail administrators and custodians claim that they have a problem with psychologically disturbed prisoners because the mentally ill are dumped in jail. While there may be some truth to this claim, it is not the whole truth. However, many are willing to see it as almost the whole truth because it fits the popular person-centered view of psychological disturbance.

Paper presented at Academy of Criminal Justice Sciences Meeting, Las Vegas, 1985. Panel #47: Contemporary Jail Management: problems and Prescriptions.

149

The person-centered explanation of the psychologically disturbed in jail leads to person-centered solutions. We can reduce the number of psychologically disturbed in jail by (1) getting a better class of prisoner, or (2) improving our current lot. The methods for meeting these objectives are also person-centered. We get a better prisoner by diverting to other places those who do not belong in jail, and we improve the mental health of our current population by (1) bringing in experts to treat individuals, or (2) sending out individuals to be treated by experts.

The person-centered view of psychological disturbances is a difficult conceptual bind to break. Many hold onto this view despite a growing mountain of conceptual and empirical evidence that personality is not the enduring characteristic we once were led to believe it was. Many will not let go even when faced with research findings which suggest that environmental congruence in jail (the match between the environmental commodities a person needs, e.g., demand for safety, and the perceived availability of those commodities in the environment, e.g., supply of safety) is more strongly associated with symptoms of psychopathology than is any personal characteristic (Gibbs et al., 1983).

Many factors bind us to the person-centered view. There are considerable cultural, personal, and political investments in this conception of psychological disturbance. It is reflected in the organizational charts of our penal institutions, and finds its way into practice in our jails in the division of responsibility for the psychologically disturbed. Treaters treat them. Custodians keep them.

Mechanics and Attendants

Some of the corrections officers I know have gladly and fully bought into the person-centered view of psychological disturbance. This view is based on an oversimplified version of the traditional medical model of mental illness. It stipulates that something has gone wrong or was never right with the individual. It may be the hardwiring or software or both, and the individual will not function properly until it is fixed. Doctors and other people mechanics (e.g., psychologists) fix people. Guards do not fix people. Jail guards and administrators run people lots. They park them safely until they are needed somplace else—court, prison, or the streets. If people who are supposedly fixed are sent to the lot (housing blocks) and don't run right, the logical solution is to send them back to the shop (hospital).

What I have presented is, of course, a caricature of the medical model. No one really sees mental illness or psychological problems as completely explained by defects in the individual. But for purposes of organization and classification within the jail, some people act as if this model of psychological disturbance matches reality. It undoubtly makes life easier for some custodians to see themselves in the parking business, not in the repair business. It also makes life easier for some clinicians, at least in the short-run, to see themselves in the repair business, not in the parking business. And it certainly makes it easier to run a jail when you can neatly separate functions into repair and parking.

The truth of the matter is, of course, that most psychological disturbances are not exclusively the products of personal defects. Even the most interior moods can be influenced by fluctuations in the environment. The point is that problems and disturbances do not occur in a vacuum. They are the products of people interacting with environments. They emerge or are played out in some context or situation. Indeed, it is difficult to think about a person without thinking about the person in a situation.

A first step in dealing with the problem of psychologically disturbed prisoners is to provide both custodial and treatment staff with the opportunity to realize that (1) they are in the people business, not the parking or repair business, (2) problems and disturbances are the product of individuals interacting with environments or human climates, and (3) custodians and treaters, but mostly custodians, are an important part of the jail environment.

I used the word realize above in the context of helping jail personnel reconceptualize their roles. By this I mean more than an intellectual understanding. It would be insulting the intelligence of the staff to merely bring them into a room and lecture to them on various conceptual schemes that can be used to describe their jobs. Most staff members already understand that they are part of the environment. What they need is the chance to realize, in the sense of attain or achieve, their influence in shaping the human climate of the jail. This realization requires that they find ways to place the concepts reflected in statements such as "we're in the people business" and "we can shape the environment to help reduce problems" into operation in the real world of the jail.

Notions like "the people business" and "environments influence behavior" sound trite. They are platitudes that are responded to with sighs and jeers. They are hackneyed phrases that provoke cynicism and sarcasm. The effects of putting these notions into practice, however, are anything but trite. When the principles that are locked in these bromides are realized in action, they have tremendous implications. This is the kind of realization that the staff should have the opportunity to experience. It is easy to get people to understand that they are an important part of the environment, maybe too easy; it is hard to get them to realize it. And, of course, this kind of realization on the front line requires a special managerial or executive perspective.

Zen for Jail Managers

Those in direct contact with inmates are not the only ones heavily invested in the person-centered view of psychological disturbance. Many jail administrators consider psychological problems the result of neurons misfiring in heads with bad wiring, and they think that doctors in hospitals are the only ones who can and should do anything about it. In their minds, the function of jail is to confine; the function of the hospital is to treat.

When the problem of prisoners who are psychologically disturbed is viewed from the traditional fix'em — park'em perspective, the solutions that immediately come to mind are (1) hire more or better fixers, and (2) reduce the number of broken ones by (a) getting rid of those currently on the lot, and (b) not accepting new ones on the lot. Jail administrators will have the resources and will be in the political position to implement such solutions when donkeys fly.

Given this seemingly hopeless situation some of the wisdom of the ancient Zen masters, who have answered questions like "What is the sound of one hand clapping?" may be instructive.

A basic premise of Zen is that each person already possesses everything he needs to see the absolute truth. Indeed, each of us already knows the truth, but we have to remove the obstructions (illusions) to seeing what we already know. We have the wherewithal to solve our problems. All we have to do is use the means that are already available to us.

Illusions are created by our attachment to static and limiting views of ourselves and the way the world operates. These views restrict our spontaneity, creativity, and adaptability.

Enlightenment is the result of breaking through illusions. It is achieved by relinquishing the conventional view of self, the world, and their relationship. This letting go allows one to see problems in a new light, and results in a perspective that is characterized by openness and creativity.

The general strategy for dealing with the psychologically disturbed in jail that will be discussed in the remainder of this chapter is similar to the Zen approach. The assumption is that many of the resources that are needed to deal with the problem are already available. What needs to be done is to recognize the problem for what it is and use what already exists to address it.

A first step is to let go of the exclusively person-centered explanation of psychological disturbances and the idea that psychiatrists and other mental health professionals are the only ones who can do anything about them. Mental health professionals are certainly important. But they can't do it all by themselves. They need the help of officers. It is the officer who observes prisoners interacting with jail environment. The guard is the one who helps men deal with the stresses of confinement on a daily basis. His opinion should count. He is the environmental specialist. He knows because the bottom line is he is a large part of the environment.

The successful use of the ecological approach, which will be discussed more fully later in this paper, requires that treatment and custodial staff recognize (1) the environment can create and ameliorate psychological problems, and (2) guards are an important aspect of the jail ecology. If a substantial number of staff members refuse to relinquish the view that doctors should fix them and custodians should park them, programs based on the human services and ecological approaches are doomed to failure.

The Zen literature is filled with exhortations to recognize what is, accept it, and deal with it. This is solid advice to jail managers and administrators. In a different world, the mentally ill would not be confined in jails. In a different world, jails would not be harsh environments that contribute to psychological disturbances and human breakdowns. In the world we live in, jails are dumping grounds for many social and psychological casualities. In the world we live in, jails are stressful places that can be unsettling even for veterans of confinement. And the world we live in is here and now, and will be here for some time.

Research in Action and Action Research

Existing research findings, especially surveys of the opinions of corrections officers, administrators, and mental health professionals (see Toch and Grant, 1982), can be an important first step on the road to re-conceptualizing the problem of the psychologically disturbed in jail. There is research available which shows that (1) those who work in jails

154 *Sneaking Inmates Down the Alley*

consider the psychologically disturbed a serious problem, and (2) psychological disturbances are linked to the jail environment.

It is not difficult to convince those who work in jails that the psychologically disturbed are a major problem. A survey of New Jersey jail wardens and social service providers support the view that those familiar with jails see psychological disturbances as a serious and growing problem. More than four-fifths (n = 35) of the survey participants responded affirmatively to the question: "Do you think there has been an increase in the percentage of jail prisoners who have social and medical problems rather than criminal justice problems in the last few years?" and the problem of prisoners with psychological disturbances was surpassed only by overcrowding (Gibbs, 1983).

When presented with the above information, most jail administrators and corrections officers will wholeheartedly concur, and go on to explain the problem and solution in person-centered terms. There are, however, some research findings available that can be used to suggest to them that the jail environment can play a role in psychological disturbances.

In a recent study funded by the National Institute of Justice, my colleagues and I examined the influences of the jail environment on psychopathology (Gibbs et al., 1983). The SCL-90, a symptom checklist consisting of 90 items, was used to measure symptoms of psychopathology before confinement, during the first 72 hours of incarceration, and after 5 days of imprisonment. The SCL-90 items cluster into 9 scales or symptom dimensions: Somatization, Obsessive-Compulsive, Interpersonal Sensitivity, Depression, Anxiety, Hostility, Phobic Anxiety, Paranoid Ideation, and Psychoticism. The average item score on the SCL-90 is known as the Global Severity Index (GSI), which is considered ". . . the best single indicator of the current level or depth of disorder, and should be utilized in most instances where a single summary measure is required" (Derogatis, 1977:12).

We compared the retrospective ratings of "street" symptoms (how they felt the week before they were arrested and jailed) of jail prisoners (N = 339) with symptom ratings by samples of psychiatric outpatients (N = 1002) and "normals" (N = 937). The comparisons supported those who assume that the jail receives people who already have a relatively high level of psychological disturbance. Jail prisoner "street" ratings were significantly and substantially greater than "normal" ratings. On the average, jail inmate ratings for symptom dimensions were 96 percent greater than those of "normals," and GSI score for jail prisoners on the street was 77 percent greater than that of normals.

Although those who were confined reported higher symptoms levels when they were on the streets than did "normals," their symptoms levels were not as great as those of psychiatric outpatients. On the average, psychiatric outpatient ratings for symptom dimensions were 117 percent greater than those of jail prisoners, and the GSI score for psychiatric outpatients was 129 percent greater than that of jail prisoners on the streets.

We made the following comparisons using SCL-90 responses to determine how time and setting influence symptoms:

(1) a comparison of jail prisoner "street" symptoms (outside symptoms) with symptoms reported during the first 72 hours of confinement (inside symptoms); and

(2) a comparison of jail prisoner inside symptoms with symptoms reported after five days of confinement (follow-up symptoms).

The symptom pattern that emerged from these comparisons was an inverted J curve. Symptoms increased sharply from street to jail and diminished much less sharply after five days of confinement. For inmates on whom symptom data were collected for all three points in time (N = 102), the inside GSI was 69 percent greater than the outside GSI and the follow-up GSI was 20 percent less than the inside GSI. The most dramatic changes were for depression. Depression symptoms increased by 132 percent upon incarceration and declined 24 percent after five days of confinement.

The data we collected suggest that jails receive a relatively disturbed group of people who become even more disturbed in the jail environment, especially during the initial period of confinement. These findings are consistent with the research on self-injury in jail and the observations of jail prisoners and personnel.

One of the purposes of our study was to examine the influence of perceptions of the jail environment on symptoms of psychopathology. This required the measurement of environmental demand and supply. Data were collected on the needs of prisoners and the resources they perceived available in the jail environment to satisfy these needs. The theory tested was that symptoms of stress or psychopathology would be more in evidence when supply did not meet demand (resources $\geq$ needs).

The measure of environmental need developed was the Jail Preference Inventory (JPI). The JPI uses a comparison-by-pairs format and measures seven dimensions: Privacy, Safety, Certainty, Assistance, Support, Activity, and Autonomy. The measure of environmental supply used was the Environmental Quality Scale (EQS). It measures the same dimensions as the JPI, but not from a demand perspective. The EQS is a supply-side instrument. It is intended to measure how much Privacy, Safety, Certainty, Assistance, Support, Activity, and Autonomy the inmate sees available in the environment.

Needs (JPI) and resources (EQS) were measured at two points in time—within the first 72 hours of confinement and after five days of confinement. On the initial administration of the JPI, our respondents scored highest on the Assistance dimension (14.7, the highest possible score was 24) followed by Support (14.2) and Certainty (14.0); Activity (12.7) and Safety (12.5) were in the middle range, and Privacy (8.8) and Autonomy (7.9) had the lowest average scores.

These findings supported our predictions that: (1) the disruption and disorganization that result from entry into jail promote dependence on outside links and strong needs for Assistance and Support, (2) doubts about one's status with the courts and control over events in the street, which are still very much a part of one's world, would result in a strong desire for Certainty, and (3) the lack of programs in jail and the boredom of the jail cell in conjunction with intrusive thoughts about pressing problems create a demand for activity.

A comparison of the initial administration of the JPI with the follow-up administration suggested that the environmental concerns of jail prisoners remain fairly stable over time. Although generally needs increased, demand for any of the environmental commodities did not increase or decrease by more than three percent, and the concordance between the rank order of the dimensions for the initial and follow-up distributions was substantial (W = .96).

The supply-side picture (EQS) looked very different from that of environmental demand. Autonomy (10.3, the highest possible score was 15) was considered the most abundant environmental commodity, and there was a relatively ample supply of Privacy (9.1) available. Certainty, Support, and Safety (8.9) were tied for the third rank, and Assistance (8.1) and Activity (7.1) were in short supply.

The distribution of ranks for the EQS average dimension scores and the JPI scores were not very similar (W = .16). The environmental commodity that was most in supply, EQS Autonomy, was least in demand, JPI Autonomy. The quality that ranked first in need, JPI Assistance, ranked sixth in perceived availability, EQS Assistance. These findings suggest that in jail, what you want, you can't get.

A comparison of EQS initial and follow-up scores suggested that supply changes more than demand. The concordance between the EQS initial and follow-up rank orders of dimensions (W = .73) was not as high as that reported for the JPI (W = .96), and there were substantial changes in the prisoners' perceptions of the availability of some environmental commodities. The perception of the supply of Activity increased by 50 percent. The supply of Certainty, Autonomy, and Support decreased by 26, 20, and 13 percent. There was little change in Privacy, Safety, or Certainty.

In our study, we proposed that stress symptoms or symptoms of psychopathology are linked to the environment. We expected that prisoners who expressed a need for an environmental commodity (demand) and perceived that commodity in the environmental (supply) would report lower symptoms levels (SCL-90 dimensions) and stress (GSI) than those who expressed a need and did not see the commodity sufficiently available in the environment.

Environment congruence categories for each JPI-EQS dimension were developed to test the congruence hypothesis. The first step was to create a high and low category for each EQS and JPI dimension by dividing each distribution of scores as close as possible to the median. This placed half of the sample in the high category on a JPI dimension, e.g., Privacy, and half the sample in the low JPI Privacy category. Likewise, half or near half of the sample was in the low EQS Privacy category, and the other half was in the high EQS Privacy category.

Once the scores for each dimension were classified into high and low categories, a 2 × 2 environmental congruence table was constructed for each of the seven environmental dimensions:

Environmental Congruence Categories

JPI Category	EQS Category	
(demand)	**Low**	**High**
Low	Concordant — Neutral	Discordant — Neutral
High	Discordant — Negative	Concordant — Positive

Figure 1

The following values were assigned to the possible outcomes:

Discordant — Negative = 0
Concordant — Neutral)
                  and   ) = 1
Discordant — Neutral)
Concordant — Positive = 2

The subjects received a congruence score from 0 to 2 for each dimension, and the scores for all dimensions were summed to a total score (range = 0-14). We divided the distribution of total scores at the median to form two Total Environmental Congruence (TEC) categories (high and low). We examined TEC in conjunction with SCL-90 dimension scores (classified into high and low symptom level by dividing at the medians) and the Global Severity Index (high and low categories). The analysis was done for both initial and follow-up scores.

We found that Total Environmental Congruence was associated with the SCL-90 Global Severity Index in both the initial ($x^2 = 10.36$, p = .002, y = -.37) and follow-up ($x^2 = 11.64$, p < .000, y = -.62) samples, and TEC was at least moderately related to most SCL-90 dimensions. The consistent pattern was that those subjects with relatively low congruence scores had relatively high symptom scores.

The research findings just described can be used to help break the conceptual bind that restricts thinking about psychological problems to persons only. The information can be used to promote conceptual expansion to include environmental factors. The purpose of presenting the research to practitioners is not only to persuade but also, and more importantly, to stimulate thinking. If administrators, officers, and mental health professionals can validate the research findings with their own experience, a powerful force for change has emerged.

Once the environment-centered approach has been adopted, the research findings presented can become the starting point for program development and program-related research. After the jail administration is committed to the expanded view of psychological disturbance in jail, a group of mental health professionals and custodians can be brought together as a study team to develop programs based on the concept. The purpose of the team would be to (1) review the existing research for relevant data and program ideas, (2) design projects to collect any additional information they need to develop programs, (3) develop innovative programs based on (1) and (2), and (4) propose strategies for implementing and monitoring programs.

Bringing together custodial and treatment staff to conduct research and explore solutions is an important first step in helping jail personnel move away from seeing the problem of the psychologically disturbed in jail in the traditional compartmentalized way—people mechanics fix them and custodians keep them until they are needed elsewhere. The information collected and the experience of working together should help destory stereotypes and get both custodial and mental health personnel thinking about the problem of the psychologically disturbed in new ways. Working together on a project should also result in the formation of professional links that will last beyond the duration of the research project. These links can be the basis for the kind of network that is needed to provide inmates with special problems with the care and services they need to psychologically survive. The network should be a reminder to guards and the mental health staff that they must depend on each other and share responsibility for the mentally ill prisoner.

Another advantage of having both custodial and mental health staff participate in research and program development is that participation breeds commitment. People are willing to pledge their support to programs they have developed, and they are willing to work to implement programs they consider practical and useful. If they have conducted the research on which the program is based, they will know how the program is linked directly to solving a problem in the real world. There will be no question that the problem exists and the program is relevant.

It is naive to think that a group of custodial and treatment staff members can be brought together and immediately form an effective research and program development team. There is usually some conflict existing between members of these groups, and before a working relationship can be established, the conflict should be resolved, or at least, addressed.

Some of the conflict may be rooted in mutual misconceptions about roles and attitudes. There are several ways they can be brought out into the open and dealt with so the research and program development team can get on with the task at hand. One fruitful approach to group conflict was used by Blake, Mouton, and Sloma in addressing union-management differences (Blake, Mouton, and Sloma, 1969). Their eight-step program consists of the following phases: (1) orientation, (2) development of self-image and counter-image, (3) exchange of images across groups, (4) clarification of images, (5) intragroup diagnosis of present relationship, (6) exchange of diagnosis across groups, (7) consolidation of key issues and sources of friction, and (8) planning the next step.

Another approach used by Hammond and his associates has been described by Toch and Grant (1982). In this approach, the groups hold separate, tape-recorded problem-discussing meetings, and exchange tapes. The expectation is that ". . . after a small number of such exchanges, the groups voluntarily [request] to work together on their common problems (Toch and Grant, 1982:260).

Group meetings to resolve conflict, conduct research, or plan programs hold the interest of the participants because the meetings are something new and different and they make the participants feel like a special group. Once the programs based on the group efforts become routine, interest and motivation will wane. The group should explore ways to maintain interest and motivation.

Some way to measure performance is essential for sustained interest and motivation in a program and for evaluation and modification of the program. Participants need some way to know how they are doing. They have to know if their efforts are having the intended effects. A positive response will encourage them to keep working. Even a negative response can be valuable because it will tell participants that they must change something in order to succeed.

The most crucial factor in the success and continuation of programs based on the environment-centered perspective is the support of top management. Toch and Grant (1982) refer to the kind of program suggested in this paper as "innovation ghettos" or "enrichment ghettos." They stipulate that the survival of such programs requires organizational protection in the form of commitment from and links to top management. Otherwise, programs become shortlived and hollow exercises.

Expected Results

The exploration of the problem of the psychologically disturbed in jail from an environmental perspective is expected to lead to the discovery that corrections officers are an important feature of the jail ecology. The view of the guard as an important force in shaping the environment is part of the human services perspective. This is an approach that is familiar to some guards, if not in name, at least in the way they operate in the jail. Even the most distant and custody-minded guards sometimes provide basic human services to inmates because it is in their (the guards) best interest. A properly timed question about a problem here and a kind word there can be the difference between a quiet tour of duty and eight hours of bedlam.

The discovery of the human service perspective by guards is a beginning in changing their conception of their jobs from parking lot attendants to resource specialists who are responsible for the well-being of the human vehicles in their charge. The human services perspective includes the traditional custodial functions like rule-enforcement and security but instead of viewing them as oppressive features of the environment, they are seen as having the potential to reduce stress:

. . . security and rule-enforcement practices also contribute to providing safe environments, to providing stable and nonarbitrary environments, and to defining the boundaries within which freedom can be exercised (Toch, 1977; Johnson and Price, 1981; Lombardo, 1981). For at least some inmates these activities are associated with the reduction of stress. As with all human services work, it is not the general context of the correctional officer's role that matters to the inmate. It is the individual officer's interpretation of that role, and the application of the interpretation to individual situations that affect the inmate's experience of stress (Lombardo, 1982:293).

Having officers explore their importance in shaping subenvironments within the jail is one way to start them thinking about expanding their human service role. Human services training that decreases tension and increases the officer's sense of control is training that is relevant and likely to be given a chance by officers. Johnson and Price have sketched the aims of such a training program for prison guards. These same goals are relevant to training jail staff.

Through training, correctional officers can be made aware of (a) the general ecological dimensions, (b) the possible presence of niches in various locations within prisons, and (c) ways in which ecological resources can be cultivated and deployed to reduce stress. Ecological patterns vary over time, are affected by transfers, turnover, program changes, and alterations in inmate groups and activities. Training thus should provide officers with a perspective enabling them to identify ecological dimensions and niches, rather than with a resource map depicting specific dimensions or niches characteristic of a given prison at a particular point in time. Moreover, training should enable officers to see their own experiences and characteristics, as well as those of their inmates, as environmental attributes. Correctional officers who see themselves and their wards as elements of the prison's ecology can play active roles in providing sanctuaries for inmates in stress (Johnson and Price, 1981:367).

Programs that are based on the human services model and environmental perspective are programs that enrich the officer's role. And if officers participate in the development of programs, the quality of officer work life and the quality of inmate life should benefit. Toch and Grant see the benefits of participation as follows:

Why does quality of service improve with participation? For one, decisions 'are simply more likely to be implemented'. . . Participation also unleashes worker creativity. . . Participation also (1) brings to the surface obstacles to performance in the form of difficulties that have been swept under the rug, (2) provides a sense of mission and collective sense of ownership, (3) yields self-respect, as one's views are respected and decisions are based on them, (4) creates new knowledge by pooling workers' experiences and judgments, (5) provides group support for the tackling and resolution of problems, and (6) decreases the climate for burnout (Toch and Grant, 1982:115).

The Myth of the Neanderthal Guard

One perceived obstruction to the adoption of human services model and the environmental approach and participatory program is the myth of the Neanderthal guard. Many officers, administrators, and treaters may see the custodial subculture as an impediment to change efforts. In many jails and prisons there is a myth, often perpetuated by the guards themselves, that most guards have a hard core, conservative, custodial perspective. It is assumed that many guards will have difficulty seeing the value of the human services approach, and they will resist any effort to move them in this direction. They see an obvious and deep-rooted clash between the custodial perspective and the human services perspective.

When we start to consider individual guards in the context of their daily lives on the tiers, the myth begins to break down. Reducing stress for some inmates by providing basic human services makes sense because it makes an officer's life easier. Situations that could result in tense moments and outright explosions can be avoided through the proper use of the human services approach. Despite the conservative, callous stance of some guards, many officers are not blind to gains they can make by adopting the human services perspective.

The notion of a pervasive value system derived from a strong turnkey perspective may be more apparent than real. Klofas and Toch (1982) surveyed 1,739 officers working in New York State prisons and found ". . . that most officers were interested in expanding their roles through the addition of human services functions to their jobs" (Klofas and Toch, 1982:241). However, they also discovered that when they asked officers to predict how their fellow officers would respond to questionnaire items, "officers consistently overestimated their peers' alienation and underestimated their professional orientation" (Klofas and Toch, 1982:242-243). These findings indicate that there is a pluralistic ignorance among guards, and they support Toch's observation of 1980:

> If pluralistic ignorance exists among guards. . ., the officer subculture becomes imaginary. In other words, the brave [officers who assume that they are alone and at risk in providing human services to inmates] can afford to be braver than they suspect, because consensus

on such premises as "never talk to a con" or "never rat to a sergeant" is falsely assumed, and no guard group really cares whether officer Jones lets a depressed inmate show him pictures of his unfaithful wife, or runs a counseling group in the protective segregation gallery (Toch, 1980:29).

The findings by Klofas and Toch indicate that the guard subculture is not entirely fiction. In the typology they constructed using responses to questionnaire items, one category was called "Subculture Custodians." These respondents were 17 percent of the sample, and they were described as ". . . the bellringers of the mythological subculture" (Klofas and Toch, 1982:247). These officers showed a strong custodial orientation on the questionnaire, and they inaccurately assumed that peers were also custodially inclined. The most common type, however, was the "Supported Majority" (34.7%). These guards saw themselves as professionals and felt that their fellow officers also had a professional self-image (Klofas and Toch, 1982:247).

The findings of the Klofas and Toch (1982) study suggest that as a whole prison guards have a professional orientation, and they are as a group more professional than they, as individuals, expected. The same could be true of jail guards, and the hypothesis should be tested for two reasons: (1) to see if the hypothesis is supported by the empirical facts, and (2) if the hypothesis is supported, to use these facts to dispel the myth of the pervasive and powerful custodial subculture. In other words, the findings should be shown to the participants and officers, as Klofas and Toch did (1982:243), to demonstrate the extent of pluralistic ignorance.

Conclusion

The analysis of problems and recommendations presented in this chapter are based on the premise that a realistic approach to the problem of the psychologically disturbed in jail requires that we broaden our perspective to include not only the disturbed individual but also where the disturbance occurs — the jail.

Our usual approach to the problem is person-centered. We assume that we have a large number of psychologically disturbed people in jail because a large number of psychologically disturbed people are arrested and sent to jail. We think if we can get a better class of prisoner our problems will be solved.

What I have just described is of course an oversimplification of the person-centered view. Most mental health professionals agree that there

are forces in a person's current environment that help shape his psychological disturbance. The problem is that we know that the environment
can be a powerful influence, but we act as if we don't know it. Our
person-centered view makes us myopic. It blinds us to a wide range of
resources that are available to address the problem of the psychologically
disturbed in jail.

A major theme of this paper is that many of the resources needed to
deal with the problem of the psychologically disturbed prisoner already
exist within the jail. Their recognition requires a reconceptualization of
the problem; and development of these resources requires the participation and commitment of the custodial and treatment staffs. The way
suggested to elicit the participation and commitment of the jail staff is to
involve selected members in action-research programs.

I am aware that there are major impediments to the formation of
such teams, especially in overcrowded jails with high staff turnover. The
benefits to be derived from the adoption of an ecological approach,
which is based on the human services perspective, are so sizable and
tangible for both staff and inmates, that it is worth the effort to try in the
face of strong resistance.

The ecological perspective will not solve the problem of the mentally
disturbed in jail, but neither will waiting for the legislature to change
civil commitment laws, hoping that the police will change their practice
of dumping the psychologically disturbed in jail, or complaining that
more mental health staff need to be hired for the jail. These reflect long-
term measures that will not completely solve the problem anyway. An
environment-centered approach will not cure mental illness. But it can
reduce stress to the point where an unmanageable crisis becomes a
manageable problem for the disturbed inmate, and this can have implications for the person's ability to cope with the next crisis which may occur in the community.

The environment-centered approach is not intended to replace the
person-centered approach. They are both part of the same approach —
one that deals with people in context. I emphasize the ecological perspective over more traditional person-centered approaches because the
influence of environment is not evident in the way we deal with the
problem of the disturbed in jail, and I think it has great potential, especially if used in conjunction with current approaches.

I do not think we are in danger of ever losing our person-centered
perspective, so I payed very little attention to this approach in this chapter. I do think we are in danger of never realizing the value of the human

services approach and the ecological perspective, so they were given top billing.

The foundation of the recommended approach is that the environment contributes to psychological problems in jails and it can contribute to their solution. This does not mean that ecological manipulation should replace all of the methods that are currently used to treat the mentally ill. There is no substitute for medical intervention for some psychological disturbances. Medication in combination with other therapies is essential to the functioning of some patients. With chronically ill patients, the human services approach and the ecological perspective are merely meant to extend and enhance the time these men spend out of the hospital.

An important consequence of adopting and developing the ecological and human services perspectives through the participation of guards is that it expands and enriches their jobs. This kind of quality of work life enhancement can go a long way in reducing job burnout, stress, and alienation.

REFERENCES

Blake, R., J. Mouton, and R. Sloma (1969) "The Union-Management Laboratory: Strategy for Resolving Intergroup Conflict," in W. Bennis, K. Benne, and R. Chin (eds.), *The Planning of Change.* New York: Holt, Rinehart and Winston.

Derogatis, L. (1977) *SCL-90 Administration, Scoring and Procedures Manual-I for the (Revised) Version.* Baltimore: Clinical Psychometrics Research.

Gibbs, J. (1983) "Problems and Priorities: Perceptions of Jail Custodians and Social Service Providers." *Journal of Criminal Justice.* 11, 4:327-338.

Gibbs, J. (1982) "On Demons and Goals: A Summary and Review of Investigations Concerning the Psychological Problems of Jail Prisoners," in *Mental Health Services in Local Jails: Report on A Special National Workshop.* C. Dunn and H. Steadman, eds. Rockville, MD: National Institute of Mental Health.

Gibbs, J., L. Maiello, K. Kolb, J. Garofalo, F. Adler, and S. Costello (1983) *Stress, Setting, and Satisfaction: The Final Report of the Man-Jail Transactions Project.* Unpublished Report. Washington, D.C. National Institute of Justice.

Johnson, R. and S. Price (1981) "The Complete Correctional Officer: Human Services and the Human Environment of the Prison," *Criminal Justice and Behavior.* 8, 3:343-373.

Klofas, J. and H. Toch (1982) "The Guard Subculture Myth," *Journal of Research in Crime and Delinquency.* 19, 2:238-254.

Lombardo, L. (1982) "Alleviating Inmate Stress: Contributions from Correctional Officers," in *The Pains of Imprisonment.* in R. Johnson and H. Toch, eds. Beverly Hills: Sage.

Toch, H. (1980) "Liberating Prison Guards." *Proceedings of the 15th Interagency Workshop.* Huntsville, Texas: Sam Houston State University.

Toch, H. and J.D. Grant (1982) *Reforming Human Services: Change Through Participation.* Beverly Hills: Sage.

CHAPTER 11

CHANGING CONCEPTS IN JAIL DESIGN
AND MANAGEMENT

W. Ray Nelson

THE HISTORY OF the American jail has not been marked by notable change during the past 200 years. Since 1790, when Walnut
Street Jail introduced single occupancy cells to accommodate prisoners
being subjected to an innovative sanction of the time, (that of serving
sentences for crimes against the state) change has barely kept abreast of
evolving technology. Despite continuing exposés of jail problems and demands for reform during this period, jail design and inmate management concepts have not been particularly responsive.

However, during the past 15 years a significant change in jail design
and management has evolved and become especially visible over the
past two years in both the United States and Canada. This new concept
is popularly referred to as "new generation jails" or more esoterically as
"podular/direct supervision" has been coined to refer to the implementation of the concept in their new adult remand center.

It is the purpose of this paper to briefly trace the origins of the
"podular/direct supervision" concept, outline the behavioral principles
essential to this new approach to jail management and design, and report why this radical change is now receiving such side acceptance. This
discussion will also explore how these changing concepts in jail design
and inmate management will affect future developments in this area.

ORIGINS

The integral relationship between jail design and the techniques of
inmate management is often understated. A new facility will not

necessarily resolve a community's jail problems unless the new structure facilitates, and is accompanied by, a professional inmate management approach that will reduce violence and comply with constitutional requirements.

In examining the jail architecture of the past two centuries, most jails can generally be categorized into one of three basic architectural/ management categories. This categorization can be useful for tracing the origins of today's changing concepts in jail design and management.

The three categories are called:
— Linear/Intermittent Surveillance
— Podular/Remote Surveillance
— Podular/Direct Supervision

In each of these hyphenated labels, the first part describes the architectural style and the second part identifies the accompanying management approach.

LINEAR/INTERMITTENT SURVEILLANCE

Most jails built during the past decade as well as the past two centuries, have been linear/intermittent surveillance. The architectural style is linear, i.e., the inmate housing areas consist of rows of individual or multiple occupancy cells at right angles to the surveillance corridors. Since the patrolling officer can seldom observe more than a few cells at a time, the term "intermittent surveillance" is used to describe the management approach imposed by this architectural style.

The critical variables that determine the severity of problems associated with the linear/intermittent surveillance category are the frequency and thoroughness of patrols and aggressiveness of inmates in multiple occupancy cells. The interval between patrols is a management variable not easily controlled, given the exigencies of the jail setting and the influence of inmates on patrol frequency. In a linear/intermittent jail, inmates have the intervals between patrols to make escape preparations, fashion weapons, assault others, etc. Because destruction of fixtures and furnishings also occurs with regularity during unsupervised intervals, it is necessary to install expensive vandal-proof housing materials.

An innovation of the past decade, however, was the "podular" architectural style. The term "podular" was coined to describe facilities in

LINEAR/INTERMITTENT SURVEILLANCE

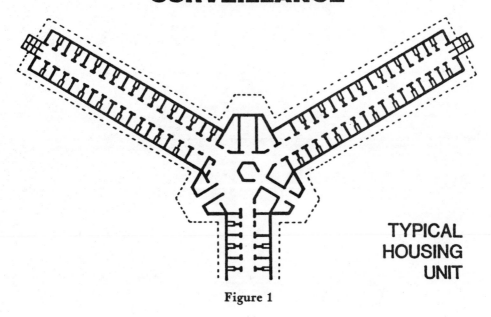

TYPICAL HOUSING UNIT

Figure 1

which the inmate housing areas are divided into manageable units composed of approximately 50 single occupancy cells grouped around a common multipurpose area in an easily surveillable arrangement. The "podular" architectural style facilitates improved inmate surveillance and supervision. The result has been reduced incidents of inmate violence.

The "podular" architectural style has been adapted to two distinctively different inmate management approaches: remote surveillance and direct supervision.

PODULAR/REMOTE SURVEILLANCE

The fundamental distinction of the "podular/remote surveillance" category is that inmates are observed from a remote, secure observation compartment and the officer has no direct contact with the inmates. Cell doors are electronically controlled from this station and communication with inmates is over an intercom system. Maximum security, vandal proof fixtures, and furnishings, are characteristic of his facility. Housing units of around 48 beds are usually subdivided into three 16-bed units or four 12-bed units. When negative inmate behavior is detected by the officer in the control room, additional officers are summoned to take the necessary corrective action.

PODULAR/REMOTE SURVEILLANCE

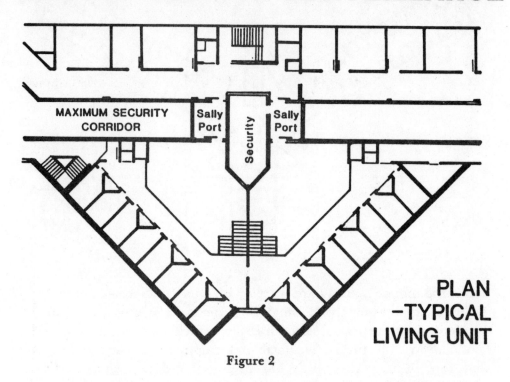

MAXIMUM SECURITY
CORRIDOR

Sally
Port

Security

Sally
Port

PLAN
–TYPICAL
LIVING UNIT

Figure 2

The remote surveillance management approach is reactive. There is an implied assumption that inmates will behave in a predictably violent and destructive manner, and management initiatives are designed to react accordingly. The costly vandal-proof materials are a reaction to the anticipated destructive behavior. The subdivision of the housing units is to facilitate the suppression of violent inmate behavior by staff.

PODULAR/DIRECT SUPERVISION

In contrast, the management approach in the "podular/direct supervision" facilities is pro-active. A staff member is stationed within each standard 48-bed housing unit to directly supervise inmates in order to prevent negative behavior. It then becomes unnecessary to install costly vandal-proof fixtures, furnishings, and finishes. The cost of subdividing the standard 48-bed units into smaller 16- or 12-bed units is also avoided. The basic management strategy is to elicit desired responses from inmates by the direct interventions of the unit officer.

The "podular/direct supervision" concept evolved in the early 1970s. It was a result of a presidential mandate to the Federal Prison System to build three prototype detention facilities. In addition to accommodating burgeoning pre-trial populations in New York, Chicago, and San Diego, these new facilities were to incorporate "state of the art" correctional concepts and technologies. They were also to serve as prototypical examples for local communities.

PODULAR/DIRECT SUPERVISION

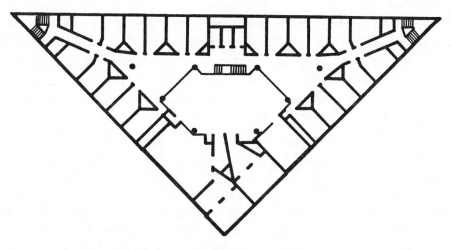

Figure 3

The planning for these new institutions include input from jail experts and a broad range of human behavior specialists. In addition, the Federal Prison System imposed several important conditions upon the designs. These conditions reflected standard operating policy in federal correctional institutions, which primarily held sentenced offenders. Probably the most significant of these conditions was the commitment to functional unit management. Introduced in the previous decade, unit management had proven effective in the delivery of services by dividing the inmates into more manageable and individualized groups. Therefore, the architects were required to design the inmate housing areas around the concept of a series of self-contained units for the general population. These areas held about 50 beds in each unit.

A second important condition, which was not considered innovative to the Federal Prison System but was unique for most detention facilities, was the practice of directly supervising the inmates. Other conditions included provisions for contact visiting, generally normalized surroundings, and a source of natural light in all living areas.

To operate within these parameters, the administration was obliged to be intolerant of any behavior that challenged the authority of the officer, or that compromised the officer's ability to manage the unit. As a result, inmates were confronted with two options: either conform to the stated expectations of management or be moved from the general population to the segregation unit. While the segregation unit meets minimum constitutional standards, it contrasts sharply with the benefits and opportunities available in the general population units.

"Podular/remote surveillance" has generally been chosen over "podular/direct supervision" as the alternative of preference to the linear style jail. The reason for this preference appears to be rooted in the reactive management approach. The remote/surveillance model is a structural and technological response to the specific operational problems and deficiencies that have plagued linear jails over the past 200 years. And, relatively speaking, the response has been successful in reducing these problems.

On the other hand, the underlying assumption in "podular/direct supervision" jails, is that the negative inmate behavior characteristic of linear jails is to a large degree the direct result of circumstances arising from the management and supervision techniques imposed by the linear architectural style. The "podular" architectural style is seen as eliminating many of these circumstances and freeing management from the necessity of functioning under the assumption of negative inmate behavior.

We must remember that for the past 200 years, jail management has been based on successfully anticipating and responding to negative inmate behavior. Given this reactive management style, it is understandable that the "podular" concept was seen by jail practitioners as providing opportunities to more adequately respond to the problems associated with the traditional linear jail. Ironically, the relative success of the "podular/remote" design, coupled with high-security furnishings and

high-security electronics, tended to mask the true potential of the "podular" concept. Few realized or accepted the fact that this new design allowed management practices that would obviate the need for most of the
reactive strategies so characteristic of traditional jail management.

It was particularly difficult for most jail workers as well as the public,
to accept that an officer's personal safety is enhanced by being in contin-
ual direct supervision of inmates. It seemed obvious that bars or other
such barriers between the officers and the inmates provided a necessary
margin of safety that could not be compromised. The fallacy of this belief lies in the fact that staff must come in direct contact with inmates for
many reasons in a traditional jail, not the least of which, is to intervene
in violent situations. It is in such situations that most staff injuries occur.
By reducing these violent incidents, staff injuries are likewise reduced.
Since staff safety is an essential prerequisite in a direct supervision setting, it must be assured in order for the facility to function. Because of
this fundamental condition along with other operational principles that
will be discussed later, staff in "podular/direct supervision" facilities generally enjoy safer working conditions than in traditional jails.

A second barrier to general acceptance of "podular/direct supervision" was that the jail did not look like a jail. Certainly it did not fulfill
the public's expectation of a jail as a place of punishment. As you know,
in most jails, over 60 percent of the prisoners have not been convicted or
sentenced. But many elected community leaders, as well as criminal justice administrators, have been reluctant to tell the public that the imposition of conditions of confinement for the purpose of punishing pre-trial
prisoners is in direct violation of the Fifth and Fourteenth Amendments.
Because of this ignorance about the role of jails as holding centers, those
jail plans that are based on non-punitive conditions of confinement are
unacceptable in many communities.

The result was that the real benefits of "podular/direct supervision"
were never fully shared with the local communities until January 1981,
when Contra Costa County opened its new detention center in Martinez, California. The Contra Costa County Sheriff's Department fully
adopted the operational concepts of the Chicago Metropolitan Correctional Center. However, they enhanced the design by incorporating
many of the recommendations from a user's evaluation, and they incor-
porated the open booking concept developed in St. Louis. The open
booking arrangement resembles an outpatient clinic waiting room
where new admissions may watch TV, make phone calls, etc., in an
open lounge setting while they wait to be booked.

During the more than four years that the Contra Costa facility has been in operation, they have experienced the same benefits as the Metropolitan Correctional Centers—and then some. They have accomplished the objectives of safe, secure, humane, and just custody. In addition, they enjoy a vandal- and graffiti-free facility. More importantly, the deputy sheriffs assigned to the jail have found that the new facility provides an opportunity for interesting and challenging employment. The Contra Costa facility not only demonstrates that a "new generation jail" can be effectively operated at the local level, but that it can also eliminate many of the personnel problems that plague local correctional operations (Frazier and Farbstein, 1985; Frazier, 1985).

PRINCIPLES AND DYNAMICS ESSENTIAL FOR PODULAR/DIRECT SUPERVISION

Those direct supervision institutions that are successful share eight general principles of operation. In the unsuccessful institutions, some or all of these principles are missing. In brief, the eight principles relate to safety, control, communications, supervision, manageability, classification, just treatment, and effective personnel. Let me offer more detail about the first three—safety, control, and communications.

The safety of staff and inmates is one of the most critical influences on jail life. Therefore, one of the fundamental principles is to assure that safety. Since self-survival is a basic instinct, when inmates find themselves in an unsafe environment, they resort to a variety of antisocial behaviors to achieve personal safety. They affiliate with gangs, attempt to escape, fashion weapons, buy protection, or generally act "bad." When staff are confronted with unsafe conditions of employment, they avoid duties involving contact with inmates, "bang in" on sick leave, or simply quit. Some have even been known to bring in contraband weapons for their protection.

We humans tend to hate those we fear and to fear those we hate. This fear-hate syndrome becomes a major source of the savagery that all too often erupts in our correctional institutions. By ensuring safety and thereby eliminating endemic fear, a fundamental systemic change occurs in the detention environment.

Much of the negative inmate behavior that causes the traditional reactive management characteristic of linear and "podular/remote" facilities can be traced to inmate and staff responses to unsafe surroundings, and to the concomitant fear-hate syndrome. The elimination of this condition is a key factor to success. By adopting a management strategy that places the correctional officer in a leadership position in the living units, the stage is set for the pro-active management of the institution and the establishment and maintenance of a safe environment.

A second critical principle is the maintenance of total control of the institution. This is achieved by dividing the population into groups of manageable size and by ensuring that the officers are in effective control of their units. Traditional jails are usually divided into two general areas: the inmate housing and the staff areas (which include secured observation corridors, offices, and other administrative spaces). Most often these two areas are physically separated by bars, grill doors, and other architectural barriers. As a result, the inmates are in control of their living areas while the staff maintain control of the perimeter, the security corridors, and other non-inmate areas.

Whenever humans are placed in a group setting where a leadership void exists, a leader, or leaders, will emerge by one means or another. In a jail setting, especially a traditional one, the process can be extremely violent. In fact, a great part of the negative inmate behavior that cannot be related to the fear-hate response can usually be attributed to this incessant power struggle within the areas controlled by the inmate population.

This kind of behavior can be effectively curtailed if jail officers are trained in the professional techniques of leadership, and if the environment is designed to ensure the officer's success in a leadership role. The "Podular/direct supervision" design has proven its ability to enhance this leadership role.

Effective communications is a third essential principle. In almost every area of society, the communication of behavioral expectations, either explicitly or implied, has a dramatic impact on performance. The jail is no exception to this well established behavioral pattern. Since the traditional jail makes a clear statement of negative expectations about inmate behavior, most inmates respond to the jail setting and procedures in a negative way. This serves to reinforce the basic assumptions upon which the negative design and procedures are based, and the result is known as the "self fulfilling prophesy."

However, what is becoming increasingly evident since the advent of "podular/direct supervision" jails, and particularly since adoption of the open booking area in Contra Costa, is that the opposite holds equally true. When the physical setting, the established procedures, and staff

attitudes provide a clear and unmistakable message to inmates that they
are expected to behave in a rational manner, about 95 percent usually
do.[1] Granted, officers who lack good communication skills will probably
have inmate management problems despite a positive environment. But
those officers trained in good communication skills will find their
management abilities greatly enhanced by a properly supportive environment.

The intention of this brief preview of the principles is simply to illustrate that the guts of the "podular/direct supervision" jail are the principles and dynamics, not bricks and mortar. Architecturally, the options
are wide open as long as the design reinforces these essential principles.

SIGNS OF ACCEPTANCE

In November 1983, the Advisory Board of the National Institute of
Corrections unanimously adopted its first position statement that read
as follows:

> The Advisory board of the National Institute of Corrections advo-
> cates that jurisdictions that are contemplating the construction or reno-
> vation of jails and prisons should explore the appropriateness of the
> "podular direct supervision" (new generation) concept of jail and prison
> design and management for their new facilities. The NIC Advisory
> Board believes that the economic, social and professional values ex-
> plicit in this concept of jail and prison design and management exem-
> plify an appropriate direction for detention of persons who require
> incarceration. Evidence indicates such facilities are cost effective in
> terms of both construction and operation.
>
> The Board instructs the Director of the National Institute of Cor-
> rections to give emphasis to the dissemination of information; the
> training of jail and prison practitioners; the provision of technical assis-
> tance; the formulation of standards and policy; and a continuous eval-
> uation of the effectiveness of the "podular/direct supervision" concept of
> jail and prison design and management, in addition to existing NIC
> programs (Corrections Digest, 1984).

Soon after the Board announced the above position statement, the
American Jail Association passed a resolution in January 1984 supporting "podular/direct supervision" as a desired form of jail management.
In July 1984, the American Institute of Architects Committee on Architecture for Justice also passed a position statement encouraging the exploration of this concept for new jail construction. In August 1984, the
American Correctional Association passed a resolution in support of the

concept of direct supervision. The Commission on Accreditation for Corrections added standard 2-5134-1 to the Standards for Adult Local Detention Facilities in 1984, which requires all new construction to facilitate the direct supervision of inmates. In view of the endorsements of the above professional organizations, the "podular/direct supervision" concept can be considered the professional "state of the art" in jail design and management.

In addition to the recognition given to the "podular/direct supervision" concept by the professional organizations representing the practitioners in the field, the judiciary has also taken notice of this design and management trend. In 1985 the U.S. District Court for the Northern District of California ordered that the Sonoma County Jail adopt the direct supervision concept in the management of inmates in their jail. This is the first judicial action of this kind that we are aware of and it is obviously too early to determine if this is the beginning of a trend or an isolated occurrence.

During the past several years, additional local jurisdictions have opened "podular/direct supervision" detention facilities and many more have elected to design and construct their new facilities along these lines. The Multnomah County Jail in Portland, Oregon, the Larimer County Jail in Fort Collins, Colorado, and the Manhattan House of Detention in New York City, have been successfully operating since 1983. Since 1984 the Middlesex County Jail in New Jersey, the Bucks County Jail in Doylestown, Pennsylvania, the Pima County Jail in Tucson, Arizona and the Clark County Jail in Las Vegas, Nevada have opened under this management concept. "Podular/direct supervision" jails are now under construction in New York City, and Buffalo, New York; Alexandria, Virginia; Philadelphia, Pennsylvania; Prince Georges County in Maryland; Miami, and Tampa, Florida; Akron, and Newark, Ohio; Topeka, and Olathe, Kansas; Billings, Montana; Flint, Michigan; and San Jose, and Santa Rose, California.

FUTURE EXPECTATIONS

Recent observations of this trend in jail design and management suggest that the concept's most critical ingredient is the management element. Both the Larimer County Jail in Ft. Collins, Colorado and the Pima County Jail in Tucson, Arizona were originally designed for "podular/remote surveillance" management. However, the Sheriffs of these counties elected to operate their new jails under the direct supervision approach and are very pleased with their achievements. In both the Florida counties of Alachua in Gainesville and Dade in Miami, the direct supervision management strategy was adapted to dormitory settings with very impressive results. The same remarkable results were achieved when the U.S. District Court ordered the Sonoma County Jail in Santa Rose, California to employ the direct supervision concept in two of their large dormitories that had been the scenes of recurring violent inmate behavior. As a result, the violent behavior was virtually eliminated. A recent in-depth review of the Manhattan House of Detention revealed that the application of the stated principles and dynamics of the "podular/direct supervision" concept were extremely effective. On the other hand, operational problems occurred where the principles were not fully operable.

Based on these recent observations, the writer believes that the principles and dynamics of direct supervision can be effectively applied to a much wider range of detention settings than the "podular/direct supervision" design. Granted, a "podular" plan designed to facilitate direct supervision may be considerably more efficient, but many jurisdictions do not have the luxury of such an option.

As the direct supervision management strategy is further developed and more generally understood,.its near universal application may be reasonably anticipated. The appeal of more economic jail construction plus professional "state of the art" recognition will not be ignored by jurisdictions building or renovating new facilities. The skill and knowledge in implementing the principles of direct supervision can confidently be expected to advance significantly in the next decade. These developments will result in less expensive and more normalized housing arrangements.

The change in jail design and management resulting from the adaptation of the "podular/direct supervision" concept is profound and widespread. It has spread across the United States and Canada with remarkable speed considering the traditional pace of change that can be expected in this field of endeavor. Representatives from Great Britain's Home Office have recently expressed interest in the concept. Should it catch on there, its subsequent spread throughout western Europe can reasonably be expected.

NOTE

[1]Information received from L.R. Ard, Chief Deputy, Contra Costa County Sheriff Department, Martinez, CA. Lecture to National Institute of Corrections Training Program, July 1984.

BIBLIOGRAPHY

FRAZIER, F.W. (1985) A postoccupancy Evaluation of Contra Costa County's Main Detention Facility. Ann Arbor, MI: University Microfilms International.

WENER, R., FRAZIER, W., and FARBSTEIN, J. (1985) "Three generations of Evaluation and Design of Correctional Facilities." Environment and Behavior, Vol. 17, No. 1, (January):71-95.

"NIC Advisory Board Endorses Podular Architectural Design for Jails and Prisons." *Corrections Digest* V15:5 (2-29-84).

OTHER REFERENCES

"Alameda County's New Generation Jail" *The National Sheriff* V36:3 (6-7-84):81.

ALEXANDER, Eugene. "Modern Jail Design" *Corrections Today* V47:2 (4/85):132-135.

Guidelines for the Planning and Design of Regional and Community Correctional Centers for Adults. 1971, Copyright by the Board of Trustees of the University of Illinois.

Illinois Bureau of Detention Facilities and Jail Standards, Jail Planning, and Construction Standards. 1971, Springfield, Illinois.

"Justice Architecture Meeting Explored, State of the Art in Jail/Prison System Design." *Corrections Digest* V14:24 (4/23):81.

LEVINSON, Robert B. and GERALD, Roy E. "Functional Units: A Different Correctional Approach."*Federal Probation* (12/73).

NEDERHOFF, Dale A. "Jail Architecture" *The National Sheriff* V36:3 (4-5-84):108, 110.

"Prison Security Consultant Claims Better Design Can Improve Security and Reduce Cost." *Security Letter,* Pt. 1 V14:23 (12-3-84).

SECKLER, Arthor J., Jr. "An Architects View," *Corrections Today,* V45:5 (10/83):60, 62.

Standards for Adult Local Detention Facilities. Second Edition, Copyright April 1981, American Correctional Association.

CHAPTER 12

JAIL OFFICER TRAINING

Goals, Techniques and Evaluation Criteria

Lucien X. Lombardo

IN THE FIELD of corrections perhaps no resource among the field's scarce resources is more underutilized, undertrained and less understood than the line-level correctional worker.[1] Nowhere is this more true than in our local jails. This underutilization of jail officer potential is reflected in training efforts directed at improving officer performance. In 1980 the authors of a report on a national survey of correctional training programs observed that correctional training programs usually proceed without knowledge of the training needs of the specific organizations or personnel involved and conclude without formal evaluation of training efforts. In addition, the authors point out that "a gap occurs in linking training to performance on the job" (Olson, et. al, 1980: vol. 2, V. 23). With regard to jail officers, there can be little doubt that one of the reasons for the "gap" between training and job performance is the lack of knowledge concerning the social and psychological dynamics of jails as correctional environments and the equal lack of knowledge concerning the social and psychological dynamics of jail officer behavior.

Only during the last 10 years has the knowledge gap begun to close with regard to **prison officers.** Research studies have begun to show that prison officers are able to and do make significant contributions to smooth institutional operation and to reducing inmate stress (Johnson and Price, 1981; Klofas and Toch, 1982 and Lombardo, 1982).

Presented at the Annual Meeting of the Academy of Criminal Justice Sciences, Las Vegas, 1985.

Other research has focused on the relationship between prison inmates, prison officers and their environments (Toch, 1975; 1977; Johnson and Toch, 1982; Lombardo, 1981). These studies demonstrate the techniques and strategies utilized by inmates and prison officers for dealing with the stress caused by conditions of confinement, and in doing so, they may inform the development of prison officer training.

When it comes to jails, however, the research is sparse. Gibbs (1978) has described the stresses of jail confinement and their relationship to inmate self-injury and Rottman and Kimberly (1977) provide insight into social relationships in jail; however, studies focusing on the relationships between jail inmates, jail officers and jail environments are seriously lacking. In fact, as Gibbs recently concluded:

> A systematic survey of the environments of jails may result in the discovery of a number of institutions, sub environments, and personnel with ameliorative qualities for inmates who are experiencing certain difficulties or who are susceptible to certain stress (1982:111).

The training process described below attempts to take Gibbs up on his challenge, i.e., to merge training and research in ways that began to systematically survey jail environments and also close the gap between training and job performance.

Training Package Assumptions

The training program described here is intended primarily for in-service jail officers. (However, with adaptations it might also be useful for pre-service training efforts.) As such, the program is not intended to be a replacement for training geared to basic orientation, security procedures, first aid, self-defense and physical training, fire prevention and safety, human relations and communications skills, and crisis intervention/emergency procedures courses most frequently offered as standard jail officer training (Olson, et. al, 1980: vol. 2, VIII-9). The program described here is intended to be "an exercise in learning about one's work and work place" in an effort to improve the quality of living for inmates and the level of job satisfaction for staff.[2]

In designing this in-service training program I make a number of assumptions:

(1) There exists within the jail officer corps of any institution men and women who carry out their formal assignments in ways that contribute to the achievement of a humane jail environment (described under goals section below);

(2) These officers do not share the techniques and strategies they have discovered;

(3) These officers do not always recognize the value of their contributions;

(4) There exists a negative group subculture that emphasizes values antithetical to humane jail environments;

(5) That this subculture rests on pluralistic ignorance;[3]

(6) That officers develop and are able to identify strategies for coping with stresses of jail work, some of which are constructive, some destructive.

These assumptions are derived in part from the research on prison officers cited above. They also reflect data gathered during the author's involvement in the design and implementation of jail officer training programs.[4] Material gathered during one of these programs will be presented in the discussion which follows.

Selection of Goals for Training

General Goals: Inmate Related

The training program described here attempts to focus on the quality of life in jails, both the conditions of confinement experienced by inmates and the working conditions of jail staff. As such it attempts to integrate the day-to-day realities of jail life and work into the training process. This quality of life focus draws our attention to four more specific goals for correctional institutions described by John Conrad as characteristics of humane correctional environments: (1) Safety, (2) Lawfulness, (3) Industriousness and (4) Hope. These goals overlap with the pains of jail confinement described by Gibbs (1982: p. 99) who writes that jail inmates

> are faced with four interrelated major problem areas: withstanding entry shock, maintaining outside links, securing stability (and sometimes safety) in a situation of seeming chaos, and finding activities to fill otherwise empty time.

Conrad's goals and Gibbs' inmate problems should provide challenges for legislators, administrators and all involved in the correctional enterprise. However, my **concern here is to demonstrate how these characteristics of humane correctional environments can provide substance for training and translate into specific behaviors for jail officers.**

(1) Safety: For the jail officer safety means not only protecting oneself but also protecting the prisoners in his or her charge. It includes creating an environment in which prisoners are less likely to suffer from the victimization of their fellow prisoners (see Bowker, 1980; Lockwood, 1980); less likely to suffer from self-victimization of suicide attempts and self-mutilation (see Gibbs, 1978; Toch, 1975; and less likely to suffer victimization at the hands of correctional staff (Barnes, 1972). To create such a safe environment is a challenging task. Officers involved in the New Jersey Training program recognized this task in their responses to questions dealing with handling conflicts between inmates. Here they identified both positive and negative officer behaviors. On the positive side they indicated that officers should (1) take preventive measures to separate inmates if they suspect the possibility of conflict, (2) discuss with the inmates possible alternative solutions, (3) refrain from stereotyping inmates in negative ways and (4) remain calm and impartial. On the other hand, these officers recognized the conflict producing impacts of negative officer behaviors of taking sides in inmate conflict, ignoring problems, running to supervisors when problems emerge, punishing without listening and behaving in loud, offensive, public ways which aggravate already bad situations.

(2) **Lawfulness:** For jail officers lawfulness is a reflection of two overlapping areas. One, ensuring that legal obligations for their positions as specified in legislation, court decisions and departmental policy are upheld. It also means that the assertion of "legal rights" by inmates is not looked upon as a "threat to authority" but rather as a request that "legal obligations" of jail officials be enforced. Where differences of opinion exist, officers should demonstrate that it is the responsibility of legally designated parties to resolve such differences (see ACA, 1982).

On a more personal level, however, the jail officer in his or her day-to-day interactions with prisoners "represents" the law, and the officer's response to rule violations by inmates represents the application of lawfulness to the jail environment. If officer behavior gives the impression that "rules and procedures" are meaningless in the jail environment then a perception of lawlessness will prevail. This may be reflected in the inmate's resort to "censorious" behavior (see Mathiesen, 1965), where officers are criticized for failing to live up to the values of justice, fairness and equality that the legal system espouses. According to the New Jersey jail officers, opportunities for such responses arise when officers reprimand inmates in public, use force or aggressiveness which aggravates problems, overreact to small difficulties, are rigid, harass inmates or ignore rules designed to regulate intra-inmate conflict. These officers also indicated that officers could contribute to the "lawfulness" of jail environment by informing inmates of rules and that the inmate is violating them; evaluating the seriousness of violations and finding out reasons for violations, exercising control without anger, using minimal force. (See Lombardo, 1981 for an exploration of the informal rule-enforcement practices of prison officers.)

(3) Industriousness: Perhaps the most difficult goal for jail administrators to achieve is industriousness. With limited resources for jail maintenance let alone inmate programming the challenge is formidable. Where programs do not exist the challenge for the jail officer becomes one of recognizing the need for activity and accomplishment (however meaningless) as a necessary condition of psychological survival in liberty depriving situations (Toch, 1975; Cohen and Taylor, 1973). Conversely, this implies a recognition that boredom and inactivity can take a heavy toll.

For the officer, the task becomes not one of designing formal programs but rather one of reducing the monotony and redundancy of jail environment, of infusing into the day-to-day life of the jail (within the officers' own sphere of operations) some variety, some on-the-spot challenges where things can be accomplished. This means that officers must be aware of their own and the institution's resources.

Where programs exist, officers should do what they can to promote inmate participation in such programs and to assist program staff in implementing such programs. The usual conflict between treatment/program staff and security staff needs to be recognized as counter productive and problem causing rather than problem solving. This is especially important where the informal emerging role of correctional officer as human services provider merges with the professional responsibilities of treatment personnel. Again, the New Jersey officers recognized this in their emphasis of the human services content of their tasks and the job satisfaction derived from contact with inmates.

(4) Hope: People need to have some reason to believe that things will get better. In jails the most common situation is that things will get worse and that life is truly beyond ones personal control (Gibbs, 1982). In many respects, especially with regard to the inmates' legal status, this is no doubt true. However, with regard to the conditions of confinement, and day-to-day jail life, this need not be the case. Again, jail officers from New Jersey have identified some characteristics of "Mature jail officers" that from an inmate's perspective provide hope. Here the officers focused on the human services content of their work and described what they felt were "mature coping officers": such officers are honest, take time to listen, follow up on requests, identify problems and evaluate their legitimacy, try to be prompt, know problems are of immediate concern to inmates, classify requests and if cannot solve, pass requests up, follow up on requests made to superiors. Such officer actions should not be considered extraordinary, but rather they are the "stuff" of correctional work. Such actions give inmates hope by demonstrating that the world can be responsive to individual needs and that socially destructive ways of handling problems are not always necessary.

Specific Training Tasks: Officer Related

Given the assumptions and general goals of training described above, the following specific tasks become the focus of our training exercise design:

(1) To surface the complexity and variety of jail officer tasks;
(2) To surface successful and unsuccessful strategies for performing these tasks;
(3) To demonstrate how the individual needs of different officers interact differently with jail officer job assignments;
(4) To surface sources of jail officer stress and positive and negative strategies for coping;
(5) To share and sharpen skills of environmental analysis and resource utilization;
(6) To feedback information developed by officers to reduce pluralistic ignorance.
(7) To enhance the development of a positively oriented jail officer subculture.

To complete these tasks, it is necessary to design training activities which permit jail officers to study and build upon their own experience and expertise. In this way, **the specific substantive material discussed in training is derived from day-to-day experience and real life problems.** In addition, this allows the training to begin implicitly from a needs assessment by the officers involved and links the training effort to specific and problematic task analysis, two factors found to be important in the evolution of "useful" training courses (Olson, 1980, Vol. 2: VIII-24).

The **training process emphasizes learning;** i.e., that both trainers and officers are involved in the learning process. Emphasizing individual response and small group and large group discussion in response to a series of specific task oriented questions, the training process involves officers (1) thinking about the issues discussed; (2) writing their observations on survey/feedback forms; discussing their individual responses in small groups and when possible, reaching consensus; (3) summarizing and sharing their concerns and information across groups. In this way, discussions are task oriented and focused; they involve a great deal of discussion and analysis. (These were characteristics of training courses identified as "useful" in the 1980 national survey. See Olson, 1980: Vol. 2, VIII-17). In this way, the training program also serves as a research program, generating data about the environmental and social characteristics of jails and the responses to these characteristics of jail officers and inmates.

Specific Training Exercises

Training Exercise #1: Jail Officer Tasks

This exercise focuses on the tasks of jail officers. Here officers are asked to explain what jail officers do to someone who knows very little about the operations of jails. In addition, they are asked to indicate which jail officer tasks they most and least prefer and why and which locations in the jail they most and least prefer and why.

This exercise is designed to elicit information on the nature of correctional officer tasks as the officers perceive them. It also surfaces the diversity of officer needs and the relationship between individual needs and the correctional environment. (This will be the focus of training exercise 4 described below).

Training Exercise #2: Stress and Coping

This exercise is designed to surface factors related to **stress among jail officers.** Officers are asked to describe the **most difficult** thing about their jobs, the **biggest problem** they have doing their job, and the **worst** thing about their jobs. In addition, they are asked to indicate how they cope with each of the forces they identify. The officers are also asked to indicate what they find to be the **most rewarding** aspect of their work.

This exercise is designed to get officers thinking about problematic areas in their working lives, and to help them identify both constructive and destructive ways of coping. Since officers will be sharing experiences, the exercise aims at expanding each officer's repertoire of constructive coping skills.

Training Exercise #3: Jail Officer Characteristics

This exercise focuses on behavioral aspects of jail officer tasks and to draw out characteristics of "mature copers" and "immature copers" in three day-to-day work situations. Here officers are asked to describe how officers they would **most like to work with** and those they would **least like to work with** would handle: (1) inmate requests for assistance (2) inmate rule violations and (3) conflict between inmates. In addition, officers were asked to give two concrete examples for each situation. In addition, officers are asked to estimate the percentage of their fellow officers who exhibit these characteristics, as well as the percentage who agree with their characterization of "mature copers" and "immature copers."

The purpose of this exercise is to generate descriptions, analyses and evaluation of day-to-day work strategies. In addition, the exercise generates data which is helpful in illustrating the concept of "pluralistic ignorance" and moving toward the development of a "positively oriented jail officer subculture."

Training Exercise #4: Environmental Mapping

This exercise is designed to test and develop officer skills at analyzing jail environments and resources, and relating these environments and resources to the satisfaction of specific inmate needs. Here, the officers are asked to play the role of inmates while utilizing the knowledge they have gained as officers. They are presented with a list of "environmental concerns" (Privacy, safety, structure, support, activity, freedom, social stimulation and emotional feedback) and their definitions (Toch, 1977:16-17).

They are asked to identify the needs that would be most important to them if they were prisoners. Subsequently, for each need they are asked to indicate the **places** where these needs will most least likely be met. Next, they are asked to identify **particular officer assignments** most and least likely to contribute to satisfying this need. They are then asked to **identify specific resources** (things, programs, activities, people) that can help them meet their concerns. Finally, they are asked to indicate **what officers can do** to help them satisfy their needs and to describe the conditions that prevent officers from helping them meet their needs.

From this exercise, officers should learn to relate inmate behavior to resources and environments of individual jail settings rather than to the peculiar psychological characteristics of inmates. In addition, it should sensitize officers to the need to constantly assess their own working environments in relation to specific inmate needs. In this way, officers should be able to contribute more effectively to the creation of more humane institutional environments.

Evaluation

Perhaps the most complicated and difficult task associated with jail officer training is the evaluation process. Evaluation implies judgment of success or failure, and accountability. Evaluation puts into the open the weaknesses and strengths of specific programs and in doing so, has serious political implications.

In reviewing evaluations of correctional training Olson, et. al. (1980: Vol. III, X-8) observe:

> . . . Several characteristics occur with predictable regularity. Most evaluations in corrections are not written into program plans and are thus conducted ex post facto—virtually eliminating the possibility of controlling experimentally or statistically many of the variables that influence training, learning and performance. A majority are conducted by outside consultants, the most costly and transition kind of evaluation (transitory in that the evaluation is not continual, providing feedback for on-going program improvement, and thus likely to be weak and transitory in its effects). Evaluation too often is a one-shot, post hoc deal, pertaining only to the group of trainees studied. Rarely, is the training program and its evaluation designed simultaneously before hand, as they should be. There is generally a failure to link training with on-the-job performance; to access transfer of learning and skills from the classroom to the job. Most evaluation results point to the need for the establishment of clearly defined organizational and training program goals and objectives, regular inspection of the skills and abilities required to perform the job, and continuing monitoring and feedback of the implementation of recommendation. Assessment of how interesting and how enjoyable the training has been is far more common than attempts to establish whether or not the training has fulfilled on-the-job needs (if, indeed, needs have been identified).

This observation has a number of implications for the training program described above. First, it implies that the organizational goals of developing a jail which attempts to provide safety, lawfulness, industry and hope are accepted goals of the organization utilizing the training program. Second, it means that the inservice training program described above must become part of the on-going training within the organization, involving officers as trainers as well as targets of training. This approach is described by Toch and Grant (1982) as change through participation. They write

> We are hard put to separate "organization change" and "person change." We know that people including people in organizations— learn to grow and fulfill themselves as they become involved. Often, the **product** of focused involvement is **change.** To put it differently,

when persons become concerned with efforts to improve their environments — particularly, their work environments — the inhabitants and their environments are liable to benefit. (p. 14)

Thus the jail officer training program must have as a necessary component, the training of officers to be trainers for other officers. This will increase the resources and skills of not only the officers involved but also the organization as a whole.

Finally, Olson, et. al.'s (1980) observations mean that training and evaluation becomes part of overall organizational assessment. Assessment, in the terms described here, relates to the degree to which the organization approaches the four goals described above.

The implications of these observations for evaluating the training program described above should focus our attention on evaluation criteria related to

(1) Jail officer behavior;
(2) Jail officer job stress;
(3) Organizational change and climate.

Olson, et. al. have pointed out the methodological problems in attributing changes in any of the above to training programs, and these problems are important (Vol. III). However, by focusing training on specific officer behavior, specific stress producing conditions and specific organizational issues, the monitoring of indicators related to each of these areas should provide at least some gross indication that the training is effective. (Remembering that training and individual and organizational change are on-going processes.)

For jail officer behavior, evaluation should focus on (1) rule enforcement practices (2) human services provision and (3) extent of institutional conflict. Here jail staff should monitor (1) both the number, type, institutional location, and staff involved in formal rule enforcement, (2) the utilization patterns for services provided (e.g., sickcall) by the jail organization, inmate self-injury, and suicide attempts, and (3) the types, location and staff involved in interpersonal conflict (either staff-inmate or inmate-inmate violence.)

For job stress, evaluation should focus on absenteeism rates, sicktime utilization, and turnover rates, officer involvement in violence and inmate disciplinary problems.

Conclusion

The jail officer training goals, process and evaluation described here envision an actively involved jail staff and administration. The processes of goal setting training, and evaluation must be on-going and long-term. If the program described here has maximum effectiveness, it should expand the role of jail officers and contribute to the reduction of jail officer stress and create a climate of humane correctional treatment. It will do so by tapping a vast reservoir of resources located in the indigenous correctional officer ranks. (See Lombardo, 1985.) In the long-run, such training will be cost-effective and reduce the likelihood that jail conditions have to be improved through the process of litigation.

NOTES

[1] The author is indebted to Dr. Robert Johnson of American University for his insights into the training process and for his colleagueship in the two training programs described below.

[2] See C. Cherniss (1980) for a discussion of the importance of the "learning" component in the organizational design of human services tasks.

[3] Klofas and Toch (1982) have found that those guards that hold progressive views feel themselves to be in a minority (though, in fact, they were the majority). Those who hold non-progressive views (reflecting the negative subculture) feel themselves to be in the majority (though, in fact, they are in the minority). See also Lombardo (1985).

[4] The author was involved in the design and delivery of two jail officer training programs. One for the New York City Department of Corrections in April, 1983 and another for New Jersey jail officers in September, 1984. Both programs were sponsored by the National Institute of Corrections.

REFERENCES

American Correctional Association (1982), *Legal Responsibility and Authority of Correctional Officers*. College Park, MD: ACA.

Barnes, H.E. (1972), *The Story of Punishment* (2nd Edition). Montclair, NJ: Patterson Smith.

Bowker, L.H. (1980), *Prison Victimization*. New York: Elsevier.

Cherniss, Cary (1980), *Staff Burnout*. Beverly Hills: Sage.

Cohen, S. and Taylor, L. (1973), *Psychological Survival: The Experience of Long-Term Imprisonment*. New York: Vintage Press.

Conrad, J. (1982), "What do the underserving deserve?" in R. Johnson and H. Toch (eds) *The Pains of Imprisonment*, Beverly Hills, CA: Sage.

Gibbs, J.J. (1978), *Stress and Self-injury in jail*. Unpublished doctoral dissertation, Suny, Albany.

Gibbs, J.J. (1982), "The First Cut is the Deepest: Psychological Breakdown and Survival in the Detention Setting," in R. Johnson and H. Toch, *The Pains of Imprisonment*. Beverly Hills, CA: Sage.

Johnson, R. and Toch, H. (eds) 1982, *THE PAINS OF IMPRISONMENT.* Beverly
    Hills: Sage.

Johnson, R. and S. Price (1981), "The Complete Correctional Officer: Human Ser-
    vices and the Human Environment of Prison," *Criminal Justice and Behavior,* vol. 8,
    No. 3: 343-373.

Klofas, J. and Toch, H. (1982), "The Guard Subculture Myth," *Journal of Research in
    Crime & Delinquency,* vol. 19, No. 2: 238-254.

Lockwood, D. (1980), *Prison Sexual Violence.* New York: Elsevier.

Lombardo, L.X. (1982), "Alleviating Stress: Contributions from Correctional Offi-
    cers," in R. Johnson and H. Toch, *The Pains of Imprisonment.* Beverly Hills, CA:
    Sage, 285-298.

_____, (1981), *Guards Imprisoned.* New York: Elsevier.

_____, (1985a), "Group Dynamics and the Prison Guard Subculture," *International
    Journal of Offender Therapy and Comparative Criminology,* vol. 29, No. 1: 79-90.

_____, (1985b), "Mental Health Work in Prisons and Jails: Inmate Adjustment
    and Indigenous Correctional Personnel," *Criminal and Behavior,* vol. 12, No. 1, 17-
    28.

Mathiesen, T. (1965), *Defences of the Weak,* London: Tavistock.

Olson, H.C., et. al., (1980), *National Evaluation Program Phase I: Assessment of Correctional
    Personnel Training Programs, vol. 2, Conceptual and Empirical Issues,* Bethesda, MD:
    Advanced Research Resources Organization.

Olson, H.C., et. al., (1980), *National Evaluation Program Phase I: Assessment of Correctional
    Personnel Training Programs, vol. 3, Evaluation Issues and Strategies.* Bethesda, MD: Ad-
    vanced Research Resources Organization.

Rottman, D.B. and Kimberly, J.R., (1985), "The Social Context of Jails" in R.
    Carter, D. Glaser and L. Wilkins, eds., *Correctional Institutions* (3rd ed.), New
    York: Harper & Row.

Toch, H., (1975), *Men in Crisis.* Chicago: Aldine.

Toch, H., (1977), *Living in Prison.* New York: Free Press.

Toch, H. and Grant, J.D., (1982), *Reforming Human Services Through Participation.*
    Beverly Hills, CA: Sage.

Toch, H. and Klofas, J. (1982), "Alienation and Desire for Job Enrichment Among
    Correctional Officers," *Federal Probation.* xxxxvi, No. 1, 35-47.

CHAPTER 13

HARNESSING HUMAN RESOURCES IN LOCAL JAILS

Toward a New Generation of Planners

John Klofas,
Steven Smith, and
Edward Meister

ABSTRACT

Numerous examples of participatory management in industrial settings are available in the literature. Far fewer efforts have been documented in the human services. This paper reviews one such example
used in the planning of a new local jail. Drawing on the work of Hans
Toch and J. Douglas Grant, the program combined individual and organizational development strategies in developing policies and procedures for the new facility. Aside from the completed products of the
program, the benefits of the process can be seen increased training, improved morale, new links to the community and innovative practices.

Introduction

A POPULAR ARTICLE in Harvard Business Review several years
ago (Guest, 1979) began with the suggestion that business leaders
would be astonished by one corporate executive's program of involving
assemblyline workers in decisions that had traditionally been reserved
for management. At the Tarrytown General Motors Plant, groups of

Presented at the Annual Meeting of the Academy of Criminal Justice Sciences, Las Vegas,
1985.

workers were setting up and designing their own jobs with the blessing of both management and union officials. If such a program was astonishing in private industry it would seem all the more unusual in human service organizations, and especially in criminal justice, even today. In this paper, however, we will examine one such program used in the planning of a new county jail.

Experiments in worker participation have frequently occurred in private industry and are enjoying a strong revival in interest today (Whyte, 1983). In the automobile industry the Quality of Work Life movement has involved managers, union officials and frontline workers together in addressing noncontractual issues ranging from job and factory design to company sponsored recreation and educational opportunities (Davis and Sullivan 1980; Duckles et. al., 1977; Jenkins, 1983). A growing fascination with Japanese management practices has spawned Quality Circles in businesses from ship building to supermarkets (Law, 1980). These programs tap employee's knowledge about their work and draw on ideas that are born of the experience of doing a job. In the process they may increase job satisfaction and productivity by giving workers some say about their work (Mills, 1979).

The efficacy of these programs continues to be supported in studies documenting changes in the American work force. Along with increased education, todays workers have brought new demands to the workplace. They seek new opportunities for growth and development and new ways of contributing at their jobs (Sheppard and Herrich, 1972; Cooper et. al., 1979; Toch and Grant, 1982:25).

In the human services, experiments in participatory management remain rare. Concern with increasing efficiency and effectiveness in the delivery of human services often produces pressures for greater control of frontline staff (Lipsky, 1980:21). Such reforms as computerized activity reports in policing, sophisticated teacher evaluations and numerical classification devices in probation and parole may smack of pre-world war II Taylorism on the assemblyline when frontline staff are not involved in their development and assessment (Grant and Toch, 1984:231). Lack of attention to the effects of these changes and to the changes in todays human service work force can reduce job satisfaction and hamper productivity (Cherniss, 1980).

Today's technical advances in correctional architecture may have similar implications for prison and jail staff. We are now in the midst of the largest wave of prison and jail construction in history (Gettinger, 1984). As we replace the antiquated fortresses of the past with new correctional facilities we should also reconsider the managerial practices of the past. As with other American workers, jail and prison staff are changing (Toch and Klofas, 1982; Cheek and Miller, 1982). They too seek new challenges at work and desire to make new contributions. If managers fail to recognize the new needs and interests of staff, the potential contributions of a new generation of correctional architecture may be limited by old generation management ideas.

A Model of Participation in Human Service Organizations

One example of innovative management practices in the human services can be found in the work of Hans Toch and J. Douglas Grant. Toch and Grant have combined organizational change and individual change in participatory reform efforts in the human services. In Oakland, California, they utilized police officers with records of confrontations with citizens to analyze police violence and devise training programs for new recruits (Toch, Grant and Galvin, 1975). The program not only changed the behavior of the violence prone participants but also addressed department wide needs. In school intervention projects, teachers and students used the democratic model to jointly address problems ranging from employment opportunities to school violence (Grant and Toch, 1984). Most recently, groups of prison officers in New York analyzed their work and proposed adding new and enriching dimensions to their jobs (Toch and Grant, 1982).

The work of Toch and Grant provides a foundation for developing similar programs elsewhere in the human services and provided the framework for the project in the Peoria County Jail. Drawing on a model with its roots in the war time studies of Kurt Lewin (Marrow, 1969), their interventions suggest three concepts central to the use of this method in planning the new jail: participation, information and productivity.

Participation concerns both to the breadth of participants as well as the content of their contributions. Participation may range from simple consultation of employees to the sharing of decision-making power by managers. Suggestion boxes or hand picked groups of front line planners limit opportunities for input and may be seen as insincere or paternalistic gestures (Dachler and Wilpert, 1978:17). While the model does not suggest abrogation of management it does require abrogation of classic top-down control (Toch and Grant, 1982:141). At a minimum, participants must be legitimate representatives of those in the trenches and they must be free to address issues which they and their peers find meaningful.

The second requirement is information. The model is one of action research in which staff have access to information about the organization and continually participate in collecting and analyzing relevant data. The method is one of self-study in which experience and new information form the basis for new ideas.

Finally, grousing or even enlightened introspection are not the goals of the process. While personal growth and development are key to the self-study model, participation must result in written products and plans for change that involve both individual and organizational goals.

The work of Professor Toch and J. Douglas Grant provided the foundation for the planning project at the Peoria County Jail. When the project began, construction was already underway on the new fourteen million dollar facility. With nearly two years before the facility was slated to open a new jail administrator sought assistance from the local university in finding ways of involving frontline staff in the process of planning the operation of the new facility.

The Project Setting

Evaluations of change efforts have demonstrated the important role of individual and organizational variables in supporting or thwarting program success. An organizational climate may not be conducive to the development of new roles for frontline staff and individual workers may be unprepared for new responsibilities (Hackman and Oldham, 1980:82). Before undertaking the project, therefore, a better understanding of the people and conditions at the jail was important.

The new jail in Peoria County was built to replace a seventy-year-old edifice that is, in many ways, a caricature of the problems associated with local jails. Decrepit physical conditions and overcrowding had made the jail a difficult place to live or to work. Roofs leaked, and plumbing malfunctioned. Even the locks on cell doors were not secure and it was common for inmates who had "jimmied their doors" to be roaming the halls after everyone had been locked back. With the exception of occasional visits and necessary medical care, all of an inmate's time was spent in his cell or on the narrow walkway of the tier. There were no exercise yards or program space and weekly religious services provided the only officially sanctioned respite from the monotony of confinement. Boredom and isolation also effected staff. With the exception of security checks and head counts, all of an officer's time was spent at a security post separated from inmates and other staff by concrete walls.

The physical conditions also had parallels in the social and psycho-logical conditions at the facility. Despite the infrequent contact, staff and inmates report high levels of conflict. Struggles with newly received in-mates were frequent as were confrontations between inmates in the holding tanks and other isolated parts of the jail. There were also other indicators of stress among staff at the facility. Turnover has been high among the officers who's starting pay is under $12,000 a year. In 1982 the superintendent of the jail, a man in his mid-fifties and the individual who had begun planning for the new facility died from a heart attack. Less than a year later his successor resigned the position in response to pressures on the job.

Beyond descriptive accounts of the facility, we also sought more systematic data on staff at the jail in an effort to assess readiness for a participative project and to provide other information which would be directly useful to the officer participants. Before the project began, university staff surveyed officers at the jail using the Correctional Of-ficer Opinion Survey (see Toch and Klofas, 1982). This instrument focussed on three concepts which were relevant to the project; officer job satisfaction, relations with inmates and perceptions of peers. Forty-five of the fifty-five (82%) uniformed staff at the jail responded to the survey. Non-responses were evenly divided between staff who were unavailable during administration and those who chose not to return the survey.

The survey data supported impressionistic assessments of the jail. Staff were experiencing significant problems at the facility but they also desired to participate in addressing these and other issues. The satisfac-tion items produced the most dramatic findings. For example, over three-fourths of the staff agreed with the item "The only thing the COs job has going for it is job security." Two-thirds felt bored on the job.

The survey highlighted a problem which seemed particularly signifi-cant for officer participation. On items dealing with communication with management, officer responses indicated considerable concern with ambiguity and uncertainty. Nearly half of the respondents agreed that "A CO is told what his job is only when he does something wrong." A similar percentage agreed with the item "We're damned if we do and damned if we don't." On items which more directly addressed opportuni-ties for input into management decisions, officer responses were also suggestive about the potential for participation. Nearly eighty-three per-cent of the officers agreed that "No one ever asks a CO for suggestions relating to his job."

Officer responses on items dealing with their relations with inmates reflected their limited contact with prisoners but also suggested interest in wider roles. Half of the officers agreed that "A CO should work hard to earn trust from inmates," and nearly sixty percent agreed that "The most satisfying jobs involve inmate contact." On the final set of items the officers were asked to estimate their peer's responses on questionnaire items. The results indicated that communication problems also extended to fellow officers. On almost all of the items, officers estimated their peers were either more dissatisfied than they were or less simpathetic to inmate concerns than was the case.

The survey of staff at the jail played an important part in assessing the organizational climate and the officers' preparedness for a participative program. The picture to emerge from the data was one of a staff, interested and enthusiastic about contributing to plans for the new jail but also somewhat skeptical about their support from managers and the interests of their peers. Suprisingly, when the data were discussed with jail managers, they underestimated both job satisfaction among the officers and interest in contributing to management decision-making.

The Program

The project began when volunteers were solicited for eleven groups which would each plan the operation of a major segment of the jail as well as draft the operations manual. Over sixty percent of the staff volunteered to participate in the groups whose topics ranged from inmate supervision to program development. The groups ranged in size from eight to ten and consisted of officers and sergeants from all three shifts. Only one group was active at a time. The officers would meet once a week for three or four months. All of the groups completed their work over the course of eighteen months. In addition to the group meetings, officers worked between two and five hours a week writing drafts of policies and procedures for the meetings. Since the groups involved officers from all shifts and crossing all scheduled days off, most of the participants contributed between two and seven hours of uncompensated time per week to the participatory program.

The first task in each of the groups was a review of the survey highlights. This feedback of data reinforced the important role of the planners and gave them insight into the problems perceived by their peers. After this, the first meeting involved orientation and setting the goals of the group. In terms of process, participation was always the goal and the first meeting frequently turned into a shouting match as officers listed on index cards all of the topics that the group would cover. Even at this stage, the detailed knowledge gained in working the job was an obvious ingredient in the officers' expertise as planners.

From the second meeting the object was to produce drafts of policies and procedures. At first, the writing was a group effort that took place in the meetings. As the officers became more skilled in the process, more and more work occurred in clusters of two or three, away from the group. The meetings then served as an opportunity for the participants to present their material and critique the work of others.

A staff of three people managed the project. A line officer organized and managed the meetings. He prepared written agendas and produced copies of the policies and procedures as the planning groups developed them. As he developed competence in managing the groups, he also took over the primary responsibility for running the meetings themselves. The second member of the project staff was the superintendent of the jail. The superintendent attended all of the group meetings where he functioned much as any other group member. He made this role clear at the beginning of each group. As he told the participants, the quality of ideas rather than rank was the chief concern of the group members. In a larger, more bureaucratic organization a manager's presence may have hampered participation but in this setting the superintendent encouraged an open, problem solving atmosphere in the groups and his presence was seen as continued support of the officers. He was also the chief advocate of new ideas, continually challenging officers to examine new ways of doing things rather than simply transplant the old methods to the new jail.

The final member of the project staff was not from the jail. The role of this university professor was one of outside consultant. He monitored the groups and trained team members in participatory methods. His chief role in the meetings was one of devil's advocate, challenging team members to think through ideas and encouraging both quality and quantity production.

Participation in Planning

The product goal of the planning program in Peoria was to develop the policies and procedures under which the new jail would operate. In less modest terms the goal was to provide a forum for officers to analyze and contribute solutions to the significant problems of a local jail. This meant that front line staff were to make decisions regarding not simply how the jail should run but why particular policies should be implemented. While the groups discussed technical issues such as the need for an accounting of silverware after meals and how cell blocks should be cleaned, they also dealt with more complex concerns, concerns which would have a significant impact on the lives of the officers and inmates at the jail. For example, should officers mix with inmates in the cell blocks or be permanently stationed behind protective barriers? Should newly admitted inmates be placed in separate cells or be allowed to mingle in the cell block to reduce adjustment problems and lessen the chances of suicide?

At times, however, the routine topics were the catalysts for the most significant contributions in the planning groups. On one occasion the discussion focussed on the seemingly mundane issue of whether officers should be encouraged or even allowed to participate with inmates in sporting activities or recreational games. Arguments about possible conflicts of interest and the corruption of the guard's authority immediately surfaced and were debated for some time. Then, without warning, one officer who had been uncharacteristically silent, rose to her feet, silenced the group and gently chastised her colleagues:

> I think of them like that, animals in cages with a lot of animosity. And that's what they are in the old jail, with nothing to do but give us a hard time and all we do is take our catwalks (security checks) and stare at them. But if we don't change our attitude we will get the same thing at the new jail and it doesn't have to be that way. We need to stop thinking about how it is now and see if we can change some things. If we don't we'll just have the same thing at the new jail.

When the discussion was over the group members endorsed limited involvement with inmates but they also had a keener understanding of the dynamics of interacting with their charges as well as a clear perception of their responsibilities as planners.

The willingness to analyze and reconsider past practices played an important role throughout the project. Among the innovative developments of the project, the officers redesigned the disciplinary process to bring it into line with due process requirements established by the courts. They developed programs where there had been none and they built, from scratch, a classification system which would meet facility needs and increase safety for inmates.

Prior to the program inmates were separated only by sex and they were all subject to the same high security environment, with close confinement and few possessions. Not only did the new system provide for the separation of offenders by such criteria as length of criminal history and sentenced versus awaiting-trial status, as required by case law and professional standards, it also recognized the need to ration security resources. The planners devised a sophisticated system of three security ratings in which privileges and freedom of movement depend on assessment of inmates' potential to be violent or disruptive.

Concern with offender classification did not end with the description of the system. The officers also recognized the need for clearly delineated objective criteria for classification decisions and rejected dependence on intuition or attitude related indicators. The most interesting discussion, however, centered on expectations about the number of inmates appropriate for each category. Initially the officers estimated that fifty to sixty percent of inmates would be in maximum security. Between meetings, however, they were asked to review the inmates currently in the jail. At the next meeting there was general agreement that fewer than ten percent of the inmates would need maximum security and that virtually all incoming inmates should be assigned to the medium security level.

The planning efforts of officers were not limited to concerns with inmates, however. The groups also demonstrated the usefulness of participation in addressing a range of personnel related issues. Officers wrote all of the job descriptions for the new facility and conducted a staffing analysis in order to recommend overall staff levels. One of the most interesting discussions centered on shift patterns for the new facility. At the old jail officers worked four, ten hour shifts per week, assuring them of a three-day weekend. Interest throughout the jail peaked when one group considered the merits of a five-day-a-week schedule. The group's members found themselves in a unique role. More than any previous groups, these officers took on managerial responsibility. They had to consider what was best for the organization and the officers as a group rather than simply their individual preferences in this "bread and butter" issue.

The topic was discussed briefly at several meetings and finally took over the agenda of one full session. The group was divided on the plan they endorsed. At the meeting each side presented lengthy and well researched arguments. They provided data on the costs of each plan, the number of job assignments that could be covered and the preferences of officers not in the group. At the end of the discussion all but one officer supported the five-day work week. As each officer reported the reasons for their final decision it was apparent that they were uncomfortable with the new role but recognized the need to consider the organization as more than the collection of the individual interests of the officers.

The struggle over the shift pattern not only demonstrates the range of topics appropriate for participatory planning, it also highlights the breadth of officer participation in the project. Although a group of ten officers formulated the plan, there was continuous discussion with the rest of the jail staff. Group members even produced a newsletter to aid the process of informing staff of their progress. In each group officers conferred with their peers and it was common for the groups to postpone decisions until they could discuss the topic with other officers. In one group an officer was even chastised by the members for his inability to report the specific interests of other officers on his shift.

Participation and Information

Planning implies expertise. Planners must be able to define problems and identify resources for the future (Cushman, 1980:41). The novice jail planners brought to their task the expertise gained by working a job. This is reflected in the detail of the policies and procedures they produced. But their expertise did not stop with their experience as correctional officers. The model is one of action research and the planners collected and analyzed information relevant to their task.

One source of information was contained in the professional standards available as a blueprint for jail management. All of the participants studied and referenced the standards promulgated by the American Correctional Association and other relevant organizations. When more specific information was needed, the officers also designed and carried out their own research programs. They collected data needed for classifying inmates for the new jail and determining appropriate security levels. In one example, the group addressing program needs at the facility surveyed inmate interest in various kinds of program opportunities. The data changed significantly the plans of the group.

Officers in the new programs group assumed that inmates would be interested chiefly in recreation and entertainment programs including sports and movies. Since there were virtually no programs at the old jail these assumptions had never been tested. As the group began designing recreation programs for the jail, a survey of inmate program interests was suggested. The officers designed an instrument which asked inmates to rank their interest in a wide variety of programs ranging from education to sports. During the next meeting, the members of the planning groups used the same instrument to try to predict the responses of the inmates. The officers were flaberghasted to find that the inmates

ranked education, vocational training and substance abuse programming as the most important areas for program development. Recreation
and entertainment programs were viewed as the least important.

The findings of the research disconfirmed stereotypes and redirected
the efforts of the planners. Before the group could continue a clearer discussion of the goals of jail programs was required. From the start, the
group saw programs as contributing to a humane and constructive atmosphere at the jail but were sensitive about the term rehabilitation and
rejected the idea that the jail should claim any responsibility for reforming or failing to reform individuals. Rather than dismiss the potential for
rehabilitation, however, the officers arrived at a policy statement in
which programs are to be a resource to assist individuals who are, themselves, motivated for change. This solution set the agenda for the group
and delineated their information needs. Since jails often detain people
for relatively short periods of time, the group put a high priority on developing programs which offenders could continue after their release.
This expanded the planning program beyond the walls of the jail.

Another important source of information was also tapped by the
planners. Each group consulted experts in their area. Representatives
from the county prosecutor's office discussed the legal requirements of
booking and inmate processing. University faculty instructed the officers in job and staffing analysis. Physicians and dentists addressed requirements for quality medical care in a secure setting and group
members concerned with booking procedures even sought guidance
from local programs for the blind and physically handicapped.

The group that relied most on outside resources, however, was the officers involved in planning the new programs. Their emphasis on links to
the community meant heavy reliance on existing community programs.
Each week representatives from educational, religious, substance abuse,
counselling and other social service programs were invited to the group
meeting to discuss their programs. Fears that volunteer programs would
be difficult to attract were soon dismissed as nearly twenty program managers indicated interest in the new jail. The meetings provided valuable
insights for the officers and outside program staff as well. After brief
descriptions of the programs, jail staff, together with the outsiders, delineated the available resources which would enhance the program as well
as obstacles which might hamper its development. Through this method
of collaborative force field analysis, officers learned details which would
have been available only to inmate program participants and program
staff learned of concerns unique to secure settings.

The benefits of these exchanges often went beyond simple information. For example, at one point, two representatives of a drug awareness program sat patiently through the officers' discussion of the use of volunteers at the jail. The planners unanimously agreed to exclude ex-offenders from eligibility, viewing them as a potential threat to facility security. Following their discussion of the drug program the representatives suggested the officers contact another member of their staff for future planning since they were both ex-offenders. The officers were so convinced by the empathetic presentation of drug problems and the difficult road to recovery that they immediately reopened discussion of the policy on volunteers and unanimously agreed to permit ex-offenders (who were properly screened) to participate.

Assessing the Program in Peoria

The re-examination of ideas and values has been an important part of the Peoria project and demonstrates the potential of programs which link organization and individual development. The threshold test of the success of the participatory model, however, is in its productivity. Over a period of eighteen months the groups of frontline jail staff met and wrote the policies and procedures under which the new jail operates. These documents illustrate the experience of the planners as correctional officers as well the expertise gained through their self-study and research. In many ways the products are imaginative and innovative and a clear break with the traditions of the old jail. This is most obvious in their developments in prisoner classification and programming.

Still, the gains of the program must be assessed alongside its costs. Participatory models require considerable resources. In this case, a year and a half of compensated and uncompensated time, the energy and time of many people not directly linked to the jail, and the risks that managers were willing to take must all be counted among the resources dedicated to the project. Had the policies and procedures been written by managers or a hand picked panel of staff, the project may have been completed in several months with considerably less drain on resources. To determine the value of participation, however, we must also consider the ancilliary gains.

One benefit can be seen in the impact on staff. In all, thirty-nine of the fifty-five (70%) officers at the jail were active participants in the project. Although several officers dropped out for personal reasons or schedule conflicts, all of the rest participated fully in one or more of the groups. When the project began few of the officers had been exposed to the professional standards or legal requirements of jail operations. By the end, nearly all of the staff had a general knowledge of them and a detailed understanding of at least one aspect. Similarly, the officers were exposed to all facets of jail management and had the benefits of conferring with experts in many areas. These contributions to training and professionalism were made possible through the process of participation.

There have also been more measurable contributions. A follow-up survey was administered after the first year of the project. The data suggest improvements in two areas. Job satisfaction had increased, particularly in the area of support from supervisors and opportunities to contribute ideas. For example, at the beginning of the project only fifty-three percent of the staff agreed with the item "Supervisors care about our morale." In the second survey agreement had increased to over eighty-five percent. Surprisingly, there were no significant changes in attitudes towards inmates. There was however, an increase in the accuracy with which officers were able to predict the attitudes of their peers. The overestimation of dissatisfaction and animosity toward inmates, which was detected in the first survey, was no longer evident. Although there are many possible explanations for these findings, the increased communication brought on through participation clearly made a contribution. The groups brought together officers who had been isolated previously from one another on different shifts or days off and provided a forum for exchanging ideas and clearing misunderstandings.

The survey findings are also supported by annecdotal data from the group members. Each group meeting ended with an evaluation of the session. Written comments provided little detail, however, since each meeting was rated high by the participants. After the last meeting of each group, however, officers spoke about their expectations and the reality of the program. The most common comments were that officers did not really believe they would actually research and write the policies. Instead, they had expected to simply be consulted or asked for suggestions. These officers commonly linked increases in their own morale to the sincere opportunities to contribute to as well as learn more about their work. Another set of comments dealt more with social considerations in the groups. Many officers indicated that they enjoyed the opportunity to discuss work-related issues with officers from different shifts or assignments, officers with whom they had little contact before the program. The opportunities to discuss and contribute to jail policy were seen as significant enough for several of the groups to propose a continuing process in which groups of officers will periodically assess and rewrite policy and procedures at the jail.

An additional benefit to the program also merits attention. The old jail in Peoria was isolated from its surroundings, exposed only to staff and inmates. The program of participation has forged new links to the community. Those links include new access to local university resources as well as links to grass roots social service programs. More importantly, these links are not simply at the managerial level. Individual officers have developed interests in substance abuse and religious programs and services for the handicapped. Citing the importance of community resources, one group even developed a plan for a permanent community advisory group. Representatives of programs and community resources will meet regularly with jail staff in an effort to improve jail and community services. The relationship between the jail and the community has changed and the jail is on its way to becoming an agency with meaningful and productive connections to its community.

Conclusion

Participatory management practices have been implemented and evaluated in a large number of industrial settings. The resulting literature provides directions for similar experiments in the human services. Differences between human service and industrial work, however, suggest the need for unique considerations and models that differ from those in industry.

A jail is not a gypsum plant and jail officers differ from other workers. In a book entitled Street Level Bureaucracy, Michael Lipsky (1982) examines the differences between human service work and other occupations. Since police, social workers and correctional officers have wide discretion in the manner in which they carry out their tasks, Lipsky concludes that, unlike industrial workers, these street level bureaucrats inevitably make organizational policy. The policies these workers project may vary widely. Alienated teachers may view their roles as primarily custodial (Packard and Willower, 1972) and psychiatric attendants may see themselves as the primary providers of mental health services (Simpson and Simpson, 1959). Correctional officers may consider themselves as vigilant centurions or human service professionals (Lombardo, 1980:144).

Another difference also distinguishes human service work. Policies and procedures effect clients rather than the inanimate objects of production. Hospital patients may be alienated by bureaucratic medical practices (Mechanic, 1976:55) and a jail may become a dangerous and hostile environment.

Jail officers have broad discretion and their policies and procedures effect the lives of jail inmates. These considerations effected both the process and product of participation in Peoria. They also highlight the importance of developing participation models in the human services which combine individual and organizational development strategies.

Human service work is changing. Workers have new expectations of their jobs and technological advances and the demands of professionalism are changing the nature of their tasks. In the midst of these changes managers must also re-examine their roles. Participatory management practices provide an alternative which may meet the needs of workers and contemporary human service organizations. As in industry, there is a need to experiment with these practices and to document the efforts.

NOTE

*This project was partially supported by a grant from the National Institute of Corrections. The opinions expressed are those of the author and do not necessarily reflect the views of the United States Bureau of Prisons.

REFERENCES

Cheek, F. and Miller, M. (1982) *Prisoners of Life.* Washington: AFSCME.

Cherniss, C. (1980) *Staff Burnout: Job Stress in the Human Services.* Beverly Hills: Sage.

Cooper, M.R., and Morgan, B.S., and Foley, P.M. and Kaplan, L.B. (1979) Changing employee values: deepening discontent. *Harvard Business Review, 57,* 117-125.

Cushman, R.C., (1980) *Criminal Justice Planning For Local Governments.* Washington: U.S. Dept. of Justice.

Dachler, H.P. and Wilpert, B. (1978) Conceptual dimensions and boundaries of participation in organizations: a critical evaluation. *Administrative Science Quarterly, 23,* 1-38.

Davis, L.E., and Sullivan, C.S. (1980) A labour-management contract and quality of work life. *Journal of Occupational Behavior, 1,* 29-41.

Duckles, M.M., and Duckles, R., and Maccoby, M. (1977) The process of change at Bolivar. *Journal of Applied Behavioral Science, 13,* 387-399.

Gettinger, S. (1984) *Time to Build?* New York: Edna McConnell Clark Foundation.

Grant, J.D., and Toch, H. (1984) Harnessing human resources in the public sector. *Economic and Industrial Democracy, 5,* 227-248.

Guest, R.H. (1979). Quality of work life: learning from Tarrytown. *Harvard Business Review, 57,* 76-87.

208   *Sneaking Inmates Down the Alley*

Hackman, J.R. and Oldham, G.R. (1980) *Work Redesign,* Reading, MA: Addison-Wesley.

Jenkins, D. Quality of working life: trends and directions. In H. Kolodny and H. VonBeinum (eds.), *The Quality of Work Life in the 1980s,* New York: Praeger.

Law, J.M. (1980) Quality circles zero in on productivity, *Management,* 2-6. Lipsky, M. (1980) *Street Level Bureaucracy.* New York: Russell Sage.

Lombardo, L.X. (1980) *Guards Imprisoned.* New York: Elsevier.

Marrow, A. (1969) *The Practical Theorist: The Life and Work of Kurt Lewin.* New York: Basic Books.

Mills, T. (1979) Quality of work life: what's in a name? *Civil Service Journal, 19,* 50-54.

Packard, J.S. and Willower, D.J. (1972) Pluralistic ignorance and public control ideology. *Journal of Educational Administration, 10,* 78-87.

Sheppard, H.L. and Herrick, N. (1972) *Where Have All the Robots Gone?* New York: Free Press.

Simpson, R.L. and Simpson, I.H. (1959) The psychiatric attendant: development of an occupational self-image in a low-status occupation. *American Sociological Review, 24,* 389-392.

Toch, H. and Grant, J.D. (1982) *Reforming Human Services.* Beverly Hills: Sage.

Toch, H. and Grant, J.D. and Galvin, R. (1975) *Agents of Change.* New York: Schenkman.

Toch, H. and Klofas, J. (1982) Alienation and desire for job enrichment among correction officers. *Federal Probation, 46,* 35-44.

Whyte, W.F. (1983) Worker participation: international and historical perspectives. *Journal of Applied Behavioral Science, 19,* 396-407.